D1509091

MODELS OF MARKETS

MODELS OF MARKETS

Edited by ALFRED R. OXENFELDT

Contributing Authors

WILLIAM J. BAUMOL, KENNETH E. BOULDING,

RALPH CASSADY, JR., GEOFFREY P. E. CLARKSON,

REAVIS COX, MARK S. MASSEL, DAVID W. MILLER,

ALFRED R. OXENFELDT, RICHARD E. QUANDT,

MARTIN SHUBIK, RICHARD B. TENNANT

Columbia University Press   NEW YORK AND LONDON 1963

To the Memory of *John Maurice Clark*
whose recent death leaves us
with very few wise and temperate
students of modern markets

Copyright © 1963 Columbia University Press
Library of Congress Catalog Card Number: 63-18435
Manufactured in the United States of America

PREFACE

This volume contains the papers and formal discussion presented at two conferences sponsored by the Graduate School of Business, Columbia University, under a financial grant from the Sperry and Hutchinson Company. These conferences and this volume were designed to serve as an inventory and situation report on the state of economists' knowledge about markets and competition.

The past twenty years have seen increasing use of formal models as analytical tools, in economics, as in other spheres. For example, the growing field of econometrics has made extensive use of mathematical models of economic relationships, especially those involved in the functioning of the economy as a whole. Operations research has applied formal models to the successful solution of a wide variety of decision problems in the management of business and government.

While this model-building activity has progressed and has received increasing recognition and approval, the much older economic models of markets have had no such progressive development and have received no such recognition and approval. This is not because of lack of apparent importance or lack of widespread knowledge about them. The subject matter of these models is clearly important, for they attempt to explain the behavior of business firms and entire industries. Furthermore, generations of economics students have been instructed faithfully in their properties. Yet a general feeling of dissatisfaction exists. Even though the market models concern some of business's most important decision problems, businessmen seem largely to ignore them. Even though they relate to fundamental issues in industry structure and behavior, only limited areas of antitrust policy and enforcement appear to make use of the market models. Many economists protest serious weaknesses in the models and use them little, but are not notably successful in providing something better.

It was against this background of dissatisfaction and apparent lack of progress that two conferences were held. Economists from universities, government, and business sought to explain the general attitude of dissatisfaction with the standard market models and to arrive at more explicit evaluations of the contributions they make or could make, their weaknesses, and the opportunities for improvement.

The Conference on Appraisal of the Market Models of Price Theory, took place at Arden House, Harriman, New York, on April 2, 3, and 4, 1962. It was organized around the major uses to which price and market theory are actually put. Specifically, business decisions, antitrust policy, industry research, and economic theory were identified as the chief areas of interest. A separate paper was devoted to assessing the value and possible applications of price theory in each one. For purposes of this first conference, price theory was defined as the state of thinking about prices and markets that existed at the end of World War II. A strong effort was made to separate an examination of traditional economic theory from that of recent mathematical developments.

At this conference, following traditional practice, two formal discussants were assigned to each paper. The main papers were distributed well in advance of the conference, as were some of the discussants' remarks. At the conference itself, those who prepared major papers commented on what they had written but did not summarize their papers, and the discussants spoke. Following the two discussants, a brief period was allowed for questions. The group of about forty was then divided into three small discussion groups for approximately an hour and a half. The main group then reassembled to hear summaries of the discussions in each small group.

Reactions to the small group discussions and to the recapitulation of those discussions varied. The consensus was that they were illuminating and productive—but not of any conclusions. In most groups, the discussants' views did come closer together, though they rarely met.

Due to the obvious lack of consensus, it was decided, near the end of the conference, to make whatever lessons could be learned from the conference as clear and explicit as possible. The result is the long final paper prepared by Professors Tennant and Oxenfeldt. As the introduction to that paper indicates, Tennant and Oxenfeldt, representing somewhat divergent views, have drawn upon whatever was presented at the conference, plus their further reflections, plus the fruits of their discussions, in order to present a common view on the value and applicability of the market models of price theory.

On September 6 and 7, a second conference was held, entitled Contributions from Mathematical Models to an Understanding of Market Performance. This conference differed from the first in that it was designed to increase understanding of new techniques for studying markets and competition, rather than to explore applications of familiar models. The techniques covered include the dual solution of linear programming, heuristic programming, game theory, and simulation.

This conference was much smaller than the first and met for a day and one half at the Biltmore Hotel, New York City. The authors of the papers constituted an interrogatory panel. Each paper was discussed and reference was made to the issues of the first conference. By reason of the subject matter, however, the discussions did not lead to the kinds of broad open issues and mixed agreement and disagreement characteristic of the first conference. Oxenfeldt and Tennant have appended a brief second paper relating the papers of the second conference to the combined purposes of the two conferences.

A few words may be in order on the subject of the value of such conferences and the lessons learned about how to maximize their potential value. The following conclusions are set down without discussion or defense.

1. Conferences designed to take stock of what we know in a major area of economic thought, what we don't know, and how we might learn more are potentially very valuable and arouse great interest and not inconsiderable emotion and controversy.

2. Organization of subject matter around "applications" is productive, for it permits a mobilization of experience by those who have tried to put economic doctrine to specific use.

3. Small group discussion, especially when the main paper has been distributed in advance, is valuable; indeed, it is the part of a conference most likely to increase understanding. However, the meetings must not be rushed, and the same members should be retained in each small group, session after session (unless there is an obvious mismatch).

4. Using the device of a paper to reexamine the subjects discussed at the conference seems to be worthwhile, if the conference proceedings have been diffuse or inconclusive. It appears essential that diverse viewpoints be represented in any such reexamination, but one consequence is that the task becomes more onerous and the conclusions may be somewhat blurred.

It is with pleasure and gratitude that I acknowledge my debt to the many persons who contributed to the two conferences and assisted in the preparation of this volume. Professor Reavis Cox deserves chief credit for having seen the value of attempting, via a conference, an assessment in depth of our understanding of markets. Moreover, with Professor William Baumol and Dr. Eugene R. Beem he actively participated in formulating the program for both conferences.

Dr. Richard Tennant has contributed many constructive suggestions to the preparation of this volume for publication. I wish to acknowledge also the cooperativeness, open-mindedness, and good humor he displayed in the preparation of our joint essay.

Finally, I wish to acknowledge the generous financial support provided by the Sperry and Hutchinson Company, which made both conferences possible and thereby provided the basis for this volume, which seeks to share the fruits of the conferences with persons not in attendance.

ALFRED R. OXENFELDT

June, 1963
New York City

CONTENTS

Part 1. Arden House Conference: Appraisal of Market Models of Price Theory

Some Things We Know and Some We Do Not Know about
Markets and Market Models

REAVIS COX   3

The Role of Economic Models in Microeconomic Market
Studies

RALPH CASSADY, JR.   20

Comments

RICHARD B. HEFLEBOWER   53

JOEL B. DIRLAM   57

How Well Existing Market Models Meet the Needs of
Businessmen

ALFRED R. OXENFELDT   61

Comments

DAVID J. JONES   93

RICHARD B. TENNANT   96

Models of Value Theory and Antitrust

MARK S. MASSEL   101

Comments

IRSTON R. BARNES   131

EWALD T. GRETHER   137

MYRON W. WATKINS   143

The Uses of Price Theory

KENNETH E. BOULDING   146

Comments

EDWARD H. CHAMBERLIN   163

JOHN M. CLARK   166

Toward the Construction of More Useful Models
WILLIAM J. BAUMOL 172

Interpretations and Conclusions
ALFRED R. OXENFELDT AND RICHARD B. TENNANT 189

*Part 2. Biltmore Hotel Conference: Contributions
from Mathematical Models to an Understanding
of Market Performance*

Dual Prices and Competition
WILLIAM J. BAUMOL AND RICHARD E. QUANDT 237

The Relevance of Game Theory
DAVID W. MILLER 265

Simulation and Gaming: Their Value to the Study of Pricing
and Other Market Variables
MARTIN SHUBIK 307

Interactions of Economic Theory and Operations Research
GEOFFREY P. E. CLARKSON 339

Interpretations and Conclusions
ALFRED R. OXENFELDT AND RICHARD B. TENNANT 362

Appendix: Arden House Poetry
KENNETH E. BOULDING 369

PART 1. *Arden House Conference*

APPRAISAL OF MARKET MODELS

OF PRICE THEORY

SOME THINGS WE KNOW AND SOME WE DO NOT KNOW ABOUT MARKETS AND MARKET MODELS

BY REAVIS COX, PROFESSOR OF MARKETING,
WHARTON SCHOOL OF FINANCE AND COMMERCE,
UNIVERSITY OF PENNSYLVANIA

The inspiration for the following papers lies in a situation that we must find very strange. Many of the academic men who work with businessmen and government agencies as consultants or advisers on managerial and regulatory problems think of themselves as being economists. They associate with economists. They belong to associations of economists, perhaps with some qualifier attached, such as "applied" or "business." And yet they seem to have an almost universal conviction that they cannot effectively apply to the problems with which they struggle the concepts, methods, and doctrines of formal microeconomic theory. There is reason to believe that the executives with whom they work hardly know that price theory and market models exist. Those who do know about them apparently never—well hardly ever—use them in their day-to-day activities.

Even when an executive employs economists as consultants he may make little use of their formal analytical tools. In moments of frustration I sometimes think that a consultant's most important function is to serve as a combined court jester and father-confessor. In a setting where the courtiers must be prudent in what they say to the monarch and the monarch must be reticent in talking to those about him, each type of functionary provides a very useful safety valve. The jester can get away with the most outrageous remarks because no one has to admit that he is taken seriously. The confessor can be told anything because he is disciplined to keep what he hears to himself. Each would lose much of his capacity to serve if he tried to move over into the management of affairs.

The attitude of indifference, if not outright hostility, toward the formal analyses of the theorists extends into the graduate schools. Students of applied economics all too often study pure theory for the same reason that they study foreign languages—only because someone requires them to pass an examination. Once they have scrambled over the hurdle, they forget the whole business as quickly as possible. A good many graduate schools have accepted the facts of life about languages and have softened or abandoned language requirements for the doctorate. Few of them—perhaps none of them—have been willing to revise their requirements in theory so drastically.

We shall, first of all, try to arrive at some judgment as to the extent to which it is true that economic theory plays little part in the management of affairs. If it is true that theory is largely ignored in management and regulation, we shall try to see why it is true and whether there is any reason for anyone to be concerned that it is true. Should we agree that the judgment is true and that the situation is unfortunate, can we also agree as to what should be done by way of correction?

The substance of what is thought about the use of market models will be found in the following papers. My function here is to provide a setting for them. Let me start by considering some of the things we know about markets as they look to those of us who have put most of our effort upon the applied fields as teachers and consultants.

Kinds of Markets

One of the first things we learn if we go out to look at markets "in the flesh" is that the term "market" means many different things.

Models that are valid enough portrayals of, or abstractions from, what one man has in mind when he uses the word have no relevance at all to someone else's concept. Thus we may think of a market as nothing more than a place where trading goes on—the city market to which farmers and artisans bring their wares, the proverbial fair, on the downtown shopping center. Or it may be an area or a region within which a sales manager concentrates his efforts to find customers by sending out salesmen, broadcasting his advertising, and persuading distributors to stock his goods. It may be a facility, such as an auction warehouse or a building in which individual sellers rent stalls. Perhaps a seller will see it as nothing more than a group of people, those who actually buy his product or those whom he may call potential customers—all sufferers from diabetes for example, if he is a manufacturer of insulin, or those children who are both old enough and young enough to enjoy pull toys, if he makes playthings. Such concepts of the market are quite different from the view, so familiar to economists, that a market is a set of abstract forces that come to a focus in an abstract price, price level, or price structure, or "the environment in which a group of close substitutes is sold." [1]

These various ways of defining markets are not mutually exclusive. Some are more superficial than others. Some lend themselves readily to empirical research, whereas others do not. For our purposes, the significant point is that businessmen, who do the work of marketing, lean toward a preference for the concrete definitions, whereas economists, whose activity is confined to thinking about and analyzing business activities, tend to prefer the abstractions. Here we have one of the basic reasons for the difficulty managers meet in trying to use the market models of economists. At some point the manager must come to grips with tangibles, with real people and goods. It is not always easy for him to recognize the people among whom he spends

---

[1] Stephen H. Sosnick, "A Theoretical Scaffolding for Analysis of Market Structures," *Journal of Farm Economics*, 43 (Dec., 1961) 1346.

his working life in the disembodied abstractions of the model builder. Nor does he always realize that he may be abstracting when he thinks of himself as dealing with the practicalities of his work.

The inhabitants of the markets in which the businessman sells are not sharp, clearly defined, easily identified entities of the sort theory needs and often finds in the work of the economists. If a businessman thinks at all about firms, enterprises, industries, and channels, he is likely to look upon them as fuzzy around the edges, hard to identify, and difficult to count or measure. The buying and selling units with which he does business are not monolithic, homogeneous, and stable in their relations to one another. No person can be taken as wholly committed, in every aspect of his behavior, to any one unit. His relation to others is a constantly shifting mixture of cooperation and rivalry. The decisions he makes and carries into effect if he can are not separable into neat, little pieces of buying and selling and pricing, each distinct from its fellows, each analyzed and dealt with as a unit. The decision maker cannot restrict his analysis to an arbitrarily limited set of variables; he has to take his world as he finds it. Life is a continuum. Dividing it mentally into segments has its uses but can be done only at the cost of more-or-less seriously distorting the problem to be handled.

About markets as they see them, business managers have available a vast body of information. A logical purist may find that they really know much less than they seem to about their markets, even as they see them; but at least they think they know a great deal about them. About markets as theorists see them, they know little or nothing and probably will argue that they can know little. How much they really use, in a systematic way, the information they have, is anyone's guess. The larger companies have research staffs whose assigned responsibilities include the task of working these data into more or less rational analyses of the problems to be solved.

With or without the formal blessing of economic theory, decision theory, and the like, these managers get a great deal of business done. They negotiate innumerable transactions and deliver enormous quantities of goods and services to end users. They act rather than observe, and, rightly or wrongly, feel that in a real sense they control the affairs in which they participate. Admittedly, they take into account the environment in which they operate; but they most emphatically do not think of themselves as helpless creatures responding blind to impersonal forces that sweep over them.

This is true in spite of the fact that they sometimes seem to do nothing more than play an adult variety of follow-the-leader. They spend two or three or four percent of their projected revenue from sales for advertising, because they believe that is what other people in their particular trades do. They set their prices where they do in order to meet competition. They give cash discounts because people have always given cash discounts and customers expect them.

Often their decisions are made not by individuals but by committees or teams. Sometimes it is difficult indeed to discern any specific decision maker. Decisions do emerge. At least the entity concerned makes or lets things happen; but the untidy way it does this seems to have little in common with cerebral robots casting dice, for which they have carefully computed the probabilities (objective or subjective) in order to learn where (within precisely formulated confidence limits) lies the path toward maximizing minimum gains or minimizing maximum losses. Almost entirely missing is the precision of computing machines that manipulate mixed systems of linear and curvilinear equations, plus some inequalities, and spew out solutions in a few succinct digits. Rules of thumb abound.

Often, too, there seems to be nothing that can be called a real decision. People act as they do because it is their routine. They govern by habit and custom as much as by calculation, and they may have very little curiosity as to how the routines get established.

All of this makes it look to businessmen as if they live in a world wholly different from that in which the model builder pursues his trade. But the two groups confuse one another by using the same words to describe quite different things. A classical example, of course, is "competition." To the economist, competition is a sharply

defined limiting case in an array of market structures. To the businessman, it is rivalry, or more properly, institutionalized rivalry, although
he probably would never think of the term. It is rivalry held within
bounds by more-or-less well-defined rules of the game.[2] The brooding
economist may see him as a monopolist or an imperfect competitor;
but he finds himself in vigorous combat at all times, always in danger from flank attack if not from frontal assault.

Kinds of Models

It is also clear that models, like markets, are of a good many sorts.
Any one of them may be good for a particular purpose but wholly
unsuitable for another. The difficulties businessmen encounter when
they try to apply economists' models to their analyses may indicate
not that there is something basically wrong with the models but only
that they are being misused. Certainly the basic objectives of economists and managers in building models are quite different.

As I have said, the economist, considered narrowly and specifically
in his role as economist, is essentially an observer rather than a par-
ticipant in the affairs he wants to analyze. When I was a graduate
student at Columbia, Professor E. R. A. Seligman, who was then
chairman of the economics department, remarked to a group of us
that, in his judgment, the economist should remain aloof from what
we now would call management or decision making. He should keep
himself, as it were, on a mountaintop from which he can look at
what goes on in the valley with benevolent cynicism, He does not
take part; he merely looks and ponders. The questions he asks are:
What happened? Why did it happen? What is going to happen
next?

The manager, down on the plain, may find helpful the reports he
receives from the economist as to how things look from his vantage
point, but he most emphatically is not a mere observer. He is a doer—

[2] See, in this connection, the percipient article on competition by Walton H.
Hamilton, *Encyclopaedia of the Social Sciences* (New York, Macmillan, 1931),
IV, 141–47.

in his own mind, at least, a controlling doer. The question to which he seeks an answer is: What shall I do? Any models he uses must help him answer that question, or they serve no purpose in his thinking as a manager.

Given this difference in point of view and purpose, the differences among models become extremely important for the matters at hand. At the very least, we can say that there are several different aspects of model making and that each of these raises difficulties for the would-be model user. Since most of the models that concern us nowadays are mathematical, the troubles begin in the nature of mathematics and mathematical reasoning.

The purely mathematical approach to managerial problems gives statements of the form: If x, then y. Such a formulation has nothing to do with the world of objective reality. One is reminded of Bertrand Russell's famous tongue-in-cheek definition of mathematics:

Pure mathematics consists entirely of such asseverations as that, if such and such a proposition is true of anything, then such and such another proposition is true of that thing. It is essential not to discuss whether the first proposition is really true, and not to mention what the anything is of which it is supposed to be true. . . . Thus mathematics may be defined as the subject in which we never know what we are talking about, nor whether what we are saying is true.[3]

Purely mathematical model building partakes of this characteristic of pure mathematics. Any axioms, definitions, and rules of reasoning one wants to use are acceptable. The only test of truth that applies is that the system shall be consistent with itself. If it can be proven to have no internal contradictions, it is true; if upon analysis, it turns out to lead to contradictions, it is false. Whether it has any relation to the empirical facts of the external world is irrelevant.

To one who works primarily in the world of management, much of the model building of economists seems to be an exercise in pure logic or mathematics. He sees economists spending enormous

[3] Quoted in James R. Newman (ed.), *The World of Mathematics* (New York, Simon and Schuster, 1956), p. 4.

amounts of time tinkering with one another's constructs as they seek out little inconsistencies or endlessly proliferate the assumptions from which they build. He may concede that by their endeavors they have built a most impressive monument to pure reason, although he is more likely to have little knowledge and less interest in the whole undertaking. If he does know anything about it, he is not likely to see in what the models say much that bears upon the real world in which he makes his living.

As a start toward closing the gap between those who do and those who observe, a student can take his model to be an analogy rather than a direct description of fact. That is, to the statement we have already made he can append another: It looks as if x, therefore y. Presumably no test for truth arises when we reason by analogy, but we do need to test for applicability if we are to use the results in management, and the basic test is relevance to the empirical world. The useful (if not the true) becomes whatever formulation agrees with observations, more or less. Unfortunately, there are no universally accepted rules as to how close an agreement between model and observation is necessary before the model can be adopted as a guide to behavior. There must always be dissatisfaction with reasoning by analogy, because of the danger implicit in it. By definition no analogy can be perfect; it must break down sooner or later.

Alternatively, therefore, our student may try to prove x to be true by empirical research and also to prove by empirical research that whenever x is true, y also is true. Then he can say simply: x, therefore y. Once again the test of truth is relevance, but, as before, there are no general rules to say when one may conclude safely that the model agrees with the observed facts closely enough to warrant accepting it as empirically true, i.e., relevant to what we can measure and count in the real world.

Still another possibility is to speak in terms of probabilities rather than certainties. Here the statement would take a form somewhat like the following: There is a 99 percent probability within 5 percent confidence limits that the following relationship holds: x, therefore y.

In this form the statement is considerably more modest, but it does not answer the fundamental question. "How close must the model come to what we observe in the real world before we can accept it as a guide to action?" Relevance is still the test of truth, and we still have no logically unassailable rules to guide us in deciding how closely the model must agree with the empirical evidence in order to justify action based upon it.

The executive who wants to use models for purposes of control adds some additional difficulties to the situation. In his thinking, y is likely to become something that he wants to happen, a goal or an objective; x becomes the action he must take in order to achieve y. Thus x becomes in some sense the cause of y. What we have been thinking about is simply correlations between x and y. Now, implicitly, if not explicitly, y becomes something that happens because of x. Perhaps the manager also thinks not so much of the degree of probability that y will follow x as of the degree of precision with which doing x achieves y. The statement now becomes something on the order of: If I do x, then the chances are w out of z that I shall achieve a reasonable approximation of y. I have enough confidence in this reasoning to put some of my money or some of my company's money into a venture based upon it. The test is still relevance, with all the problems it raises, and these are complicated still further by the fact that statistical tests may be impossible because the statistical run will be short. Perhaps the case will be unique.

Furthermore, the significant test for the executive may be something quite different from determining whether statistical evidence supports reasonably well the conclusion that by doing one x he can achieve a fairly close approximation of one y. Around him lie many x's and y's. What he really wants to know, therefore, is which of the goals open to him he should try for, as well as which of the courses he shall take to any given goal. He must consider not only complete alternatives but degrees of achievement under each alternative that looks promising.

His difficulties arise not only when he looks forward to see what he should do, but when he looks backward to see what he has achieved. Looking backward raises an almost unanswerable problem of evaluation. In effect, he has to set the real world of what happened against the hypothetical and infinitely extensible world of what did not happen. So he has no completely reliable test as to whether he did really maximize or optimize the quantity by which he intended to be governed. Even after the fact his tests of any models he uses must remain uncertain.

Another set of difficulties arises from the inherent characteristics of statistical generalizations. We may draw an analogy from physics. The statistical nature of the laws or formulas of physics has been much discussed. Many of them summarize the aggregate effect of random behavior by enormous numbers of individual particles. Back of them lies the concept of a statistical universe in which random movements by a multitude of parts add up to a predictable aggregate. The movements of the individual units—the so-called Brownian movements—are themselves completely unpredictable.

Here again enters the contrast between the observer and the doer. The statistical view of the world of business may be acceptable to anyone who takes the role of outside observer—the economist, for example, or some other social scientist. He may be statisfied, even though the number of units in many specific situations is far too small to make possible safe statistical predictions. To the individual businessman, the view is not at all acceptable insofar as his own operations are concerned. He is the Brownian particle that engages in Brownian movements. He does not think of what he is doing as moving about at random, especially when he is trying to make use of models to guide his behavior. He has purposes and he believes that what he does has some influence upon the extent to which he achieves, or falls short of achieving them. What he needs is ways of judging the probable effects of his individual actions.

Fallacies and Difficulties in Model Building

It should be evident by now that there are a great many points at which the processes of model building and model using can go wrong when they are applied to the world of affairs. First, the mathematics may turn out to be erroneous. A lapse in the rigor of the mathematical reasoning it embodies may make the formula, If x, then y, fail the test of internal consistency. That is, the set of primitive terms, postulates, definitions, and operating rules may lead to mutually contradictory theorems.

Much of the work done in pure economic theory consists of searching out fallacies of this sort in the published work of economists. It may merely demolish some formulation or go on to set up alternative formulations designed to eliminate the observed flaw. If the theory is defective in this way, it obviously must fail as a model to be tested in the world of empirical fact.

The theory may be accurate enough as far as it goes, but incomplete. Perhaps x is only one of several factors that imply y. Perhaps y is only one of several conclusions implied by x. Obviously the utility of any model is greatly affected by the extent to which it approaches the form: If and only if x, then y and only y. It can be acceptable, of course if it takes the form: If and only if x_1, x_2, x_3, then y and only y.

The mathematics may be wrong in another sense. Much of the mathematics which model builders, especially those who work with variants of classical and neoclassical economic theory, have used, was devised in the course of efforts to answer problems encountered in physics. We have no reason to suppose that the entities of the economic world correspond in their essential characteristics to the entities of the physical world. There are many situations, for example, in which assumptions that decisions can be made at margins involving infinitely small increments or decrements simply are not valid. Perhaps better prototypes can be found in other sciences—notably biology, psychology, and sociology—for which new systems of mathematics are required. Perhaps mathematical thinking is not applicable at all, as is sometimes argued in an admittedly fuzzy way by those who say that the understanding and, even more strongly, the managing, of affairs must be more an art than a science.

If its mathematics is valid and appropriate, a model still may fail because it cannot be tested empirically. An excellent example is the enormous but largely unsuccessful effort that has been made to derive demand curves statistically. Conceptually, the demand curve of neoclassical economics—the schedule of quantities that a consumer or a group of buyers would take, at each of a set of prices, at a given instant in time—is neat and clear and exceedingly useful. Trying to use it in practice, however, one comes up against the hard fact that he has no data except the price at which something moved and the amount that moved. All the rest of the data lie hidden in the world of the never happened. Valiant, devoted, and knowledgeable efforts have been made to get around this difficulty by assembling price-sales data for successive dates and then using statistical techniques to compact them into a timeless schedule.

Curves can be plotted that give a respectable average of where demand has been over a period of years, but the businessman needs to know what the demand for his products is when he sets his price, not what demand has averaged over the last generation. Furthermore, he needs such schedules for much narrower categories of goods than the statisticians ordinarily use in their computations. He wants to know not only what demand is now but what it would be under each of several assumptions as to possible changes in his product, modifications in his advertising, and variations in the ways he can quote a given price or make a given change in his price. He may have to think not only of the demand curve among ultimate consumers of his product but also of how this demand will be transmitted back to him through a far-from-perfect communication channel made up of retailers, wholesalers, brokers, salesmen, and researchers. And he may want to find some way of breaking one demand curve into several by segregating his markets and differentiating his prices among them.

Should the model be accurate enough, the manager may find that it requires him to take actions that simply are not feasible. It is all very well to tell him that he can govern his advertising by counting the number of present users who will drift away from his product week after week if he does not advertise, the number who will drift to his product from competitors without advertising, and the percentage of change in each drift he can induce by advertising. He normally cannot have such figures to work with, perhaps not even when he is willing to spend large sums for the purpose, and he cannot be sure that if he has them for some past period they still hold good for his present situation. Furthermore, he cannot be sure that a particular advertisement or a particular advertising campaign will even approximate the averages his model uses to guide him.

Sometimes one has reason to believe that the model cannot be used because even though x will be followed by y within acceptable confidence limits, x is too expensive to be justified by the desirability of y. Working out the model and collecting the data can be very costly. They may be warranted only if the result is to be applied to a major question of policy. Running the model through a computer to deal with any specific case may also be costly. A company that is hesitant about setting long-term policies, or never gets around to thinking about them, will not find the model approach very helpful under these circumstances. Perhaps it should, but it will not.

More difficulties that arise in the application of models to the management of affairs grow out of the fact we have already mentioned: that a model ordinarily shows correlations but not causes. It follows that even if x is correlated closely with y it may not be the best instrument with which to control y. Considered as exercises in pure mathematics, most models are invertible. Considered as exercises in management, they may not be invertible at all. The sequence in which things must be done to produce the results sought may be quite rigid. Changing some variables in order to affect others may distort the model itself, no matter how accurate it may be as a description of what a mere observer sees in the situation.

The problem can be illustrated by considering a misuse of national income accounts that is fairly common. Although such a system of accounts is ordinarily cast into the form of numbers, many people who use it assume that it is closely analogous to an intricate system of pipes, pumps, and tanks through which a homogeneous fluid flows. It is hardly an accident that a good many efforts have been made to draw pictures of the system of national accounts in such terms. At least one physical model using this analogy has been constructed.

There is nothing objectionable in these efforts per se. They may be quite helpful as learning or teaching devices. But they may lead to a misunderstanding of what can be done to control the flows if they are not used with great sophistication. In a water supply system, it makes no difference where new units of water are inserted. They presumably will flow freely and in due course produce the expected effects upon the amounts moving through every measuring point. In a system where what flows is a tremendously complicated and constantly changing assortment of goods and services (as when we consider national income) the comfortable assurance that pumping new units into the system at one place will produce effects exactly like those produced by pumping in at another place does not hold.

It may be that the aggregate amounts computed in dollars will rise everywhere as planned; but the individuals affected and the assortments of goods they receive will vary a great deal, as between any two ways of inserting expenditures into the system or removing them from it. So, also, the qualitative aspects of market models may far transcend their quantitative aspects in practical importance. The particular kinds of advertising done, for example, may have more effect upon the results achieved than will the amounts spent. Yet the effects of these aspects of advertising may be almost impossible to predict or even to measure, after the fact.

It may also be impossible to separate out x and use it as an instrument of control over y. Or the side effects of x may be unacceptable even if the particular y produced is what management wants. In marketing there is a good deal of talk about the marketing mix. Students and managers of marketing are often told that they must work out and apply judicious combinations of actions in pricing, packaging, advertising, personal selling, financing, and so on. It is not sufficient to do a superb job of advertising and forget to get goods into the stores or to design them so that customer satisfaction will not lead to repeat sales. So, also, we may speak of a management mix in which the executive combines an assortment of quite imprecise instruments into a program compounded in considerable part of guess and hope, as distinct from calculation. In such a setting, if he does x, he may produce effects upon the whole mix that are undesirable.

There is no doubt, too, that the whole apparatus of models is often too slow and clumsy to be usable in a fast-moving situation. The variables a company meets in its operations are many and often unpredictable. They may or may not have been included in the model to be used. There may or may not be time to add them if they are needed. Since much of what goes on in the market is a form of combat, opponents will introduce as many surprises as they can. There is thus no nice, orderly world in which all that it would be desirable to know is known, or can at least be reduced to calculable probabilities and risks, before the model is devised.

Finally, it may be impossible to work out models that cover enough variables to make them useful. There is much talk nowadays of system analysis in marketing. Much has been written to illustrate what can be done with efforts to treat business organizations and situations as systems of interrelated variables rather than as models in which one or two values are permitted to vary, in order to isolate their effects, everything else being held equal. There is little evidence that such analyses are being very widely used in the actual management of affairs by the decision makers, as distinct from their staff advisers. Where they are used, they seem to be much more effective in the control of physical processes than in the intangible processes of buying and selling.

Justification of Model Building

Although some part of the reluctance of managers to use sophisticated models in their work undoubtedly stems from the attitude expressed by one company president with whom I have worked ("I

just don't like algebra") much of it also grows out of the limitations
of models we have been discussing. The models are not always good
enough to force their way into the kit of managerial tools over the
objections that arise from mental blocks against mathematics.

If the students with whom I come in contact are a fair sample,
I venture to predict that the coming generation of managers will not
completely or quickly change this situation. They listen politely and
struggle manfully with models and with the underlying mathematics.
I believe it is fair to say, however, that many of them are still not
convinced that this is the way management is done or should be
done. Those who find themselves able to work with these instruments
effectively probably will be attracted into staff rather than line positions.

Why should we bother about whether models work well or not?
For all its limitations, model building has become extremely fashion-
able of late. This is true not only in academic ivory towers but among
consultants and staff research people who work with managers, helping them to solve their daily problems. The development is obtrusive
and intrusive. No one on the campus of a collegiate school of business can escape it. No one who reads any journals on the rapidly
growing list of business publications can avoid it. He must learn at
least enough about model building to be able to reject it intelligently,
if he feels that he must reject it.

There is some justification for "practical" men to dismiss the whole
effort as a sort of academic drug addiction. Unquestionably, for certain turns of mind it is easier to work with abstract formulations of
problems than it is to go out into the dusty market place and struggle
with the empirical facts in all their confusion. Many of the students
who are developing the methodology of model making seem to be
content to spend their time playing with the models themselves. It
will not do, however, for the businessman to seek an easy way out of
his discomfort by ridiculing the "egghead." There are too many indi-
cations that we may be on the verge of major breakthroughs in the

application of systematic methods of analysis—probably mathematical in form—to the management of affairs.

So we come to the justification for the effort in which these papers are, engaged. We shall do well to look systematically at what has been accomplished in three separate areas by efforts to apply the models of microeconomics to the making of decisions by businessmen and government officials. These three areas are business management in general, marketing research, and the regulation of monopoly. In addition, we shall give some attention to the contributions made to economic theory itself by efforts to improve the available models.

THE ROLE OF ECONOMIC MODELS IN MICROECONOMIC MARKET STUDIES

BY RALPH CASSADY, JR., PROFESSOR OF MARKETING
AND DIRECTOR, BUREAU OF BUSINESS AND ECONOMIC
RESEARCH, THE UNIVERSITY OF CALIFORNIA,
LOS ANGELES

The term "model" as applied to economic phenomena is not easy to define because it may connote different things to different people. Thus, the term may mean something very precise and explicit or it may mean something imprecise and implicit. There may be, however, certain things that all economic models have in common, and if so, these should be incorporated into a definition of a term which would serve as a point of reference.

According to Webster's, the term "model" is the diminutive of the word *modus* meaning the way of doing something. In one sense the word means "that which exactly resembles something; a copy," or a "miniature representation of a thing; sometimes, a facsimile. . . ." [1] For the purpose of this discussion, economic models might be defined as simplified replicas of actual systems, or segments thereof constructed with a view to discovering or demonstrating possible economic results under given conditions; or more broadly, any "blue-

---

[1] *Webster's New International Dictionary* (2d ed., unabridged). Webster's further defines the term "model" as "5. An archetype. 6. Anything . . . that serves, or may serve, as an example for imitation. . . . 7. Something intended to serve, or that may serve, as a pattern. . . ."

print" or overall plan of procedure which is to serve as the framework of a study. Such models may or may not be quantified; thus, we are taking a very broad approach to the subject.

Economic models may be used: 1) As analytical devices to serve as foci for intensive empirical investigation into actual market situations, not only for the purpose of supplementing market knowledge but, perhaps, even for the purpose of improving the existing model; 2) As essentially complete but simplified mechanisms in accordance with which "dry-run" tests can be made in order to predetermine economic results; 3) As guides to policy determination, even in the absence of any empirical investigation; 4) As abstract plans which would serve as bases for the building or rebuilding of an economic system or segment thereof; 5) As pedagogical devices to assist in communicating abstract principles or ideas to others.

Economic models may be of widely varying types. They may involve the gross national product, labor requirements and availability, interaction of demand and supply, and so on—we, of course, are interested primarily in models which are related to market behavior, including pricing and pricing results. Such models involve mainly (a) the nature of consumer demand, (b) the supply of product-services, and (c) the competitive structure and behavior. While other participants are studying these phenomena from different points of view, my concern with models is, of course, their use in research activities, and in such circumscribed use the employment of models, understandably, may be limited.

For the balance of this paper an attempt will be made to illustrate the relevancy of models in the type of microeconomic studies in which I have special interest—mainly, those in which various competitive situations have been "placed under glass." The exposition, then, is largely related to a reexamination of projects already completed, to determine to what extent, if at all, models have played a part in the methodological scheme.

The methodology involved in this analysis is not complex. The issue concerns the relationship of models to empirical research. The specific question is, to what extent do economic models have applicability in market investigations involving price and competitive behavior. The answer to this question should throw some light on an important methodological problem.[2]

Use of Models in Earlier Research Investigations

In planning the substantive aspects of this paper, my first thought was to brief the literature to discover to what extent, if at all, models had been used by those conducting market studies. But, it was soon apparent that I had all I could do to determine what use had been made of models in my own studies. This section is devoted to studies conducted in earlier years, and the following one is devoted to more recent studies, one of which is still in process.

IMPACT OF INNOVATION ON GROCERY WHOLESALING

Fifteen or so years ago a microeconomic study was made of grocery wholesaling, in which an historical model was employed.[3] The principal question here was what effect, if any, did the development of the chain store, with its integrated wholesale and retail operations,

[2] It is suggested that the reader refer to my exposition of market research methodology, "Market Measurement in a Free Society," *California Management Review* (Winter, 1960), pp. 57–66. This study brings out the fact that the methods available to the researcher for obtaining market data are observation (direct and indirect), interrogation (structured and depth), and experimentation (simple and controlled), with particular emphasis on the observational and interrogational procedures. This, of course, has to do essentially with the data-gathering function. Thus, sources from which necessary market data are derived include direct observation of market phenomena as well as published reports by market observers or participants or other investigators, including the government (which may be designated as the direct and indirect observational methods) and actual field studies designed to obtain factual as well as motivational information directly from those who have such knowledge (which may be designated as structured and depth interrogational methods). While various methods are employed, like the anthropologist I rely most heavily, where possible, on information secured from primary sources (i.e., observing market phenomena and interrogating marketing functionaries).

[3] Ralph Cassady, Jr. and Wylie L. Jones, *The Changing Competitive Structure in the Wholesale Grocery Trade* (Berkeley and Los Angeles, University of California Press, 1949).

have in the grocery field. Subquestions which followed were: To what extent did competitive factors withdraw from the trade and others come in during the period of the study? What changes developed in operating methods by those who remained? What effect, if any, did all this have on the cost of marketing groceries at the wholesale level (i.e., on wholesale margins)?

The method was to make a detailed study of the evolution of operating conditions from one era to another. More specifically, a decision was made concerning the starting date of the period under study (1920) and the ending date (1946), and intensive investigation was made of the competitive conditions, including types of competitors and operating methods, existing in the earlier period (before the effect of innovation had a chance to make itself felt), and those found in the later period (when the effects were finally consummated). The final stage of the study involved an intensive analysis of changes in the number of competitors and the operating methods, year by year during the twenty-six year period. In other words, use was made of a quantified model based upon a changing competitive structure.

Thus, we started with a particular market competitive situation as of a certain time—and subsequently some vendors dropped by the wayside, some changed their methods, and some new entrants arrived on the scene. Finally, we arrived at the year 1946 with a new competitive structure, which had evolved in a few short years through the struggle of forces contending for survival. Such a study is largely exploratory in nature. The method involved here was mainly indirect observation [4] of all developments regarding the problem under consideration (i.e., changing competitive institutions) from one period of time to another.

Incidentally, the study revealed tremendous changes in operating methods over the years. Moreover, a comparison of the margins, or

[4] The term, "indirect observation," applies here because the researcher obtained information from others (through trade papers, court records, and interviews) who were either participants or direct observers. See "Market Measurement in a Free Society," *California Management Review* (Winter, 1960), p. 60.

the prices paid for wholesale distribution, for the earlier and the later periods revealed a staggering difference. Thus, in 1920, percentage margins of wholesale grocery concerns were about 12 percent, while in 1947, grocery wholesalers (at least some of them) were operating at a cost of only a little more than 3 percent of sales, thus revealing a tremendous increase in efficiency combined with some reduction in the amount of service rendered. It may be concluded, then, that the historical method, if properly used, may yield interesting and valuable competitive data and that an historical framework might be considered as a kind of model.

COMPETITION AND PRICE MAKING IN RETAIL GASOLINE DISTRIBUTION

Much may be learned about the usefulness of models by reviewing the research methodology utilized in a microeconomic study of the Los Angeles gasoline trade, conducted about ten years ago.[5] In approaching this study, certain possible consumer- and competitor-behavior patterns were determined, in addition to the specific market-area and retail institutions to be placed under study. Then the existing structure was quantified, in so far as this was possible. At least two phases of the project appear to be relevant here.

Pricing under normal competitive conditions. In a study of this type the author makes use of a complex of analytical tools, including a study of the nature of the product-service, demand for and supply of the product-service, and the nature of competition in the particular field under study. Use was also made, here, of the "pure" competition model as a bench mark, the elements of which include, of course, numerous traders, homogeneity of product-service, prevalence of market information, and ease of entry.[6] One may utilize the latter

[5] Ralph Cassady, Jr. and Wylie L. Jones, *The Nature of Competition in Gasoline Distribution at the Retail Level* (Berkeley and Los Angeles, University of California Press, 1951).

[6] "Pure" competition and "perfect" competition are examples of fairly precise economic models. In the latter we assume that if (a) traders are numerous (so numerous that there would be no substantial influence by any one factor on the market), (b) competitors are well informed (so that they know much about offerings and market opportunities), (c) product-services are homogeneous (so

model by considering the effects on price making of fewness of traders, differentiation of product-services, absence of adequate market information, or difficulty of entry.

One of the most interesting findings of the gasoline study, in relation to the subject of this paper, is the fact that the product of the majors and that of the independents, so-called, are differentiated in the minds of consumers so as to justify or require differing pricing strategies. This differentiation—based partly on product-service differences and in part on an absence of consumer market knowledge— gives rise to substantial price differentials between the offerings of certain types of gasoline outlets. Thus, the independents (or aggressive price competitors) must price their merchandise at 1½ to 3 cents less than that of the majors (or conservative competitors) in order to induce patronage. This major–independent differential may, at times, give rise to an intensive price struggle (as it did recently in one market) between forces favoring narrow, as against those favoring wide differentials.

One of the first questions one might ask at this point is, to what extent, if at all, are gasoline prices set on the basis of the relationship between marginal revenue and marginal cost, which, again, is a kind of model. According to the marginal hypothesis, of course, prices would presumably be set in such a way as to maximize net revenue in short-run terms. Without attempting to set off another controversy,[7] I must state that price making is simply not conducted in

---

that offerings are perfect substitutes for one another), and (d) traders may move in and out of the market if it appears advantageous for them to do so (so that supply and demand are easily equated), certain price results will obtain.

We can then use this as a model either to predict results, given "perfect" conditions, or to make prognostications when variations from such conditions are assumed to prevail. It should be noted that we may use a model in order to predict market conditions without deciding that we ought to reconstruct the economic system to conform to the model—a fact that some economists seem to have lost sight of. Also, such a model should not be considered immutable by market researchers who should always be on the lookout for additional market factors or refinements which might strengthen the model.

[7] See, for example, R. A. Lester, "Shortcomings of Marginal Analysis for Wage-Employment Problems," *The American Economic Review* (March, 1946), pp.

this way in any real situation about which I have knowledge. Therefore, little confidence can be placed in the application of this model
to pricing studies.

In empirical studies of price making one cannot rely on this model,
as stated, because too little is known about actual price-quantity relationships (i.e., demand) and cost behavior to continually adjust
prices in accordance with changing demand and cost conditions.
Even if we did have more knowledge about such relationships, the
marketing institutions which resell the goods would not want to
purchase from vendors whose prices were constantly in a state of flux,[8]
and their customers, in turn, require a certain degree of stability.[9]
But even if we did know enough about demand, and customers did
not mind fluctuating prices, it would be foolish to attempt to maximize net revenue on every item in every transaction. The business
concern is not interested in maximizing profits in short-run terms or
on all items but, rather, in longer-run earnings on the total product
mix.

However, when new products are added to a line, a kind of marginal analysis is employed by those responsible for price making.
This is based on estimated added revenue from the new item in relation to estimated added cost occasioned by the handling of the new
item, assuming prices and percentage margins remain constant and
allowing for any adverse impact on substitute items. But even here
one must consider that competition may force the stocking of the
item regardless of the estimated net revenue, and it is often not so
much a question of the profit that can be made on this item as a

---

63–82; Fritz Machlup, "Marginal Analysis and Empirical Research," *ibid.* (September, 1946), pp. 519–54; and R. A. Gordon, "Short-Period Price Determination
in Theory and Practice," *ibid.* (June, 1948), pp. 265–88.

[8] In any case, one could not expect to retain customers if he arbitrarily cut
them off when profit conditions were not ideal (e.g., the drop of temporarily
unprofitable fuel oil customers in winter!)

[9] Businesses simply cannot be run on a basis of continual price adjustments to
fluctuating demand conditions, if only because retailer-customers would find such
unstable conditions intolerable. The point here is that fluctuating prices make for
serious inventory problems which endanger profitable operations.

question of the best alternative use of shelf space.[10] It should be noted, in addition, that despite "losses" on a particular item, its promotion might aid in the sale of other items and thus be quite profitable when considered in broader terms.[11]

Pricing under abnormal competitive conditions. Price wars—which are basically a manifestation of a shift in emphasis from impersonal striving for success (competition) to a more-or-less personal attack on rival vendors (conflict)—are more prevalent in the gasoline industry than in any other.[12] In studying price warfare one tries to find out (a) how such conflicts start (including the basic as well as the proximate causes); (b) what, if any, price behavior patterns result therefrom; (c) the extent of the transmission of the conflicts from one market area to another; (d) how long wars last; (e) how they are concluded; and so forth.

At this stage of our knowledge, price-war studies are largely exploratory, and the research method on which one has to lean most heavily is that of the examination of reports of such "wars" (including those in trade papers), supplemented by interrogation of participants or observers. It is important in seeking information on price warfare (as in other types of investigations) that preconceptions be avoided. It is equally important to avoid bias developing out of interviews with participants holding strong views for one side or the other.[13] On the positive side, one might find it helpful, in conducting

---

[10] If one were to approach the problem from this point of view, of course, one would simply determine the prospective net revenue to be earned on two or more alternative items and decide on the one that had the greatest profit potential.

[11] See the discussion of loss-leader pricing pp. 39–41.

[12] See Ralph Cassady, Jr., *Price Making and Price Behavior in the Petroleum Industry* (New Haven, Yale University Press, 1954), particularly "Retail Price Wars in Gasoline Distribution," pp. 262–80; and Cassady and Jones, *Nature of Competition in Gasoline Distribution*, particularly pp. 148–55, 172–75.

[13] There is a methodological problem here which is interesting but not easy to solve. Should the researcher, who is in a position to do so, interrogate participants while a price war is going on (and thus possibly derive biased information and even condition the behavior of such individuals), or wait until later (and take a chance that some of the nuances of particular moves and countermoves, and even feints, would be forgotten)?

price-war studies, to have in mind, as a model, the nature of normal competition in the trade under study.

In a microeconomic analysis of price warfare, one might try to find out who made the initial price move and why the move was made, as the first step in a behavioral-pattern model covering all stages of the war. We usually find that when a price move is made by one major-company vendor it is done as a result of competitive squeezing, perhaps by the independent fringe, say, which has been gaining business at the expense of the national-brand stations. Moreover, the underlying conditions which are conducive to price warfare, such as a "sloppy" supply situation, make it possible for independent stations to acquire supplies of gasoline at bargain prices, thus widening margins and permitting price reductions at the retail level. It would seem that the practice of granting subsidies to warring dealers by suppliers also has some bearing on the prevalence of wars in this field.

As we all know, a genuine price-war situation is one in which successive reductions and counter-reductions result in inordinately low prices during the period of the war. By its very nature, price behavior under price-war conditions becomes somewhat irrational and hence unpredictable. Therefore, one would probably be able to make only limited use of conventional models under price-war conditions.[14] However, it is possible to employ the concept of international conflict as a model for price warfare.[15] Moreover, one may effectively utilize the overlapping trading area model in evaluating the transmitted effect of price changes made by one firm on others located some distance away.[16]

[14] As Professor Edward H. Chamberlin has stated, theory probably more effectively explains why price wars do not break out more often, than why they break out at all.

[15] See Ralph Cassady, Jr., "Price Warfare and Armed Conflict: A Comparative Analysis," *Michigan Business Review* (November, 1956), pp. 1–5; and "Taxicab Rate War: Counterpart of International Conflict," *The Journal of Conflict Resolution* (December, 1957), pp. 364–68.

[16] See the discussion of overlapping trading areas in relation to price warfare in Ralph Cassady, Jr., "Price Warfare—A Form of Business Rivalry," in the second edition of *Theory in Marketing* (Homewood, Richard D. Irwin, in press).

HYPERINTENSIVE PRICE COMPETITION IN
DEPARTMENT STORE OPERATIONS

While intense competition prevailed for many years between R. H. Macy & Company and Gimbel Brothers department stores, self-restraint in price making was usually practiced by both parties, so that, ordinarily, price conflict did not break out. Normal competitive conditions were temporarily interrupted in late May, 1951, when Macy's announced price cuts on several thousand items which had been price-fixed [17] but which were now price-free, as a result of the Schwegmann decision.[18] The moves and counter moves which followed these reductions resulted in open warfare in the New York department store field.

The basic conditions making the 1951 Macy-Gimbel price war possible appear to have been a change in legislative circumscriptions, ample supplies of goods, and the animosity between Macy and Gimbel top executives, particularly on the part of Gimbel's against Macy's.[19] The conflict was triggered by the Schwegmann decision, which vitiated the nonsigner clause in connection with fair trade contracts in interstate commerce, and the moral responsibility of Macy's to reduce prices because of its constantly reiterated complaint that it could not reduce prices on fair trade merchandise, implying strongly that it would do so if the law permitted it.

Many interesting discoveries were made as a result of the investigation of competitive behavior in the Macy-Gimbel price war. For example, something was learned about (a) the nature and purpose of the first move, (b) the proportion of items reduced in such situations (a relatively small number), (c) types of items which were price cut (well-known brands),[20] (d) the depth of cuts (seldom below invoice

[17] Ralph Cassady, Jr., "The New York Department Store Price War of 1951: A Microeconomic Analysis," *The Journal of Marketing* (July, 1957), pp. 3–11.
[18] *Schwegmann Bros. v. Calvert Distillers Corp.*, 341 U.S. 384 (1951).
[19] It is interesting that Macy's slogan had been for years "We endeavor to save our customers at least 6% for cash, except on price-fixed goods," while Gimbel's motto was "Nobody—but nobody—undersells Gimbel's."
[20] Consider the model of a well- and favorably-known brand in competition with a little-known or unfavorably-known brand with a substantial price differen-

cost) and (e) the length of time of such a conflict (several weeks at most). Less was learned about other aspects of the price war, including the method of bringing the conflict to an end.

But, again, the employment of an orthodox competitive model does not appear practicable in such an investigation and, indeed, such use might be dangerous, especially if the researcher went into the study with preconceived notions and the attitude that little could be learned because he already knew how competitors would behave, on a basis of the assumptions of some model.[21] Such an attitude is fatal to effective research effort. Actually, the most valuable tool of analysis in any research investigation is the sincere feeling, at the outset, that we know little, if anything, about the problem to be studied, and must therefore keep our minds completely open if we are to avoid conditioning research results.

DISCRIMINATORY PRICING IN MOTION PICTURE DISTRIBUTION

About fifteen years ago, I began some work in the field of price discrimination and, after considerable exploratory effort, published a series of articles on various aspects of the subject, including the taxo-

---

tial between the two. See Ralph Cassady, Jr. and E. T. Grether, "The Proper Interpretation of 'Like Grade and Quality' Within the Meaning of Section 2(a) of the Robinson-Patman Act," *Southern California Law Review* (April, 1957), particularly pp. 259–62. But note that the normally higher priced product is precisely the one which is used as ammunition in price warfare which may break out between retail merchandising institutions, and that the less popular and hence lower-priced substitute item may not even be reduced in price.

[21] To take an example: The locality discrimination model, so often referred to in discussions of the way the old Standard Oil Company eliminated rivals and in which a predatory concern allegedly drops prices in the market area where competitors exist and raises them in the areas where competition has been eliminated, is not nearly as practicable as it seems. See Ralph Cassady, Jr. and William F. Brown, "Exclusionary Tactics in American Business Competition: An Historical Analysis," *UCLA Law Review* (January, 1961), pp. 91–95. The reasons for this are that in some fields, at least, competitors may be very difficult or, indeed, impossible to get rid of, and even if they were eliminated raising prices would almost certainly attract others. This does not mean, however, that a firm might not compete harder in some markets than it does in others, but only that the simple locality-discrimination model might serve as an intellectual trap for the unwary.

nomic structure of price discriminatory activities.[22] I was then, and am now, familiar with the Joan Robinson theoretical solution to the problem of discriminatory pricing in two or more markets with varying demand elasticities, but never have found the highly theoretical (and, in fact, unrealistic) approach very enlightening or useful.[23] It is not surprising, therefore, that it was not included in my kit of analytical tools when the study of the pricing of motion picture films was initiated in 1957.[24]

As we know, profit enhancement is theoretically possible through price discrimination because we are able to obtain higher prices from those having higher incomes and more intensive desires (thus, lower price elasticities), but at the same time, we are able to tap lower-income groups (which possess higher elasticities) without disturbing the rest of the market. The ideal end of all discriminatory pricing is, of course, the attainment of the individual buyer's full demand price for the product-service. In the motion picture industry this is the

[22] See my "Some Economic Aspects of Price Discrimination Under Non-Perfect Market Conditions," *The Journal of Marketing* (July, 1946), pp. 7–20; "Techniques and Purposes of Price Discrimination," *ibid.* (October, 1946), pp. 135–50; "Legal Aspects of Price Discrimination: Federal Law," *ibid.* (January, 1947), pp. 258–72; and "Legal Aspects of Price Discrimination: State Law," *ibid.* (April, 1947), pp. 377–89.

[23] Mrs. Robinson has said that in a price discriminatory situation involving two markets, "Output will be determined by the point at which the aggregate marginal revenue curve cuts the marginal cost curve, and the amount sold in each market will be the amount for which marginal revenue is equal to the marginal cost of the whole output." Joan Robinson, *The Economics of Imperfect Competition* (London, Macmillan, 1959), p. 183. One might add (assuming the soundness of this contention) that the prices in the two markets would be determined by the intersection of a vertical line running through the marginal revenue curve for each product at a point determined by the crossing of a horizontal line running through an intersection of average marginal revenue and marginal cost.

[24] See Ralph Cassady, Jr., "Impact of the Paramount Decision on Motion Picture Distribution and Price Making," *Southern California Law Review* (February, 1958), pp. 150–80. For a case study of competitive conditions in this industry in an earlier era see Cassady, "Monopoly in Motion Picture Production and Distribution: 1908–1915," *Southern California Law Review* (Summer, 1959), pp. 325–90, in which a monopolistic combination is analyzed and the economic factors which brought about its dissolution are depicted in minute detail.

amount the exhibitor is able and willing to pay, as evidenced by the estimated gross earnings less operating costs, in relation to the intensity of need for the particular film (Fig. 1). Thus a kind of model is available in this area of analysis, also.

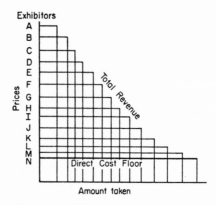

Fig. 1. Conceptual illustration of the potentialities
of discriminatory pricing of motion picture films

That opportunities exist for discriminatory pricing in the leasing of motion picture films should be obvious when it is realized that grossing potentialities of various theaters vary from a few hundred dollars to considerably in excess of $100,000 per week. That price discrimination is practicable, is easily demonstrated by the relatively high value of each transaction (which permits individual investigation and bargaining), the overt nature of theater operations (with their simple price structure and easily-computed consumer response), and the complete control of the product by the vendor through the retention of title to the actual film (which permits limitations on leasing rights by the lessor).

The main point, here, is that in the motion picture industry the estimation of the full demand price is not too difficult because exhibitors operate, figuratively, in a goldfish bowl—that is, the admission price is plainly displayed, customer counts are possible, and those in the know are able to accurately judge the intensity of the need for the particular picture offered the theater for the particular clientele served by the prospective exhibitor-buyer.

This means that each buyer can be dealt with individually and an attempt can be made to exact a rental price which will approximate the full demand price of each (although this ideal will not necessarily be attained). A model based on the factors which enter into the price paid by an individual theater for a film would reveal that such a price is governed by (a) the grossing potential of the theater in relation to operating costs, (b) the competitive position of the buyer's theater in the community, (c) the number of alternative films available to the theater at the time of the negotiation, (d) the number of pictures required by the theater operator, (e) the type of picture offered in relation to the particular market served by the theater, (f) the buying power of the purchaser, (g) the price paid by the theater previously for a certain type of picture (i.e., precedent), and (h) the astuteness (or even sharpness) of the traders. A publicly acclaimed picture such as *Ben Hur* is, in a real sense, unique while a mediocre picture may have numerous substitutes. It does happen, however, that some pictures may be very popular in one type of community but may "lay a bomb" in another.

The resulting motion picture rental price is basically dependent on the relative strength of the bargaining positions of the buyer and seller. A vendor will strive for all the traffic will bear and a theater operator will try for the lowest terms possible. Thus, the "horse-trading" may result in entirely different terms for various exhibitor-buyers, a part of which difference, admittedly, results from differences in the priority of showings. It is an interesting fact that even if the percentage terms given different exhibitor-buyers were the same, the rentals paid would differ tremendously among theaters because of the differing grossing potentials of the various theaters. For example, the terms might be 50 percent of the gross to the distributor and 50 percent to the theater. One theater, for example, might gross $500 and another $50,000, and thus one pays $250 and the other one $25,000 for the same picture.[25] Therefore, it should be obvious that price discrimination is inherent in any percentage-leasing arrangement.

Mention was made above of factors which influence the rental price paid by individual theaters for motion picture films. Among these was the relative bargaining power of the parties involved in the transaction. As regards the seller, this would include the desirability of the particular motion picture involved in the deal—whether he is offering *Ben Hur* or some cheaply made potboiler. But as regards the buyer, a very important factor would be the degree of buyer competition for the product offered, and this involves the number of exhibitor-buyers in the community or area.

In any one submarket there may be several buyers, or two, or, indeed, one. If there is only one—a "closed town," as it is known in the trade—or if, in other words, a monopsonistic condition prevails, the bargaining strongly tends to favor the buyer. This conclusion can be inferred from an implied competitive model which would indicate that the buyer faced with no competition from other buyers would be able to "write his own ticket."

However, in this situation—as in so many model situations—a conclusion based merely upon structural conditions is not entirely tenable. Let us say that a theater operator owns the only theater in town, or that he owns all (of several) theaters, so that a monopsonistic condition prevails, as a result of which the buyer apparently could practically set his own price. But this conclusion may be vitiated by

[25] In the case of theaters with small grosses, fees for the use of film are usually set on a flat-rental basis, thus permitting small exhibitors with low gross potentials to obtain films for their theaters. The result is that film rentals, in the United States at least, typically vary from as little as $25 per week (or less) to $25,000 per week (or more). It may be noted, however, that an individual distributor might have a policy which precludes service to exhibitors who are not able or willing to pay some stipulated minimum amount (such as $25), on the grounds that it would not be worthwhile to service the print, ship the picture, perform the bookkeeping work in connection with the rental, collect the payments, return the print to the exchange, and inspect it, for less than this.

the fact that the picture is one that the exhibitor *must* screen or lose the good will of his customers and the astute distributor, of course, knows this and behaves accordingly. Hence, the exhibitor is not as independent as he might seem to be.

But, this is not all. Just as important is the fact that a motion picture distributor might withhold pictures from a "closed town" and thus lose revenue in short-run terms but gain revenue in long-run terms because of the better rental prices gained from the maneuver, when the monopsonist capitulates. It may be, also, that a distributor would encourage another exhibitor to enter this territory in order to provide the competition necessary to establish a satisfactory price.[26] One may conclude from this that models are useful in empirical price discrimination studies, at least to a limited extent.

The Applicability of Models in Later Studies

Consideration thus far has been given mainly to the methodology of studies made in past years. Attention now will be focused on several aspects of a study, just published, on competition and price making in supermarket operations,[27] as well as on a study of auction pricing which has been in progress for some time but which is not yet completed.

COMPETITION AND PRICE MAKING IN SUPERMARKET OPERATIONS

Recently I worked for several years on a study of the nature of competition and price making in supermarket operations. The basic question here was, how do such institutions behave competitively? The method of investigation utilized was first to select the market area and the segment of the market structure to be studied, and then to seek answers to specific questions relating to competitive behavior. This suggests some reliance on implicit models, at least.

[26] Before the 1946–48 decree which forbade integration of distribution and exhibition operations, a distributor might simply have established another theater in a "closed town" or have threatened to do so, with somewhat the same result.

[27] Ralph Cassady, Jr., *Competition and Price Making in Food Retailing* (New York, Ronald Press, 1962).

Multiphase pricing. One discovery that was made fairly early in the supermarket study (although it may be surprising how long this actually took!) is that pricing at the retail level is not a single problem but is really a multiphase activity. That is, the price is not simply made once and for all but must be made and remade at various times during the retailing process. The problem here is that the investigator must search blindly, with little to guide him but his own imagination. When one does not even know what he is looking for, the use of models is, to say the least, limited.

It is interesting that no one in the industry seemed to fully realize the multiphase nature of retail pricing. We stumbled onto the possibility that this was so when my research assistant brought in what appeared to be conflicting answers, from different respondents, to the question, "What are the actual steps that the supermarket price maker takes in the pricing of the product?" In pondering this apparent dilemma, I considered that the pricing process might consist not simply of a single act at all but may involve several actions which may differ substantially at different phases of the marketing process.

With this multiphase hypothesis in mind, therefore, I began to think in terms of the possible varying circumstances which require price-making decisions. The first differentiation which suggested itself was between the pricing of a newly stocked item at the time the product was initially acquired and the repricing of the product for promotional purposes in connection with week-end specials at some subsequent time. Later, two other quite different circumstances requiring price-making decisions were thought of: the pricing of various products at the time the institution was first established (i.e., the use of penetration pricing) and pricing at the time semipermanent price increases or decreases became necessary. Once this simple model was constructed, the rest was easy.

In my view, limited use can be made of models in the study of retail pricing in its various aspects. In this analysis of multiphase pricing, for example, what was necessary was not so much preconceived notions about how competitors behave, but fresh insights relating to additional information about actual competitive behavior. Even here, guidance may be derived from a model (e.g., oligopoly), assuming, of course, that such models are considered only as hypothetical in nature. In addition, new models can be constructed for the solution of special problems.[28]

There is even, as has been pointed out, some applicability here for a marginal approach to pricing (in itself a kind of model). For example, one problem that arises in connection with the pricing of new products is the decision as to whether to purchase or not to purchase a particular product. The basic question in considering the addition of a new item is whether the marginal revenue earned will exceed the marginal cost incurred. But this analysis must be pushed further. One must include in the final calculation marginal cost–marginal revenue information regarding other alternative uses for the shelf space which would be needed for the new product, and an estimate of the effect of the various alternative items on sales of other products in the complex of commodities offered. Thus, even in this situation there may be opportunities for the application of a kind of modified marginal revenue–marginal cost model.[29]

Variable-margin pricing. In the investigation of price making in food retailing, one begins very early to hear about what is called sliding scale pricing, or variable-margin pricing. This concept is based on the fact that retail margins on grocery items vary considerably from one another (from 2 percent or even a minus figure to as much as 50 percent of sales), depending, to some extent, evidently, on the sales rate of the items.

However, the term "sliding scale" erroneously suggests that the retail vendor marks up goods on a basis of some sort of variable

[28] See particularly pp. 38, 41, and 42.
[29] The marginal analysis is practicable in this instance because in applying it (a) one does not have to know too much about consumer demand, (b) price changes will not be expected to occur with every fluctuation in market conditions, and (c) it is not assumed that sales will be limited by the short-run profit considerations relating to the individual item.

markup chart, and that this chart becomes an instrument used by the price maker in his price-making activities. Actually, the variable margins are the result of historical fact which in turn is based on competitive moves and countermoves in the past, and while the individual vendor may be guided by previous margins, he keeps one eye on relevant competitors so that he will not be undersold. Thus, variable margins are not so much the basis of retail pricing as they are the result of prices which are determined in other ways (see Table 1).

TABLE 1. SELECTED MERCHANDISE ITEMS CLASSIFIED ON A BASIS OF PERCENTAGE MARGIN AND DOLLAR MARGIN EARNED, FOR THE 12 WEEKS, FEBRUARY 25–MAY 18, 1957

High percentage margin, high dollar margin				High percentage margin, low dollar margin			
Item	Percent margin	Dollar sales	Dollar margin	Item	Percent margin	Dollar sales	Dollar margin
Lettuce	35.7	14,298	5,104	Cough drops	33.8	154	52
Luncheon meats, bulk	27.0	39,456	10,656	Lighter fluid	43.0	128	55
Orange juice, frozen	20.4	16,725	3,408	Safety pins	52.3	52	25

Low percentage margin, high dollar margin				Low percentage margin, low dollar margin			
Item	Percent margin	Dollar sales	Dollar margin	Item	Percent margin	Dollar sales	Dollar margin
Cigarettes	5.7	84,447	4,801	Buttermilk	7.9	655	88
Coffee, regular	5.7	49,064	2,813	Tomato soup	7.7	4,586	351
Milk, fresh	7.7	51,042	3,934	Watermelon	8.1	917	74

Source: Basic data derived from "Super Valu Study," (New York, *Progressive Grocer*, 1958).

Offhand, one might gain the notion that variable-margin pricing means that the retail price structure in which differing margins are found is discriminatory per se. While this may be so, it does not necessarily follow, because while percentage margins may be higher for one product than for another, the unit dollar margins may be considerably lower. A further consideration might be the variation in unit-sales volume. Thus a product with a low percentage margin might produce a large amount of dollar margin, while another product with a high percentage margin might produce only small amounts of dollar margin. As can be seen from the data in Table 1, there are wide variations in margins in both percentage and dollar terms. These may be classified as follows: (a) high percentage and high dollar margins, (b) high percentage but low dollar margins, (c) low percentage but high dollar margins, and (d) low percentage and low dollar margins.

One may easily infer from this that while percentage margins vary considerably among products, low percentage margins do not necessarily result in low profits, even leaving leader pricing out of our calculations. One may also infer that speaking glibly about price discrimination in connection with variable-margin pricing is dangerous, not only because percentage margins and unit dollar margins may not gibe, but because cost variations may offset any percentage margin variations. It would appear that there would be little opportunity for using models in research in this area.

Loss leader pricing. Another concept relating to the study of supermarket competition and price making might be worth considering at this point. This concept is based on the fact that one does not need to drop prices on his whole line of products in order to attract custom but needs only drop them on certain key items (i.e., those which are purchased often and are thus important to consumer buyers). In analyzing the loss leader problem one may (perhaps, should) employ a model of sorts. We might call this the price elasticity—cross elasticity consumer-behavioral complex, and it would, in simplest terms, involve the elasticity of demand for the product-service of one vendor, and the impact of price changes by one vendor on the amount taken of the product of other vendors, as well as on other products in the price cutter's own lines.

Leader pricing is therefore dependent not only on price elasticity but also depends substantially for success on the application of one more principle—namely, cross-elasticity of demand. That is, one must first attract custom from other retail vendors by the use of "red-

hot specials" (the impact of this on rival vendors would be an example of direct cross-elasticity) [30] but assume that the patrons of
other institutions attracted by leader items will remain to purchase
complementary items. This, then, means that the impact of the low
price of the price cutter is that of increasing sales of the price cutter's
other offerings through the principle of inverse cross-elasticity. This
gain will be offset to some extent, however, by the heavy impact on
sales of competitive brands when one brand is used as a price leader,
especially if the price cut item is a well- and favorably-known brand.
In other words, consideration must be given also to cross-elasticity
of demand between price-cut and non-price-cut brands in the price
cutter's own institution.

It becomes quite clear, therefore, that a fairly complex model may
be utilized in connection with leader pricing. This consists of (a)
price elasticity for the product-service of the price-cutting firm (b)
direct cross-elasticity of demand as applied to competitive offerings
(c) direct cross-elasticity among the price cutter's brands of the particular item which was reduced in price, and (d) inverse cross-elasticity of demand as applied to the price cutter's complementary items.
The various segments of this model (if it may be designated as such)
are illustrated in Fig. 2.

While reasonable confidence can be placed in this model, one
may hesitate to attempt to quantify it. The reason for this is that relatively little is known about the impact of various price reductions
on sales volume and, in fact, one would suspect that impacts would
vary with the type of product, the particular brand, the market area,
the time of year, the day of the week, the time interval between price
reductions on the same item, and so on. The model in this instance,

---

[30] One must be careful to distinguish between direct elasticity for the product-
service of a vendor (who reduces the price of his offering with sales-expanding
results) and the cross-elasticity of demand (or impact on competitors who do
not cut). The former may be substantial in amount (because the increase in
amounts taken is concentrated on one vendor), while the latter may be negligible
(because the impact is dispersed over a number of competitors). If so, the price
cutter may attain the double advantage of gaining increased sales without being
subjected to retaliatory action by rival vendors.

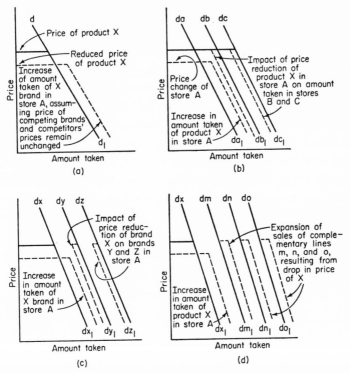

Fig. 2. Elasticity and cross-elasticity complex underlying loss-leader selling

(a) Price elasticity for product-service of store A; (b) cross-elasticity of demand for product-services of stores B and C; (c) cross-elasticity of demand for brands Y and Z in store A resulting from reduction in price of brand X; (d) inverse cross-elasticity between price-cut item X and complementary items M, N, and O.

however, indicates behavioral tendencies and thus has applicability as a guide to our thinking concerning dynamic market conditions and even to decision-making.

Increasing or decreasing shelf prices. The price maker must, from time to time, consider increasing or decreasing his shelf prices because of changing market conditions either at the supplier level or at the retail level. There may be considerable hesitation on the part of retailers to change prices not only because of the cost of repricing but because of the risk of an adverse competitive impact which might result from price changes. Some have even argued that "sticky" prices result from a peculiar demand situation developing out of oligopoly conditions.[31]

It has been argued, that the demand curve, for homogeneous prodducts, at least, produces a kink caused by a hesitation on the part of individual firms either to move up (because they might price themselves out of the market) or down (because their move would be matched by rivals and thus be neutralized). This hypothesis is illustrated in the left middle segment of Fig. 3.

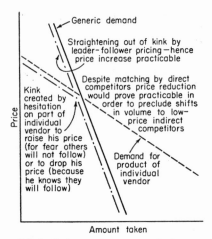

Fig. 3. Kinked demand curve and the conditions which vitiate price stability

While there probably is such a tendency present in some (perhaps most) competitive structures depicted by this model, there are offsetting factors at work which tend to weaken its validity and thus reduce its usefulness as a model. Among these factors [32] is the leader-

---

[31] See, for example, R. L. Hall and C. J. Hitch, "Price Theory and Business Behavior," *Oxford Economic Papers*, No. 2 (May, 1939), 12–45. See also Paul M. Sweezy, "Demand Under Conditions of Oligopoly," *The Journal of Political Economy* (August, 1939), pp. 568–73, and George J. Stigler, "The Kinky Oligopoly Demand Curve and Rigid Prices," *ibid.* (October, 1947), pp. 432–49.

[32] Others: (a) the product-service is not homogeneous, (b) the vendor is such a small factor in the market that his pricing moves are disregarded, or (c) the move is made secretly and thus cannot be followed.

follower pricing situation, which removes much of the risk from the raising of prices by individual vendors.[33] Thus, if an effective price leadership situation prevails, the kink would be straightened, because price makers would know that increases could be made with impunity. (See the upper right hand segment of Fig. 3.) For example, individual supermarkets undoubtedly raise prices on the assumption that others will do the same.

In considering price stability or flexibility below the prevailing price quotations, quite different considerations apply. The tendency toward stability in the downward segment is vitiated to some extent by certain other factors. One of these is the fact that under some circumstances (e.g., when reductions are only for temporary week-end "special" purposes) decreases will not ordinarily be followed. Another is that while a price decrease of a more permanent sort may be met by direct competitors (other supermarkets, say), such a move may be necessary as a defensive measure against invaders (discount-house grocery departments, for example) in the hope that inroads on sales can be averted.[34] Thus, prices are more flexible than they would at first glance appear to be, both above and below the prevailing price, and hence the kinked demand curve model loses much of its validity.

Intensity of competition. It has been over twenty years since J. M. Clark's "Toward A Concept of Workable Competition" appeared in the *American Economic Review*.[35] As we all know, this was an attempt to point out that given certain conditions competition does not need to be "pure" or even quasi-"pure" to be effective. Since the time of Clark's work much has been written on workability, and we have now come to think more specifically about the requisites for

[33] It does not remove all of the risk because there is often only one vendor who can lead others up, and if another were to try it he would fail in his purpose and be forced to retreat. See the discussion of this in Ralph Cassady, Jr., *Price Making and Price Behavior*, pp. 88–89.

[34] This same situation obtains in the gasoline industry (as in others, undoubtedly) where, along with major-brand stations, there are minor-brand outlets (i.e., an independent fringe) and individual major-brand stations from time to time drop their prices, knowing that they will be met by direct competitors, in order to reduce the independent-outlet/major-outlet differential and thus protect or regain what they consider to be their share of the market.

[35] June, 1940, pp. 241–56.

workability. Thus the factors required are said to include: (a) the existence of alternative sources of supply, (b) independence of action by vendors in seeking buyer custom, (c) absence of substantial control of supply by any one seller, and (d) easy access to markets.

This group of factors, of course, constitutes a kind of model which might be applied to actual competitive structures in order to form a basis for a judgment as to whether they are, in fact, effectively competitive. Indeed, an application of this formula was made in one of my studies several years ago, but with something less than satisfying results.[36] The source of my dissatisfaction with this model is that it is so easily misapplied. Actually, it is only hypothetical (i.e., unproved) at this stage of our knowledge and, as such, it should be mainly utilized in focusing attention on areas where microeconomic investigations may be used to confirm or vitiate the tentative conclusions. The workable competition model certainly should not, at this stage, be used as an inductively-based standard for determining the effectiveness of existing institutions or systems.[37]

But the discussion of competitive effectiveness thus far has been only preliminary to a suggestion for a further step in evaluating the vigor of competition—namely, the attempt to define and measure competitive intensity, and, in fact, to discover the source of intensive competitive conditions. In the solution of this problem one cannot employ ready-made models because such models have not as yet been developed. In fact, the basic problem is to construct a kind of model of a competitive condition in which intensity would likely be found.

I have been interested in the problem of competitive intensity for some time and have, in fact, made some suggestions along this line in the new supermarket study to which reference was made above.[38] Although these are still hypothetical and will likely remain so in-

[36] See Cassady, *Price Making and Price Behavior*, particularly pp. 335–41.

[37] See the doubts cast on the validity of the workability concept in Edward S. Mason's "The Current Status of the Monopoly Problem in the United States," *Harvard Law Review* (June, 1949), particularly pp. 1269–71.

[38] Cassady, *Food Retailing*, pp. 108–13.

definitely, they may have some relevance to the discussions here. The problem of competitive intensity involves many important subquestions, including the precise meaning of the term, the factors affecting the condition of competitive intensity, and the market results which one might expect from intensive competitive conditions.

Let us start by hypothesizing that, while competition may be effective in the supermarket field, rivalry may be intensive in some market areas, and even neighborhoods, but not in others, and that competitive intensity may vary considerably from time to time with changing circumstances, so that competition may be "easy" at one time and "tough" at another. We may go at least one step further and make some guesses regarding the circumstances which give rise to changing competitive intensity, although these are still unconfirmed. These include the presence of a new entrant who, to the extent that he acquires sales volume, gains it at the expense of others, and/or some competitor who is young and vigorous and aggressive minded and who, as a result, will, and in fact loves to, compete hard. These are only two of many possible factors which might underlie intensive competition. The "guessers" [39] among us could perhaps supply additional ones.

This suggests that it remains for empirical research to determine whether such varying-intensity situations actually exist—if so, what circumstances give rise to competitive intensity and how such conditions manifest themselves in terms of market results. It suggests, also, the possibility of using a deductively constructed model as a hypothetical tool in an actual market investigation in order to focus the researcher's attention on the relevant issues. [40] Through this method one may be able to substitute factually based theory for

[39] See the brilliant discussion of the roles of "guessers" and "accumulators" in natural science research contained in "Back to Aristotle," the first of a series of lectures by Wilder D. Bancroft on The Methods of Research [*The Rice Institute Pamphlet*, Vol. XV, No. 4 (October, 1928), pp. 167–223].

[40] Before doing this one would, of course, have to establish some criteria for competitive intensity which would be in my view quite possible, though perhaps difficult.

guesswork, and thus make some progress in model building into the bargain.

PRICE MAKING BY AUCTION PROCESS

It might be interesting to note that I have been working, on and off for some years, now, on another aspect of price making—namely, price making by auction system. My interest in this subject started some years ago, when I initiated a study of certain aspects of the fishery industry in preparation for a paper which was given at a joint International Economic Association—Food and Agriculture Organization conference in Rome, in the early fall of 1956.

This interesting method of buyer-set pricing is brought forcefully to the attention of a person studying fish marketing because auctioning is for various reasons almost universally employed in this trade at the primary distribution level (i.e., in sales by the fishermen to primary distributors and processors). This introduction to this age-old price-making scheme was followed in 1958 by a world-wide study of fish distribution, with special emphasis on the auction method of price making.

An extended discussion of this study is not in order at this time but I would like to point out the relevancy of the use of models in a study such as this, limited though it may be. While there is little chance, one would think, of employing any formal model in such studies at this time, if only because we do not know enough about this price-making process to construct one, we must not lose sight of the relevance of basic market factors in our analysis of the problem.

There is such a paucity of knowledge about auction pricing that one tends to be overwhelmed by particular questions. For example, what is the precise effect of numbers of traders per se on auction prices; to what extent does secrecy in bidding have a bearing on price results; how important is the effect of the method of auctioning—the English auction, the Dutch auction, the Japanese simultaneous-bidding scheme, the handclasp bidding method, the written-bid system—on prices; what is the significance of the catalogue in auction selling; what, if any, influence may the auctioneer himself have on auction results; and what price patterns may one expect to find during the auction-sales period? Moreover, what effect, if any, does the presence of dealers have in an auction patronized in part, at least, by consumer-buyers, or vice versa (as in an art auction)? What about the effect of certain natural phenomena (such as typhoons) on the price results (in fish markets, say)? [41]

There is little doubt that answers to these and other questions will be forthcoming as a result of intelligent use of the investigatory process. The question is: To what extent, if at all, can models be advantageously employed in prosecuting this study? In my thinking about the problem recently, in preparation for the resumption of this investigation, the possibility of a taxonomic approach—the employment of a simple supply-demand-competition model as an analytical tool—has become more and more intriguing as a starting point. This model should serve to focus attention on the relevant price-influencing factors in the full expectation that the market results would be indicated and the conditioning influences will be revealed, by the research effort so-exerted. Thus, a model of sorts is useful, even here.

Conclusions

It should be obvious that little can be accomplished by gathering data for their own sake—that is, without some purpose or plan. Thus, one should not approach a market study without some model in mind, if only the delineation of the particular market area and the segment of the market structure being placed under glass. But, in addition, there usually is some awareness on the part of the investigator of the nature of demand and supply as well as the competitive structure which one might find in the area under study, and often the model is even more explicit.[42] In considering the applica-

---

[41] It is interesting that typhoons may have the effect of raising prices (if such a storm appears imminent and there is a chance that fishing craft will be delayed) or depressing prices (if supplies are on hand but customers are unable to get to the market to shop).

[42] This can be inferred from the studies discussed above as well as from other

bility of models one might classify their usefulness in four ways: they
may be 1) very useful in all situations; 2) fairly useful in all situations; 3) quite useful in some situations but not in others; and 4)
not useful in any situation.

In this paper, consideration is given to the usefulness of models
mainly from one point of view—that of the market researcher.[43]

studies by this author which include: 1) The employment of a model consisting
of the concept of interarea competition and profit and loss-balance sheet analysis
for evaluating the small-city distribution system. Ralph Cassady, Jr. and Harry J.
Ostlund, *The Retail Distribution Structure of the Small City* (Minneapolis, The
University of Minnesota Press, 1935). 2) The actual working of a chain store's
price policy of meeting competitors' lowest prices item by item, market by
market, and day by day, by means of a model composed of simultaneous comparisons between the chain's prices and those of competitors, to determine
whether the firm's prices were in fact lower than the average in every market
area, as they should have been assuming the policy were adhered to. Ralph
Cassady, Jr. and E. T. Grether, "Locality Price Differentials in the Western
Retail Grocery Trade," *Harvard Business Review* (Winter, 1943), pp. 190–206.
3) The impact of a program of vertical integration on chain store prices and
profits on a basis of a model consisting of a comparative analysis of vertically
integrated, semi-integrated, and nonintegrated operations, and an evaluation of
the effect of each type of operation on various cost elements of the production-
distribution process (such as manufacturing, labor relations, sales promotion,
and so on). Study made for large, integrated concern, unpublished. 4)
Determining the price advantage, if any, of acquiring certain agricultural
commodities early in the season rather than on a hand-to-mouth basis during
the season, by means of a model consisting of a series of price-behavior studies
for various years depicting the daily price quotations of the particular commodity
under investigation. Study made for large integrated concern, unpublished.
5) An investigation of the world-wide demand for, and the marketing of,
tuna fish by the use of the distribution-channel model, including methods of title
transference. Cassady, "World Wide Expansion of the Market for Tuna," Food
and Agriculture Organization of the United Nations, unpublished. 6) A microeconomic analysis of certain trade-restraining activities by means of an exclu-
sionary-tactic model designed to isolate and evaluate this type of behavior. Ralph
Cassady, Jr., and William F. Brown, "Exclusionary Tactics in American Business
Competition: An Historical Analysis," *UCLA Law Review* (January, 1961), pp.
88–134.
    [43] I consider myself primarily a pure researcher, interested in seeking the truth
for truth's sake, but occasionally I put on another hat and attempt to solve a
practical market problem with profit maximization as the goal. In so doing, I
often find it useful to utilize some type of economic model. One such example
was a recent attempt to advise a franchised distributor on a Robinson-Patman
Act 2(d)(e) problem (the law requires any services or allowances made by a
firm to be granted to competitors on "proportionally equal terms"). Ordinarily,

From this viewpoint, one must admit, models do indeed serve an important purpose at one or more stages of the investigatory process —pre-data-gathering, data-gathering, and post-data-gathering.

First of all, models indicate the direction to be taken and assist the researcher in retaining perspective as he enters a new field of investigation.[44] Models, in the second place, may act as a focus for the gathering of data relevant to the solution of the problem, and thus, in a real sense, contribute to problem solving.

In the third place, they may be useful as hypothetical standards against which actual findings can be compared for evaluation purposes. A properly constructed model might, in the fourth place, serve as a kind of control or mechanism for determining market results which would obtain under somewhat different conditions than those which actually prevail.[45] Finally, even in the absence of market data,

---

it would appear to be unnecessary to grant advertising allowances to dealers miles apart. But if they are indirectly competitive with one another because of partially overlapping trading areas which transmit effects from one market area to another, they may be, in theory, at least, in competition with one another and, if so, allowances given one would have to be given the other on "proportionally equal terms." Thus, the overlapping market areas model serves as a useful tool in the solution of this practical problem.

[44] For example, the researcher can evaluate the presence or absence of homogeneity of product-service, the existence of an independent competitive fringe, or what not, which may be significant market factors in price investigations.

[45] Many of the electrical firms involved in the 1961 General Electric price fixing conspiracy, anticipating private damage suits following the government's action, pleaded *nolo contendere*, with a result that there was no testimony providing details of the alleged conspiracy. This, of course, makes for great difficulty when firms allegedly damaged by the trade-restraining activity have to prove that prices of electrical equipment were higher than they would have been without the conspiracy. Some way, therefore, has to be found to compare the prices paid and the prices which would have been paid under conditions which do not exist. The method selected for accomplishing this, reportedly, is the construction of a hypothetical statistical model of the electrical-manufacturing business, based on conditions before the conspiracy, and adjusting the data to allow for general economic trends during the conspiracy years. See *Time Magazine* (December 15, 1961), p. 80.

Some sort of model is needed by the plaintiff in any private antitrust suit which is up on merits (not on some procedural issue), because the juries, in assessing damages, must have some basis for the computation of the damage figure. Thus, a firm which is seeking damages may plan to use a model based

models may be useful in indicating tendencies which might serve in predicting market moves, as in the case of curled demand [46] or the kinked demand curve, for example.[47]

Models may be employed not only as foci for investigations but also as the subjects of investigations, per se. Models are, by their very nature, simplified mechanisms; therefore they tend to be superficial as compared with actual market conditions, and may even be invalid, in part. One problem would be that of testing the validity of the model against actual market behavior with the object of improving it. However, if the investigator possesses sufficient intellectual curiosity and perspective he can employ a model until a certain point is reached in the investigation and then proceed, without benefit of model, to probe more deeply.

And if he follows this course and comes up with new market data these can be used, in turn, to refine the model and thus enhance its usefulness for other purposes.[48] However, it will be a long time, one

---

on erstwhile earning figures (before trade-restraining activities began) or one based on present earning power of some competitive operation which is free from such restraints. Such models must be utilized by the courts in treble damage actions if damage computations are to be anything more than guesswork. For an example of the application of such models in a motion picture industry suit, see *Bigelow, et al.* v. *RKO Radio Pictures, Inc., et al.*, 327 U.S. 251, 257–60 (1946).

[46] This refers to the hypothesis that under certain conditions (e.g., if the price is somewhat lower than that of a well- and favorably-known brand) low price might be related in consumers' minds to low quality, and that the demand curve for such an item falls away to the right in the upper part of the schedule but curls back toward the vertical axis in the lower reaches. See Fig. 4(d).

[47] See Fig. 3.

[48] Consider, for example: 1) The impact of the element of time on demand and price elasticity. Ralph Cassady, Jr., "The Time Element and Demand Analysis," chapter 12 in *Theory in Marketing*, Cox and Alderson, eds. (Chicago, Richard D. Irwin, Inc., 1950). 2) The actual behavior of competitors under conditions of differentiated oligopoly. Cassady and Jones, *Nature of Competition in Gasoline Distribution*, chapters VII–X. 3) Monopolistic competition and price discrimination. Ralph Cassady, Jr., and E. T. Grether, "The Proper Interpretation of 'Like Grade and Quality' Within the Meaning of Section 2(a) of the Robinson-Patman Act," *Southern California Law Review* (April, 1957), pp. 241–79. 4) The effect of time on the dissipation of monopolistic control. Ralph Cassady, Jr., "Monopoly in Motion Picture Production and Distribution: 1908–1915," *Southern California Law Review* (Summer, 1959), pp. 325–90.

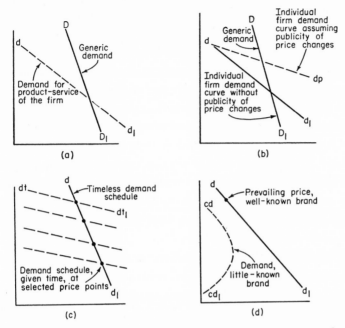

Fig. 4. (a) Price elasticities for individual-firm and generic-product demand; (b) price elasticity of demand with and without publicity; (c) relationship of price elasticity with and without time element; (d) association of low quality and low price on demand

would think, before we will be able to lean very heavily on models for precise solutions of market problems, if only because there is so little we know about actual market phenomena and the results cannot be better than the data used to furnish precision to the model. There is some question, therefore, whether human behavior can be predicted with accuracy, even where a quantified model is employed.

Despite the foregoing limitations, one might conclude that a serious researcher in the field of market competition and prices, who expects to make penetrating analyses of market phenomena and market behavior, must, to some extent, employ models. For example, he would get nowhere without the perfect-competition model and its counterpart, the nonperfect-competition model, as a guide to his observations and to his thinking. And he is just as dependent on various nature-of-demand models, including those distinguishing between generic demand and demand for the individual firm [Fig. 4(a)] evaluating the presence of publicity of market moves [Fig. 4(b)] appraising the existence of the element of time in considering impacts of price changes [Fig. 4(c)] indicating the effect of the association of low prices and low quality in the minds of buyers [Fig. 4(d)] and the like, for guidance in the consumer-behavior area.

But, regardless of the amount of help we can obtain from models in our research into actual market phenomena, we should not lean too heavily on them, because a model is barren per se. It is not a source of information but only a tool, albeit a valuable one. Even the most refined models are only instruments of analysis and will not provide the market data which are so badly needed by the empirical researchers. We must, therefore, on the one hand, abhor the rejection of the use of such tools by market researchers (who in effect would thus be "grubbing with their hands" when a more effective job could be done with proper implements), but must, on the other hand, avoid the use of these tools as though they were ends in themselves (because by so doing we would be failing in our responsibilities of adding to our rather poor stock of knowledge regarding market mechanisms).

One final point: While there is no question about the need for models in market research, the question is how to obtain sounder models which accurately reflect actual consumer and/or competitive behavior patterns. One way of doing this is to make more microeconomic studies for the purpose of verifying or vitiating presently-held assumptions and, where indicated, to replace these with more realistic models. This task may be most effectively accomplished by the market researcher and the economic theorist working in collaboration.[49] It can only be hoped that such teams can be organized for this task in the not-too-distant future.

[49] It is important to note, in this connection, that the refining of traditional models by findings from empirical investigations can probably best be done not by theoretical economists becoming empiricists or by empirical researchers becoming theoreticians, but by direct cooperative effort between the two.

COMMENTS

By Richard B. Heflebower

Taking liberties with a famous sentence of the Bard of Avon, Ralph "Antony" Cassady has come not to bury price theory but to praise it—so faintly and obliquely that had it human form, it might wish it were dead. A funeral oration over the remains of a man of note, or an appraisal of a theoretical framework, must reflect understanding of the objective of the man's career, or of the theoretical system, and appraise accurately the application of his or its tenets. Such does not characterize Cassady's consideration of "The Role of Economic Models in Market Price Studies." As a consequence, I shall be cast in the role of defending the relevance of price theory to such research, to a higher degree than I would choose were I to present a full-length paper.

Running through Cassady's paper is a confusion between economic theory and the empirical values of variables. Theory is devoid of empirical content; it specifies the empirical evidence that is relevant and the functional relationship among variables. But the estimates have to be made by the decision maker, or the analyst. Once that is done, predictions can be made and compared with observed outcomes. Most of Cassady's expressions of doubt about the use of economic models—he sometimes gives the idea that they are ready made and do not have to be checked, and possibly recast, for each problem—indicate that he is really concerned with the difficulty of estimation. This has nothing to do with the usefulness of the model. The issue, rather, is whether a model formulated out of the relevant parts of price theory, when estimates have been made of the prescribed variables, enables one to make accurate predictions.

Before turning to the problem of estimation, it is necessary to consider the time period to which the model is to apply. Dr. Cassady erroneously says that according to marginal analysis "prices would presumably be set in such a way as to maximize net revenue in short-run terms." Harrod has asserted that such a view of the firm's objective is wrong, that revenue curves of firms are far more elastic in the long run, and that the usual conclusions, in the ordinal sense, about welfare effects of imperfect markets are correspondingly wrong.[1] But Chamberlin claims that his analysis is long run. Actually, the theory of the firm is one of maximizing the present value of the firm. Only when that end is served by maximizing

[1] R. F. Harrod, *Economic Essays* (New York, Harcourt Brace, 1952), pp. 139–87.

profits (in the accounting sense) in the short run, is it rational to do so, as it is in pure and perfect competition. Otherwise, maximization of profits in the short run is apt to be inconsistent with the long run. What would rectify all such errors would be to always introduce user cost into the analysis, a particularly useful step in understanding price-war situations, and one not recognized by Cassady.

Regardless of what is being maximized, Cassady is bothered by the fact that neither the business manager nor the market researcher advising him has good guess-estimates, let alone precise values, for the elasticity of demand, for changes in demand intensity, or for other variables. How, then, can profits be maximized? Again, the confusion may stem from the vision of pure and perfect competition for (it being static also) the existing price is a datum to which the firm adjusts. But that model is not operational; markets work because they are not pure and perfectly competitive. Hence, each seller has to estimate either future prices if the market is highly but not purely competitive, or, more often, he must have some idea of what would happen if he were to raise or lower his price. Indeed, if he is engaging in loss leading, he faces the estimating problem (about effects on sale of other items and responses of rivals) outlined by Cassady. Within the range that a seller is not fully disciplined by the market, that is, does not learn of errors that in the extreme could bring insolvency, his estimates of demand elasticity and its intensity are what is relevant. To the degree that the market researcher cannot measure the values of these variables, the management's economic and business function is to "pin the tail on the donkey." Furthermore, all such considerations as to cost in money form, or "costs" that are unfavorable reactions of customers, come under this rubric. The better estimator makes more money than does the poor one, *ceteris paribus*.

Outside the clearly competitive markets (as for agricultural staples) the problem the economist has as the analyst of the market performance is that rarely can more than ordinal-type estimates be made of the relevant variables. That is particularly true of cross-elasticities among close substitutes and of the elasticity of particular types of sellers' revenue curves. This does not forestall making some fairly conclusive statements about the character and social consequences of types of rivalry, particularly if the consideration thereof is integrated with a full exposition of the organizational features of the market.

A good example of this and of the adaptation of theory is Cassady's wrestling with what I term the unit of analysis problem. That has to do with whether to center attention on the item or on a broader concept of product and, separately, with the complex of interrelationships among items that are grouped by this broader concept. Chamberlin emphasized the ultimate in a narrow unit of analysis, a particular seller's brand of a particular sub-item of a product line, but with all such products separated by small but varying degrees of cross-elasticity. What Cassady shows is that there are useful groupings of brands for the identical or highly similar product physically, which restores market, or rather market-segment, analysis—a more accurate concept, empirically, and more useful than Chamberlin's "group."

Beyond this type of unit of analysis, Cassady demonstrates that for some problems the appropriate unit encompasses a family of items that make up a product line. In some cases, notably in the distributive trades, the appropriate unit crosses commodity lines and may, indeed, be a market-basket concept. Had Cassady gone on to point out explicitly that in the distributive trades and in some manufacturing, such as meat packing, the relevant "price" is the gross margin in a value added sense, and that the margin is for the "basket" as a whole, the picture would have been complete.

This does not mean that all interest in a narrowly defined product disappears, but rather, to use a military analogy, it is relegated to the tactical level. In contrast, the strategic or more fundamental price decisions, or observed market outcomes, have to do with groupings of brands for a physically identical good, for groups of items physically unlike but in the same line, or for groupings of commodities that tend to be brought together. All these, it seems to me, are extensions and adaptations of price theory that show the understanding and skill of the researcher.

But when Dr. Cassady comes to explaining the price (or margin) relationships among market segments or items in a product or distributional line, he vacillates between finding that theory asks the relevant questions and assuming that observed facts reflect blind reflection of earlier (and perhaps rational at that time) behavior. Even though he finds a fairly stable price differential between majors' and independents' brands of gasoline, he hesitates to put this in price theory terms and talks about strategies as if they were not reflective of cost and revenue considerations. On the other hand, he finds those considerations relevant when a new product is added to the line but he cannot see how the estimates of marginal costs or revenues may be affected by opportunity costs. He then refers to Joan Robinson's classic exposition of price discrimination as unrealistic. But, he uses it in his exposition of discrimination in rental of moving pictures and highlights the problems of estimating the elasticity of demand by various categories of buyers. Then he adds, but does not place in a game-theory context, the case of the single seller, single buyer in a locality. Going back to price relationships within a category, whether among submarkets for a product or among products sold together, as in a supermarket, Cassady indicates the price-cost or margin differences that exist often are "the result of historical facts," and concludes that there "would be little opportunity for using models in research in this area." But the appropriate model would specify the variables to be estimated; all that he has shown is the difficulty of estimating the values of variables in particular situations.

Cassady could have handled price analysis more effectively had he distinguished between the study of prices with given market parameters, and the forces giving rise to changes in those parameters and the consequences thereof on price performance. Is the source of a price war a change in the supply situation or of intensity of demand? Or does it (e.g., a price war in gasoline) originate in a new structural situation such as new, or lesser, sources of supply for independent brands, or an altered cross-elasticity between them and major brands? In the wholesale grocery trade, does price theory guide the exploration of the causes of structural change from a predominant two-step to vertically integrated distribution and the subsequent limited coexistence of the two structures? My guess is that much of the explanation lies in the success of product differentiation; an empirical conclusion, but one that calls for going beyond Chamberlinian economics to study the dynamics of differentiation.

The last observation provides a transition to what I see omitted from Cassady's paper, the real deficiencies in price theory. Some of these, however, can be corrected by major additions within the comparative static methodological framework. (That is not likely to be true of the oligopoly problems for I see no prospects of a formal theory within the classical technological utility function framework.) The experience of men with first-hand acquaintance with markets, such as Cassady, could be productive of new hypotheses. Except for one brief explanation that the kink in a seller's demand curve disappears by certain conditions of price leadership, Cassady seems not to visualize petroleum refining or department stores of a shopping center in oligopoly terms, nor does he see that the oligopolistic organization of wholesaling may explain why the grocery wholesalers were so slow in meeting the chain-store innovations. But certain of the steps needed to analyze the vertical structure of firms and markets can be carried out in the neoclassical tradition. The theory can be extended beyond a single transaction step between sellers implicitly alike in degree of vertical integration and final-consumer buyers. Except where vertical integration is an uncertainty-reducing device, it can be studied in static terms. Diversity in degree of vertical integration, whether the integration is "full-fledged" or "quasi," is not solely a feature of static equilibria; it is also a device for reacting to disequilibrating forces whether the disturbance stems from new values of a variable, with the structural aspects of the market undisturbed, or reflects a change in the structural parameters of the market. Herein lies a shortcoming of the theory of product differentiation, for success in bringing it about can alter a structural parameter, say, the vertical organization of the market, or after a lag, have a perverse effect on the cross-elasticity between the well-known and the other brands of a product. That is part, but only part, of the analytical problem where the product can be made a variable. The time lags and uncertainty involved can be handled only crudely, if at all, by comparative statics of price theory. That is only one of a family of dynamic problems, many of which have to do with the meaning and usability of a particular criterion of firm motivation, such as profit maximization, a topic that must certainly recur throughout these papers.

By Joel B. Dirlam

Professor Cassady has found that the conventional neoclassical theory of the firm has been of little assistance to him in conducting his studies of market behavior. Instead, he has relied on techniques paralleling those of Walton Hamilton and other institutionalists; analytical, but without rigorous and uniform models. His dissatisfaction with the textbook model is based primarily on its inability to explain short-run pricing behavior. Cassady would apparently retain, as useful to understanding long-term trends in market price behavior or relative price levels for similar groups of products, the concepts of supply and demand, but divorced from notions of equilibrium positions of firms related to long-run average cost curves.

I assume that I am not unique in sharing Cassady's distrust of textbook marginal analysis. I am not quite sure how Cassady intends his models to be used. His purpose appears to be a limited one, which limits the depth of his inquiry. I feel that Cassady could, by some additional introspection, clarify the purpose and level of explanation of his studies.

He does not successfully resolve the question of the purpose for which his models are constructed, in his introductory discussion of the usefulness of models, in his summaries of the various empirical studies he has made of pricing behavior, or in his *ad hoc* model.

Cassady's answer to these doubts would be that he wants to organize the data in such a way that we will be able, for instance, to predict a pricing change or to be convinced that we understand it (in the context of the model) after it has happened.

But, whether such a model is satisfactory depends upon what question we want answered. There are, from the standpoint of economics, questions more important than whether certain kinds of price behavior are likely to be found in a given industry. Cassady is, in effect, assuming that an explanation or prediction of price behavior satisfies standards of economic adequacy, if it is equivalent to that possessed by an intelligent trade journal reporter or pricing executive. The market-study technique will convey the feel of the market, through interview and immersion in price series and trade annals. The purpose of the market study approach, then, it seems fair to say, is to put the economist in as good a position as the National Petroleum News to predict when rising gasoline inventories, resulting from a high rate of output of fuel oil, will lead to a price war. And he can, with some assurance, pinpoint the spot where the war will break out, though he probably won't be able to say how long it will last, until there has been a distribution of the duration of price wars. Is this feel for the market, however, all we want from an economic model?

If it is, we can dismiss the textbooks, without regret. Whether or not the retail margins on grocery items are determined in accordance with $mc = mr$, or the rentals charged to different motion-picture theaters enable the producers to reflect the varying demand elasticities and to reach equality in different markets for the same product, would be a matter of indifference. As experts in motion-picture distribution, we can ride along with developments of the motion-picture distribution market, and we are not likely to be taken by surprise. Moreover, and differing here with Cassady, we will accept sporadic price warfare, in some markets, as part of the normal behavior pattern, since warfare achieves, by other means, the goals of diplomacy.

But the Cassady-type model, in spite of its virtues as compared with models built on assumptions divorced from reality, cannot, without revision, be utilized for more demanding economic purposes. This is not because it fails to offer a guide to the businessman in making the decisions necessary to reach his goal. This I do not regard as a deficiency. Rather, it seems to me to stop at the threshold of what is required if we are to advance economics as a study of behavior. We cannot rest with a level of understanding which embraces only the more-or-less accurately expressed formulae for pricing action by business firms, against the background of historical surveys of their interactions, numbers, sizes, and marketing practices. It seems to me we must go on to something more—to develop an insight into the internal development of the goals and the significance of the organization, history, personalities, and other factors of each of the firms we are interested in. Why are some firms aggressive, and others somnolent? How do goals get set? What part do pricing decisions play in the overall framework of decision making? If the firm is playing a game, is it Monopoly, Risk, or Scrabble? I am far from convinced that Cassady's approach in its present form can give us the answers to these questions, or similar ones, and without such answers it will prove difficult to transfer experience from one firm or industry to another.

Perhaps Cassady would reject this expansion of the purpose of his surveys and would, with some justification, protest that an economist has to get some limits to his universe; he cannot be responsible for everything that influences prices. Nevertheless, it seems to me that the peculiarities we are trying to understand in pricing are merely one phase, and not necessarily an independent one, of the behavior of business firms. A theory of the firm awaits a study that will embrace all of its activities and lead to generalizations applicable to new situations for a variety of purposes.

I am fully aware of the hazards and limitations of mixing noneconomic factors, as they are conventionally conceived, with the economics of the business firm. Perhaps, in a world where businessmen are so much aware of the importance the public attaches to the way in which they articulate their goals, and where their own views of their role, or the role of their firm, may not conform to the publicly expressed view, or may even be an unconsidered stereotype, economic studies of market behavior will never be able to make significant progress toward usable generalizations. We may be left with something comparable to the sociology of William Graham Sumner, which is where market-behavior studies appear to be today.

Linear programming, operations research, and kindred problem-solving techniques do not, it seems to me, provide an alternative approach to understanding market behavior in the large. Firms do hire technicians to solve inventory, ship-scheduling, feed-mix, and media-selection problems, and certain behavior patterns emerge when they do so. It requires little insight by the economist to discover that, in such cases, behavior conforms to a rather precise, mathematical model. But the behavior is, of course, that which lends itself to decision making by these techniques, which is to say, when uncertainties are reduced to a minimum. The newer techniques will have to be worked into our summaries, but they don't appear able to rescue economists from the dilemma of depending on interviews of conscious, far from disinterested parties. Nor can they provide goals. They are not techniques for understanding behavior, but constitute the types of behavior we are studying.

The broader and more significant aspects of changing market behavior will continue to call for more comprehensive investigational techniques, in essence, those summarized by Cassady in the conclusion to his paper. Starting with some basic insights and bents determined by his training and concern with aspect of scarcity, the economist will proceed to construct hypotheses, largely tailored anew for each market, though increasingly informed by experience in similar markets elsewhere. These hypotheses will be refined and reworked in the course of the investigation until an approach to a satisfactory explanation is reached. If the questions that concern us, as economists, about the market behavior of firms in steel, automobiles, drugs, and petroleum can be answered, it will be by extending the scope and depth, as well as the number, of market surveys, of which Cassady's are representative.

HOW WELL EXISTING MARKET
MODELS MEET THE NEEDS
OF BUSINESSMEN

BY ALFRED R. OXENFELDT, PROFESSOR
OF MARKETING, THE GRADUATE SCHOOL OF BUSINESS,
COLUMBIA UNIVERSITY

Strenuous efforts to find someone to write this paper who is well versed in price theory and has also been responsible for business investment or pricing decisions uncovered very few persons with these qualifications. Almost all of these people said that they were not well equipped to discuss the usefulness of market models for businessmen because they had not "kept up with theory"—which is significant in itself. Also, the press of business responsibilities did not allow any one of them the time to prepare a paper for this conference. As a penalty for my failure to persuade a qualified person to accept the assignment, it was given to me. To compensate for my lack of direct responsibility for operating business decisions, I have interviewed most of the persons who were or might properly have been invited to prepare this paper.

Although the topic of this paper is clear, it would profit from refinement. First, the needs of businessmen which might be served by the market models of price theory must be identified—that is, in what decision areas might price theory possibly assist businessmen? Second, the form in which market models might and do help businessmen must be specified. Third, a valid standard for measuring the contribution of market models to business decisions is required.

The areas in which price theory might help businessmen will be divided, here, into three classes: price decisions, investment decisions, and "all others." This paper will be structured around this classification, which, though admittedly arbitrary, provides room for all types of decisions. Non-price decisions will not be passed over completely, though very little space will be devoted to them. Models are aids in problem solving; they most emphatically are not solutions in themselves. They are aids to understanding, rather than descriptions. Viewed in this perspective, the models of price theory must be evaluated by the following tests: 1) Do they direct attention to the relevant factors operating in the real world? 2) Do they enhance the understanding of these factors and their interrelationships? 3) Do they formulate problems in a manner that facilitates the collection of data required to make proper decisions?

A valid yardstick for measuring the value of market models to businessmen is elusive. Obviously, someone who knows price theory should not be compared with someone who consciously employs no models at all. Executives who are unfamiliar with the models of price theory almost certainly employ other models in arriving at their decisions. To assess the value of the market models of price theory, one should compare them with other models—and most particularly with those which businessmen untutored in price theory develop for themselves.

As one would expect, the models of price theory are particularly relevant to business decisions about price—and most of this paper discusses their value in price decisions. However, the other areas of business decisions to which price theory might be applied, and its value in those areas, will be sketched first.

Investment Decisions

The essential ingredients of investment decisions are: a time dimension, the expected stream of income that the acquired asset will produce over its economic life, and the expected costs that will be incurred over that period to obtain that income. The most useful concepts relevant to most investment decisions include discounting to adjust income for the fact that present income is more valuable than future income, the life-cycle changes in demand for a product or industry, and the course of technological and unit-cost changes as a product matures. These concepts lie outside the market models of price theory.

Market models admit time considerations only in a limited and contrived manner; demand for the total product is assumed to be unchanging; costs are permitted to vary only with changes in output and as passage of time admits of changes in scale; the major change admitted into the models with the passing of time is the entry or exit of firms from the market. Thus, dynamism is absent from in the traditional market models of price theory. But investment represents the concern of major executives, rather than clerks, for the very reason that markets are dynamic and are buffeted by many forces that vary over time. More specifically, the market models of price theory do not take account of the systematic changes in demand for goods, services, securities, or funds, with the passage of time. They also fail to alert decision makers to the necessity of forecasting systematic changes in demand and of expecting the unexpected.

Conditions of cost receive no more adequate treatment than does demand in the market models of price theory, from the standpoint of someone using them to make investment decisions. Changes in technology, engineering discoveries, and the perfection of production technique with the passage of time are passed over by the market models (however much the theorists themselves might know about these matters).

In other words, executives who are estimating of the pattern of revenues and costs over the life of an investment—and the length of its life—get relatively little help from the market models of price theory. These models might even encourage unsophisticated users of models to project the present far into the future—predicting perhaps the most unlikely outcome of all.

Two possible exceptions to this critical assessment should be noted: first, price theory assists in the preparation of a long-term demand or price forecast; second, familiarity with price theory might lead decision makers to ask—and possibly help them to answer—questions about the type of market structure that would develop for a product whose introduction was considered.

Investment decisions, especially those involving a commitment for a long period, inevitably rest upon long-term market forecasts. Such forecasts must be built upon an analysis of the basic-demand forces affecting the product. Although the forces involved often are non-economic, persons with training in formal economics, and particularly in price theory, apparently are more successful in long-term forecasting than persons with other types of training. One executive of a large petroleum company attributed the mistaken long-term price forecasts by high-level executives of his industry to the fact that their academic training was mainly in the field of engineering. (They hold positions in fields like finance and marketing.) He said that his own formal economics training was a significant help to him in making a long-term price forecast and in being able to present it in a manner that won acceptance by top management. Other men of equally high native intelligence with engineering backgrounds went far wrong in their forecasts of petroleum prices, for they simply projected past trends—even though the basic market forces had clearly changed. This executive believes that the investment department of every large firm should include someone who is informed about the determinants of price.

Investment decisions, when they involve new products, require consideration of the type of market structure that will develop as the product matures. Would businessmen with no training in price theory ignore this question, or would market models assist them to make such a forecast—possibly by posing questions in an illuminating manner? If an executive who had not studied price theory were asked to guess, on the basis of his business acumen, what degree and form of competitive pressure would arise for a particular item, would he do less well than a master of market models? I have neither experienced nor observed any perceptible advantage resulting from familiarity with market models in dealing with problems of this sort. What appear to be determining factors in specific cases—like the level of rivals' technical competence, the speed with which competitors might "discover" and attempt to imitate the product, the importance to customers of your having been "first," the likelihood that your firm can maintain technical leadership for a long time by virtue of its initial advantage, the number of firms that have and would be willing to risk the resources required to produce efficiently, the availability of suitable distribution outlets for other producers, and the like—again lie outside the province of market models.

In considering the use of market models in business decisions, one finds time and again that theoretical models take account of very few—and extremely obvious—forces. Their main value to someone making a concrete decision is not in calling his attention to factors that are unknown to him. On the contrary, the practitioner's models are vastly more complex and complete than the theorist's. It is rather in the way the problem is formulated and in the precision and rigor of the concepts employed that a model is likely to be of help in making concrete decisions. This type of value is very difficult to identify and measure. Specifically, with respect to investment decisions, market models appear to offer little on either score.

Nonprice and Noninvestment Business Decisions

There are not many business matters, beyond price and investment decisions, to which the market models of price theory are relevant. One stands out, however, as important and growing in importance: the use of these models in matters of public policy and public relations. More specifically, businessmen are aided materially by a knowledge of the market models of price theory in: 1) predicting the reactions of regulatory authorities concerned with antitrust enforcement and with rate regulation; 2) predicting the likelihood that a contemplated action could be justified to the satisfaction of the relevant regulatory agency; and 3) presenting justifications to the public or to a congressional investigating committee for actions or existing arrangements. Businessmen recognize that the regulatory authorities and the courts are strongly influenced by price theory; they know that it would help their cause if they could justify their behavior in terms that are consistent with that theory.

Other business decisions to which the market models of price theory are sometimes relevant include: wage determination, international trade decisions, fixing of terms with resellers, choices between sell or lease, and between make or buy.

The market models of price theory were not originally developed by persons intent upon providing intellectual aids to businessmen. Price theorists, at least until fairly recently, were concerned solely with understanding broad forces affecting the utilization of economic resources and with formulating public policy. Use of the market models of price theory for other and by-product purposes has, however, reached the point where the by-product seems to have become the main product. Useful intellectual tools are extremely difficult to fashion even when one's purpose is clear and specific. Skepticism clearly is in order when someone who has produced a cake by following a recipe for a pie also claims that it is about the best cake that could be baked.

It would be difficult and pointless to itemize all the price decisions that a business executive is called upon to make—and which might be facilitated by price theory. The following classification will, however, provide a place for all of them and should help to organize the discussion which follows:

1. Price decisions intended to endure indefinitely or for a substantial period.

2. Multi-transaction price decisions intended to prevail only a short period.

3. Single-transaction price decisions.

PRICE DECISIONS INTENDED TO ENDURE INDEFINITELY OR FOR A SUBSTANTIAL PERIOD

Included in this class are price decisions intended to prevail for a period of over, say, two months. A person making such decisions usually expects the price set to remain in effect until market conditions change substantially—and he does not know how long that will be. Moreover, he will expect to make some adjustments in these prices during short periods, in an effort to preserve them while under stress, in the hope that they can be revived when the period of stress is over. Many of these price decisions are intended to last for a season or a year and usually are described as "changes in list price." They rarely are binding upon the seller for any long period even if they are represented to be "prices for this year's models." (Important exceptions are the rate decisions of public utility executives; these often cannot be altered for substantial periods.) The safety valve by which executives relieve the damage of poor price decisions is change. Modification, if not reversal, of price decisions is commonplace.

What guidance do the market models of price theory give businessmen who make such price decisions? First, we shall consider the major types of relatively long-term price decisions that are made by businessmen, to see whether directly relevant market models exist—and whether there is opportunity to construct helpful models to fill a void. Thereupon, we shall divide price decisions into their principal elements, namely reactions of customers, reactions of competitors, and costs; the contributions of the market models to the needs of businessmen to understand and make decisions involving these elements will then be explored.

The major long-period decisions of businessmen include decisions about:

a. Differentials among items in the line

b. The number of items to include in the line

c. The specific prices to charge within the total range covered by the line

d. Items to add to or drop from the line

e. Base price

f. Terms of sale—cash and quantity discounts

The product line and the contributions of market models. The first four items on the foregoing list refer directly or indirectly to a line of products. The offering of many models of a given product each possessing somewhat different features and selling at different prices is extremely widespread—even for important industrial products. Price decisions that must be made by executives increasingly concern the range of prices covered by the whole line, the number of items in the line, the differentials in price among individual items, and even the maximum quantity of certain items that will be produced. To my knowledge, no market model has been developed specifically to assist a businessman with this type of decision. As will be shown, attempts to apply traditional market models to this problem can actually do harm. At best they give little or no assistance. Consequently, price theorists could possibly make a significant contribution to businessmen in this sphere. (Theorists might start simply by studying the models employed by businessmen who grapple with this problem.)

Price theory dictates that each item in a line of products be considered a separate product and that the businessman view his demand problem both in terms of price elasticity of demand (to take account of customer reaction) and in terms of cross-elasticity of demand (to anticipate possible rivals' reactions).

Also, strict adherence to price doctrine would lead the businessman to seek a price that would maximize the profitability of that item. As a practical matter, of course, he would want to maximize the profitability of his total enterprise, taking account of the profitability of other items in the line. How this interdependence could best be handled is not suggested by price theory; nor does price theory enjoin the decision maker to take account of the interdependence of his own several offerings. Indeed, in the absence of other models to serve this purpose, an executive might be inclined to apply existing models to each item individually.

To consider individual items in a line as separate products does not correspond to the manner in which most businessmen think about this problem. Most executives would not find it a helpful model and in some ways it is actually misleading. It would be far more useful to regard the various models as members of a team, with each item in the line carrying out a specific assignment by which it helps to sell or enhance the price of the other items in the line, rather than compete with them. A businessman must recognize the value of promotional and prestige models. The first builds traffic and attracts customer attention to the product and causes some people to think about purchasing an item that they would otherwise have assumed was "too expensive for them." Prestige models can give the entire line an aura of high quality and the manufacturer an aspect of dependability. They make it easier for the customer to spend more than he had originally intended because his purchase cost so much less than the most expensive item in the line. Models for pricing purposes must take full account of this type of interdependence. Just the analogy between a team and a line of models or products will be found very helpful by most businessmen.

One executive, well trained in price theory, stated that this training helped him considerably when he participated in the pricing of new models of a consumer product that was to be added to an already large assortment of models. In his formulation of the problem, this executive distinguished between "substitutions" (customers the firm would win away from itself, thereby reducing sales of other models in its line) and "conquests" (customers won from rivals). By setting up the problem in a matrix form, taking account of the margins on the different models offered by the firm, he was able to clarify the issues so that management guesses and research efforts were concentrated on the crucial issues. (His colleagues told him that he had greatly illuminated the problem for them and aided in its solution.) One must ask, however, whether price theory made the contribution in this case. It would appear that other disciplines, including mathematics, and even engineering, would have contributed more directly to this type of formulation than would price theory. Perhaps all of these helped less than native intelligence and an empirical bias, for the ingredients in the problem were admittedly clear to all concerned. What this executive provided was a device for organizing and computing known factors in the problem. The connection between his contribution and the market models of price theory is not clear—though he is convinced that without them he would not have been able to formulate the problem as he did.

Base price determination in long-term price decisions. If we ignore the problem of the product line and concentrate on the decision about price for a single item or a base price that is intended to prevail for a substantial period, how well do the market models of price theory serve the needs of a businessman? Specifically, do they help him by indicating the "kind of market in which he is selling" so that his thinking revolves about the appropriate issues? Would it help him, for example, to know that he was selling under the conditions of heterogeneous oligopoly with limited freedom of entry rather than in some other type of market? Would such knowledge tell the average intelligent businessman anything useful that he did not already know?

Certainly, an executive operating in an industry is acutely conscious of his competitors' existence and most anxious to know all he can about the way they think and their basic pricing and marketing policies. Also, he will have opinions about the relative merits of his product and those offered by rivals—though the validity of these opinions is rarely great. Certainly, he will be conscious of the extent to which customers regard the competitive offerings as homogeneous. What in the market models would assist him? Clearly it is not an identification of factors that he might otherwise overlook. They would help, if at all, by providing a structure which enabled him to understand them better, or to understand their relationship to one another or how they operate in combination: or helped him guard against loose thinking about any of these factors.

These possible values of models are most difficult to assess. Those trained in price theory are both impressed and grateful when others frame problems in a form that is familiar to them; in doing so, they certainly make the problems clearer and easier to solve than would alternate formulations. However, such formulations may not be helpful to persons who have not been trained in price theory. An accurate assessment of these models as aids in thinking is almost impossible.

I have gained three impressions from many discussions with businessmen about price decisions, both in general and with respect to specific decisions about price for a model year. First, businessmen's presentations of the issues in a pricing problem seem moderately disorganized to me; they clearly use a different model than the one I use to conceptualize such problems. Second, they come out at about the same place that I do in conclusions and in the reasons for decisions. Third, they tend, over time, to adopt the fairly orthodox models in their discussions of price. The conclusion I draw is that businessmen use models that are blurred and unconscious and welcome some explicit structure, especially if one is known to their associates. The market models of price theory represent structures that are quite acceptable to them. Therefore, they apparently serve a purpose. These models are not necessarily more powerful than the unconscious models that businessmen use or than other models that might be developed. After all, only economists have made a systematic effort to develop explicit market models. In the absence of any other models, businessmen apparently do find them helpful in organizing some major factors that should influence a pricing decision.

The market models of price theory are built essentially around a few market forces: customer response, the number and responses of rivals, and the entry and exit mechanism. Let us now analyze these forces individually and explore the value of individual elements that make up the market models. If these models are like most others, the whole will be much more than the sum of the parts.

The market models of price theory give a central position to demand considerations in price determination; businessmen do so also. To what extent can the price theorists help the businessmen with this aspect of price decisions? What do the market models say that would not otherwise be discovered very quickly by businessmen? What interrelations are suggested that might otherwise go undiscovered? Are any questions posed, or posed in a particularly helpful way, by price theory?

Customer market reactions have several fairly distinct aspects which ordinarily are lumped together. Much is to be gained by considering separately (a) the law of demand and price elasticity of demand; (b) methods of altering the level of demand; (c) price changes and customer perceptions; and (d) effect of price changes on resellers.

That a price reduction will ordinarily spur sales—all other circumstances unchanged—certainly was common knowledge long before Adam Smith started the study of moral philosophy. That sales were more sensitive to price reductions for certain products than for others probably was no less obvious or ancient in its discovery. That one might describe this relationship between price changes and unit sales by the term "elasticity of demand," and measure it—at least in theory—is admittedly fairly recent and the price theorist deserves credit of authorship. This notion, however, has done lots of mischief both in the classroom and, to some extent, in business; its contribution to the needs of a businessman trying to set a base price may be far below zero.

Price theorists have tended to speak of price elasticity of demand for individual products as if it were uniform over the relevant stretches of the demand curve. (They have done this despite the tendency, since 1933, to draw demand curves as straight downward-sloping lines, in order to simplify the construction of marginal revenue curves.) The fact that demand curves have different elasticity at different prices, as drawn in just about every text and in the classroom, does not alter the fact that uniform elasticity at different prices is the implication of almost every discussion of price elasticity. For example, product A will be pronounced as more price elastic than product B—without any reference to the levels of price that are considered. Indeed, economists often describe the price elasticity of the demand for some products on the basis of studies conducted quite a few years earlier—compounding the sin of assuming uniform elasticity all along the curve with the greater one of assuming uniformity over time.

The market models of price theory do not explicitly state that price elasticity is uniform over space or time; the foregoing criticism applies to the way that economists use their apparatus, rather than to the apparatus itself. However, an apparatus is faulty that is used efficiently by only a tiny proportion of those who try to do so.

Price elasticity of demand for any product probably varies considerably from one part of the demand curve to another, depending upon the availability and price of substitutes, the nature of the personal income pyramid, and resellers' traditional margins, among other things. Average revenue curves, therefore, should be irregularly shaped; marginal revenue curves should often have a crazy shape. Realism thus destroys the neat and simple conclusions (for instance, that marginal cost and marginal revenue intersect at only one point) that are so dear to every classroom teacher's heart and so vital to the mediocre student's sanity.

Most price theorists seem to consider the concept of price elasticity of demand one of the most valuable tools to teach their business students. Its value to businessmen would appear to be slight because a much more clear and directly applicable formulation exists for the businessman's needs. In place of price elasticity of demand, which is a ratio of percentage differences, the effect of price changes on sales can be expressed in absolute terms. Specifically, the effect of price reductions on unit sales can be stated as the number of added units that would be sold as a result of given dollar "expenditures" in the form of price reductions. The cost, in dollars, of a given price reduction would be estimated by taking the loss in revenue from customers who would have been willing to pay the higher price; one would associate this sum with the additional units that would be sold at the reduced price. In a specific case, one might estimate that a price reduction costing $1,000 would increase unit sales by 200; a $2,000 price reduction would raise sales by 350 units, and so on. This formulation would appear to be far more useful than the concept of price elasticity of demand, because it states the effect of price changes so that they become directly comparable with outlays for other sales-inducing measures, like advertising, personal selling, quality change, added service, credit, and speedy delivery. It requires no more information to state the effects of price changes in this way than in the form of price elasticities of demand.

The weakness of market models in setting prices that are intended to endure for a considerable period are greatest in the treatment of demand. Except for the flap in the tent opened by Professor Edward Chamberlain, when he made it respectable for economic theorists to explore the effects of promotional outlays on sales, the price theorist's models have made demand a given. Demand in market models thus represents a condition to which the seller must adapt. Businessmen, on the other hand, are mainly concerned with methods of altering the level of the demand schedule.

Market models may be said to apply after all economically justifiable actions to alter demand have been exhausted. Even if their applicability were to be so drastically delimited, the market models' treatment of demand would deserve serious criticism as a tool for businessmen.

The demand curve states that a reduction in price will increase unit sales because of an income and substitution effect. It does not take into account the effect of price on buyers' evaluations and perceptions of the product itself. The evidence is overwhelming that product quality is, more frequently than not, judged by customers on the basis of price. Consequently, price changes that alter valuations alter the level, and possibly the shape, of the demand curve. Market models ignore this possibility and necessarily do not indicate when such is the case. Similarly, experience shows that customer reactions to price changes are strongly affected by the passage of time; the deterrent effects on purchases of a price increase, for example, tend to dampen as customers become accustomed to the higher price. Perhaps even more serious, sales at any price depend heavily upon whether the seller is continuing to charge the price or whether he had raised or lowered his price to get to that price.

Ingenious economists can draw families of demand curves to take these circumstances into account; or, they can fashion phrases that explain what factors have been considered and are "already taken into account in the curves as drawn." The businessman must estimate the effect of such customer responses, a theoretical apparatus that ignores them will mislead many who use it.

A more obvious omission in market models is the failure to recognize that many producers sell their wares through resellers. Responses of resellers to price changes occasionally are the very opposite from those of the ultimate consumer—and generally are very different. Indeed, an important class of resellers—such as franchised distributors —sometimes would buy more at high than at low prices and would react more favorably, or less negatively, toward price increases than would the ultimate consumer. By constructing market models composed of the producer (with his U-shaped cost curve) and the ultimate consumer (described in downward-sloping demand curves), private theorists drop the reseller out of the price decision. This omission represents a serious weakness of market models for many sellers. Or, more constructively, it offers an opportunity to develop special models to serve a business need that is unsatisfied at present.

The concept of marginal revenue represents one recent breakthrough of price theory. How much and in what ways does it help businessmen with decisions about long-term price? My experience suggests that the concept is well-understood by noneconomists where it applies, but that it does not apply very well in many concrete business situations.

To measure the effect of a price reduction upon total revenue, it is necessary to estimate future demand conditions in the absence of the price change. The textbook method of measuring marginal revenue rests on the assumption that the demand curve will remain constant for a long period—and possibly indefinitely. Once that assumption is relaxed, the measurement of marginal revenue becomes enormously complex, and involves a consideration of factors not specifically included in the price theorist's formulation of the problem. Specifically, many of the sales that will be won today by a price reduction will represent sales that would have been made in the future to the same customers at a higher price; some will be to people who would never have made a purchase without the price reduction. Some sales would involve inventory accumulations by customers who would have bought from the firm cutting price anyway, and by customers who would have patronized another source. Also, the firm might have lost future sales by antagonizing customers who recently had made a purchase at the higher price. Consequently, one cannot measure the change in total revenue brought about by a reduction in price, even after the fact. To follow the method by computing marginal revenue in simple exercises would produce wholly mistaken results.

In situations where the concept of marginal revenue can be applied—where the level of demand is fairly constant over time—it apparently is understood by noneconomists. Persons with engineering and accounting backgrounds will say something like, "If we reduce charges, we will have a loss to make up on added consumption, because we give up income we would have gotten at the higher price."

Teachers of price theory are constantly bedeviled by students' failure to distinguish between primary and secondary demand. By sharpening this distinction, does price theory contribute to the businessman's understanding of demand and aid him in setting long-term prices? Do executives who are not trained in price theory make serious business errors because of failure to distinguish between total demand and the demand for the firm's output?

Any executive who attempted to apply estimates of the price elasticity of demand for the total product to his own firm's output would make serious errors. In the usual case, where sellers are interdependent, they are very different. Experienced business executives have considerable experience which indicates roughly, if not precisely, the demand effects of any price action they might take; consequently, they could hardly judge the elasticity of demand for their firm to be the same as that for the product they sell. Furthermore, not one business executive in my experience justified or opposed a price change by citing a measurement of price elasticity of demand—whether for his firm or for the total product.

Accordingly, ignorance of the distinction between total demand and the demand for an individual firm's output apparently has not led business executives into mistaken price decisions. However, it undoubtedly has prevented some from understanding what the company economist was trying to explain, on occasion.

Perhaps a realistic example will sharpen the points that were made about the treatment of customer responses in the market models of price theory. The formulation of the price problem faced by a typical new firm, or by an established firm offering a new item, illustrates the chief deficiencies of the market model's treatment of demand. New firms and new products represent investments; to set price, the seller must estimate changes in product cost and demand conditions over the life of the enterprise. The instantaneous demand and cost curves of price theory, thus, do not meet the needs of an executive setting price for a new product.

Also, the initial price set by the new firm is likely to influence the future demand for the product: first, its initial price ordinarily will affect the value attached to it by customers for quite a long period; second, the original price also might influence the amount of sales support given to the product by distributors at various levels, for their margins are affected by the manufacturer's price decision.

Similarly, the firm's initial price decision is likely to affect the level of its costs and those of rivals when they arise. If it establishes high prices and wide margins for distributors, these are likely to endure—perhaps indefinitely. Also, the width of margin will influence the amount of advertising and personal selling devoted to the product. These expenditures tend to be governed by the ratchet principle, so that once a firm establishes an expenditure pattern, this pattern endures for a long time. The price decisions of new firms give rise to a whole family of demand and cost curves. This view of the pricing problem faced by new firms differs considerably from the approach incorporated into the traditional market models.

In summary, then, the many weaknesses of the treatment of demand in market models should not come as a surprise. The price theorist basically is not interested in customer responses in concrete situations; apparently, he need not be concerned with them for his specific purposes. On the other hand, customer reaction is perhaps the most vital preoccupation of the businessman. Market models fail to satisfy one of his most urgent needs, mainly, perhaps, because price theorists have not really tried to satisfy this need.

Contribution of market models to an understanding of rival's responses. Thus far, we have evaluated market models by the help they give businessmen to distinguish between different types of market structure and in their formulation of customer responses to price, all for the purpose of setting long-term prices. Market models include another vital ingredient which must figure prominently in any long-term price decision: an analysis of rival interaction. This element in a price decision concerns such matters as whether, when, to what extent, and by what means rivals will respond to the price changes of one of their number. How great is the contribution of traditional market models on this score? (Game theory will not be considered here as part of traditional price theory; even if it were, the conclusions drawn would not be altered significantly.)

Price theory treats seller interdependence under two general headings: "numbers of firms" and "cross-elasticity of demand." Although these notions are, partly, different ways of saying much the same thing, they are also quite dissimilar.

As developed by price theorists, the numbers of firms concept recognizes three different types of market situations. In the first, individual firms are so small and inconsequential that their actions do not affect others perceptibly; consequently, each decision maker can ignore the actions of every individual rival and assume that they will be unaffected by his market actions. In the second type of market situation, the price actions (or output decisions) of any one firm will, or might, significantly affect one or more of its rivals so directly that they may be moved to take retaliatory action. In the third situation, the seller has no rivals at all, and therefore need not consider rivals' responses—though he might be wise to take account of potential competition. How valuable is this set of distinctions to the businessman? What is here that he would not recognize already? Are these distinctions as clear and sharp as they could be and need to be—for the needs of businessmen?

From the businessman's standpoint, it is the second type of market situation that is of paramount interest. Contrary to the views expressed by some economic theorists, the businessman finds, or at least, fears, responses of rivals, where the economist assumes there will be none. He desires subdivisions within this category in which rival interdependence exists, but the market models offer him virtually no help. "Where the product offerings of rivals are dissimilar, retaliation is uncertain," is about all the guidance that the price theorist is able to offer—and this statement is only a somewhat obscure statement of what is obvious to the businessman. The economist's belated recognition of oligopoly and the kinky demand curve might be likened to the "discovery" of an island by some explorers; from the standpoint of the natives, no discovery took place.

Perhaps if most price theorists recognized that the first and third market types (many sellers and one) are virtually empty categories, they would make greater efforts to subdivide the oligopoly box. Until they do, the businessman cannot expect to get from price theory any help with one of his most vital and vexing problems.

How much help will the businessman derive from the concept of the cross-elasticity of demand? This concept does help to make precise and at least theoretically measurable the degree of interdependence between any two firms. It states what most businessmen describe as "how much he can hurt me and how much I can hurt him."

Businessmen seem to be able to identify their chief competitors and have a fairly clear notion—and a valid one, as far as can be observed—of the degree of interdependence that exists. Their method of measuring interdependence is different from that used with the concept of cross-elasticity; they frequently make "lost-order analyses" and "lost-customer studies" which indicate the circumstances under which business was lost, to which company, and for what apparent reason. These analyses take account of interdependence based upon far more than price—as, indeed, is necessary.

The businessman, as implied several times before, is interested in changing the conditions he faces, especially when they are unpleasant, as well as in adapting to them. He wants to know what he can do to reduce this interdependence. The market models suggest that he can achieve partial success by differentiating his offers from those of his rivals. This course is limited for most firms; moreover, it does not necessarily lessen interdependence significantly. To make the point more simple and direct, businessmen mainly would like to know how to raise price in a manner that is most likely to lead their rivals to follow their example and to reduce it so that it is least likely to be followed. On these points, the market models of price theory have nothing to offer. As a result, some businessmen who are beset by what they regard as cruel and insane competition look to disciplines other than economics for guidance. One of the most promising is the field of international diplomacy and power politics, but sociology and psychology also make useful contributions. The market models, even where they may describe conditions fairly accurately, do not help the businessman much in deciding how to change them.

Contribution of market models to an understanding of costs. The supply side of market models is no less vital in explaining the behavior of markets than the demand side; however, the models mainly divide markets into selected types on the basis of supply conditions—that is, by numbers of rival firms operating in the same market. A second factor determining supply conditions is costs, and we shall consider briefly the contribution that market models make to the business-man's treatment of costs in his price decisions.

The theoretical treatment of costs by economists has a long his-tory; one of the truly classic treatments of the subject, by Professor John M. Clark, dates back to the middle 1920s—almost a decade before the development of the market models that are under review here. The U-shaped cost curve has its origins in the earliest writings about agricultural costs and in the principle of diminishing returns (and variable proportions). While our theoretical understanding of costs certainly represents a debt to the economist, it was not con-tributed by the price theorist; we err if we associate our knowledge about costs with the traditional market models.

Rather than attempt a detailed discussion of the value of cost theory to businessmen—an involved and weighty subject in itself—a few general observations will be ventured, to provoke further con-sideration.

1. Except for the systematic treatment of costs by E. A. G. Robin-son, cost theory has sadly neglected nonproduction costs. Indeed, it may be responsible for the neglect of sales costs as a social phenome-non by economists and persons concerned with public policy.

2. Cost theory deals primarily with the impact on costs of capacity utilization and the scale of facilities; it virtually ignores all of the many other factors influencing cost.

3. The marginal cost concept represents a valuable contribution, but economists probably exaggerate greatly the difference between average and marginal costs in actual cases.

4. The genuine difficulties in computing marginal costs when the price decision is to hold for many months—and hopefully, years—are glossed over by price theory and leave the businessman desiring to apply the notion at the mercy of the traditional cost accountant.

5. The problem of "creeping overheads"—a genuine conceptual one to which theorists could make a valuable contribution—is un-treated by price theory even on the rare occasions when it is recog-

nized. In short, the value of the concept of marginalism applied to costs is nominal when one is considering, as we are here, price decisions intended to endure for some time.

6. Price theory does not unravel the mystery surrounding the allocation of common costs. The argument that they should be allocated on the basis of demand is no more valid than argument for other bases of allocation and suffers the added limitation of being far more difficult to apply, as it must be, *ex ante*.

These propositions admittedly constitute a cavalier treatment of an important subject. They do suggest the lines along which one might present a more extensive discussion of the subject, and, hopefully, suggest some of the points that must be considered in an evaluation of price theory's contribution to businessmen's price decisions.

Long-term price decisions and terms of sale. The list of long-term price decisions presented earlier (see p. 67) included six items, four of which were concerned with the product line. Since we have just completed our discussion of the determination of the base price, we now can turn to the last item: "Terms of sale—cash and quantity discounts." Businessmen's decisions on these points sometimes are critically important for an entire industry; where the firm departs from common trade practice, these decisions can affect its fortunes profoundly. What help can an executive responsible for such decisions derive from the models of price theory?

The cash discount is mainly a vestige from a time when loanable funds were extremely short and sellers attempted to minimize their extension of credit. Very likely, though we cannot know for certain, the size of cash discounts originally reflected the value of liquid capital to sellers. (Since its value was probably smaller to many of their customers, the discount—really the price that the seller would pay for a loan—permitted mutually beneficial capital transactions.) Although most sellers experience no capital shortage, the price they pay to customers for prompt payment greatly exceeds the cost of funds obtained from other sources. The cash discount now exists mainly because it cannot be withdrawn by unilateral action, except by a powerful price leader. In such a case, the discount may be considered a routine reduction in base price, extended to all customers on equal terms. (It serves, but only rarely, as an emergency source of funds for buyers who are particularly pressed for funds.)

In some trades, however, where customers include many small, financially insecure, and not wholly reliable buyers, the cash discount partly represents a reserve for bad debts. More importantly, it is sometimes a device by which sellers divide their customers into separate markets on the basis of the strength of demand. Observe that the preceding discussion of the rationale underlying cash discounts did not refer to aid that businessmen might derive from market models in establishing cash discounts. Persons with an accounting or finance background would seem to be more likely than price theorists to formulate the problem in terms of setting a price for liquid funds.

Price theory includes a set of models to deal with price discrimination. These models are intended to explain conditions where demand for a firm's output is composed of several separable submarkets between which little movement by customers is possible and where price discrimination is legal. How much do these writings help the businessman who wishes to establish quantity and cash discounts? (Admittedly, the economic theorist does not offer price-discrimination models as aids in setting cash and quantity discounts; the businessman must use the model available that comes closest to meeting his needs.)

The price-discrimination models do, or could, help businessmen in several ways. First, and most important, they suggest that total demand may be composed of separate submarkets characterized by different levels and intensities of demand and that sellers would find it profitable to set a separate price for each one. Unfortunately, the apparent applicability of the price-discrimination models has been sharply delineated—or maybe simply misnamed—so that few people regard them as appropriate for conceptualizing problems like cash and quantity discounts. Second, the factors that keep markets separate and the conditions where separation is, at best, temporary, are illuminated by the models and might help businessmen to know when price discrimination is economically feasible.

The most serious limitation of the price-discrimination models is that they do not help businessmen to segment their markets in specific cases or even indicate how they might think fruitfully about the matter. The examples discussed by price theorists are simple and obvious and fail to suggest the enormous opportunities for market segmentation. The price-discrimination models could assist businessmen to formulate the issues involved in cash and quantity discount problems, even though price theorists have not recognized and emphasized this application. (If called market-segmentation, instead of price-discrimination, models, they would get much wider application.) However, if these models were used in setting quantity discounts, sellers should recognize that buyers might shift from one "class" to another by bunching their purchases through time, or by forming cooperative buying arrangements.

There are, of course, other uses than these for the price discrimination models. As one might expect, they would apply best to situations where the same product or service is sold to widely different types of customers—like residential and business customers. Also, this model could be applied, to a degree, to set prices on different models in the same line. If that were done, models offering distinctive special features could be priced to give the highest returns, while the standard models might yield little or no profit. (This formulation of the problem would be far less satisfactory, it seems to me, than one which views the entire line as a team.)

In summary, price theorists have developed some models that could help businessmen to set quantity and cash discounts. Few price theorists or businessmen seem to recognize this possible application, however. Despite their limitations, the price-discrimination models appear to be among the most powerful and useful now available. Possibly by renaming them, their broad applicability might become more widely recognized.

This discussion of cash and quantity discounts completes our review of the value of traditional market models for businessmen who set prices intended to endure for a substantial period. Some types of long-term price decisions have not been discussed. The more important omissions are: the selection or rejection of price-lines and the determination of "psychological price." It is almost self-evident that price theory contributes little, if anything, to these types of decisions.

Two other main classes of price decisions remain to be explored: multi-transaction price decisions intended to prevail only a short period; and, single-transaction price decisions.

MULTI-TRANSACTION PRICE DECISIONS INTENDED TO PREVAIL ONLY A
SHORT PERIOD

Pricing traditions and practices vary enormously among industries. Whereas public utilities ordinarily are restricted to constant prices or to rates that vary according to a regular pattern by hour of the day, day of the week, and season of the year, prices in some trades change several times an average day. Although it is perilous to generalize about all industry, firms apparently are making increasing use of short-period special prices. Such prices are plainly labeled as unusual and of short duration. Not infrequently, the period when the special price will be withdrawn is specified.

Week-end Specials and cents-off promotions at the supermarket; white sales, fur sales, and Washington's Birthday, Valentine's Day, and other sales at department stores; off-season rates at resorts and on transportation facilities; and end-of-season clearances, all are examples drawn from common experience. What may not be so well known is that most manufacturers of consumers' goods and some industrial companies employ similar price promotions. Skill in making such price decisions can greatly enhance a firm's profits. What help can business executives derive from the traditional models of price theory?

By their very nature, time is a critical dimension in these decisions.

Specifically, they revolve around questions like: when, on what items, for how long, and how much? The timing questions would appear to be almost as crucial as those involving the level of price itself.

Some price theorists confronted with these questions would respond that they are to be answered on the basis of a knowledge of demand at different times. This view gives no help to business, and does not take account of some of the most critical variables in such decisions. Among them are: how willing are buyers to shift the timing of their purchases, how many potential customers will desert "regular sources" in order to achieve a saving of short duration, how large an inventory of the item are customers willing to hold, to what kinds of short-period price promotions will rivals—and specifically, which ones among them—respond, and when? Price theory neither poses many of these questions nor suggests how to find answers. It offers basically static models which are powerless against problems in which changes over time are central. The weakness of price theory for use in making short-period multi-transaction price decisions can be illustrated by the cents-off decisions which are so widespread in the food field.

Cents-off sales almost always are proclaimed conspicuously on the product's label. This type of price arrangement is common to soap, detergents, and coffee, but will not be found on such foods as dairy items or canned fish. Why are these price reductions made in the first place? One motive is the obvious one—to divert some business from rivals. Another motive is to induce regular customers to "stock-up on the item" and therefore to be "off the market" when a competitor offers a special cents-off promotion. How important is this second motive in the minds of those who set prices? How valid is it in specific cases? It is almost impossible to answer either of these questions; however, businessmen are guided by such considerations and their decisions are put to the test in the marketplace so that, if they were in error, that fact would have become discovered in time.

Interestingly enough, rivals do not retaliate directly against such cents-off promotions except under most extraordinary circumstances.

They seem to operate on a revolving-door principle; now one firm goes through the door with its promotion, later, another's turn will come. A firm may reach a particular market with its promotion when someone else is also running a cents-off sale; in that event will have less effect than the firm had hoped; however, it will have blunted the effect of its rival's sale. When a firm is taking business away from competitors in a particular market with a cents-off sale, rivals bide their time until it is terminated; that firm probably is under pressure from its rivals in other markets because of their promotions.

To measure the effective price charged by firms in businesses where such sales are usual, one must take the list price, the number of cents-off promotions, the size of the price reduction, and the amount of product affected by the cents-off promotions. Thus it is difficult for firms to know accurately their competitors' prices. Retaliation, consequently, becomes extremely unpredictable.

Do the models of price theory assist businessmen to think through the type of promotion just described? (Perhaps it could help a businessman to decide whether it is wise to enter a business where pricing is done in that manner.) My answer is that they do not provide any help with such price problems. As partial proof, those in the business do not apply such models—even when they happen to know them very well.

SINGLE-TRANSACTION PRICE DECISIONS

The last major category of price decisions to be discussed are those that involve a single transaction. Examples of such decisions include competitive bids, auctions, special orders, and the sale of one-of-a-kind items like real estate, buildings, homes, businesses, and *objets d'art*. The number of such price decisions is large and accounts for a significant proportion of the revenue obtained each year by many firms. Businessmen would welcome assistance with these decisions. What help can they get from the market models of price theory?

Single-transaction price decisions mainly revolve around considerations of demand and opportunity cost and generally involve direct negotiations between buyer and seller. Such price decisions usually are dominated by few and fairly obvious considerations including: the highest amount that the buyer will pay at the start; what might be done to make him willing to pay more; how to get him to disclose his top price; how much rivals will charge, under negotiation, for something that the buyer considers comparable; whether the buyer will take considerable effort to seek out substitute products; the price that other potential buyers would be willing to pay for the product and how long it would take to find them; the costs of waiting for another customer; and the alternative opportunities that would be foreclosed by completing this transaction. These data are extremely elusive in any specific case, but their relevance is well known to persons involved in such transactions. However, the market models of price theory do not include many of them and do not illuminate single-transaction price decisions for businessmen.

The recently developed competitive-bidding model does contribute slightly to a conceptualization of such decisions, mainly by treating them in probabilistic terms. However, this model also represents an enormous oversimplification and seems to be inferior to the unconscious models that some businessmen employ. Those businessmen, with whom I have been personally associated, who have made such decisions seem to have conceptualized their problem effectively— without any help from the market models of price theory.

One intellectual tool, the so-called marginal engine, does apply particularly well in single-transaction price decisions. (There might be some debate as to whether it represents a part of the market models or is generic to all economic analysis; this potential jurisdictional dispute need not concern us.) The model that directs us to compute the costs and gains attendant upon the decision, and would have us organize the data under the head of added costs and added revenues, is both supremely simple and enormously powerful. My experience suggests that, surprisingly, many intelligent and academically trained business executives do not apply the marginal engine, and their conceptualization of some problems is less sharp and effective than it would be if they were familiar with its application. Moreover, when they are taught the basic ingredients of marginal analysis in a relatively few minutes, many seem to undergo an "aaahaaa experience" that suggests they understand something that had puzzled them.

No group such as this one, schooled in marginal analysis, need be told how difficult it often is to compute marginal costs and marginal revenue in concrete cases, especially when opportunity costs figure so heavily and these costs generally measure potential opportunities for profitable use of scarce resources of uncertain likelihood. Nevertheless, one would certainly want to include marginal analysis as a tool which is valuable to businessmen for both pricing and investment purposes—and, indeed, for virtually any type of decision, in or out of business, they may make. It must also be recorded that most executives do use a simple "pros and cons" or "pluses and minuses" model that comes to very much the same thing—as they apply it.

Executives who make single-transaction price decisions mainly need skill in negotiation—more than they need an intellectual model. They must, in particular, develop ruses that lead their "adversary" to disclose the strength of his desire to conclude the transaction. On this matter, they get no help from either the formal market models or marginal analysis.

Summary and Conclusions

The length of this paper can be explained by the large number of business decisions that might be illuminated by market models. These decisions are numerous and diverse, ranging from investments to foreign-trade decisions, but they concentrate overwhelmingly in the field of price. Even price decisions alone are highly diverse and devilishly complex. Businessmen would doubtless welcome assistance with these decisions. As the foregoing discussion suggests, the traditional market models of price theory make only slight contributions to business's needs for intellectual models.

Perhaps the main reason for this situation is that price theorists, at least, originally, did not have the needs of businessmen in mind.

However, many economists claim, or imply, that their market models describe reality fairly accurately, and many teach market models as if they were useful guides for executive decision. As indicated, the applicability of these models and the amount and form of illumination they cast varies greatly from price decision to price decision. Actual business experience, training in other disciplines, and the "culture" accumulated within business that is passed on to newcomers by word-of-mouth or through the trade press contain models that often are far more powerful than those of price theory.

Some consider the limited value of market models to be inescapable because business is so complicated and specialized. They hold that one can learn what one needs to know to make price and investment decisions only by going into business, or by studying realistic cases. That view seems quite mistaken. There appears to be ample opportunity to fashion models which would be more useful in business. Businessmen are not likely to develop such models for themselves, however. My experience suggests, rather, that if new and useful models are developed, they will be assimilated by executives and applied with intelligence.

The job, if it is to be done at all, will be done by academically inclined persons. They need not be at universities; business has been adding academicians to its staffs for some time now. Price theorists can doubtless make a valuable contribution to the construction of models that will help businessmen. To do so, they must believe that aid to business executives represents a worthwhile purpose. Many academic economists, like academic sociologists and philosophers, tend to consider commercial applications of their knowledge to be suspect, if not demeaning. They will need to familiarize themselves with the kinds of decisions that businessmen make and the circumstances under which they are made. (They will probably simplify their task if they try to uncover the unconscious models that currently are employed by executives to make price decisions.)

It is fairly obvious that to create useful market models for business will require a very great increase in their number. Even as general-purpose machine tools usually are far less productive than specialized machines, so, too, are broad and general market models low in intellectual productivity.

The direction in which operations research is moving currently illustrates the path that applied economics probably must take to meet the needs of businessmen. Operations researchers have developed dozens of special models to handle the inventory problem alone; they have special models to deal with allocation problems and decisions that are basically spatial. The foregoing review suggests that special models could be constructed to conceptualize product-line pricing, quantity discounts, short-term, multi-transaction price decisions, and various types of oligopolistic interdependence, among other decisions.

The situation could hardly be otherwise. Industry is enormously varied, complex, and changing. To expect the diverse needs of those engaged in industry to be met by few and relatively simple models is almost naïve. The fact that the needs of price theorists—for the purposes of economic theory—are so simple and few should not mislead others to conclude that businessmen can get by with a tool kit that contains a few unspecialized tools.

The men I have interviewed in connection with the preparation of this paper are in general agreement about the value of market models for businessmen: they find them simple and therefore not directly applicable. However, they believe that price theory does help them, to a small degree, with business decisions, though they are not wholly clear about the nature of that help.

Recent years have provided me with many opportunities to observe and test the applicability of market models to business decisions. The negative conclusions presented here are confirmed for me by this repeated experience. I have taught the essence of market models to many highly sophisticated business executives during the last few years. Their reactions have been strangely similar. To my constant surprise, they are extremely interested in the subject and become highly intrigued; most make great efforts to understand the market models and some develop a near mastery. All, or nearly so, end up by treasuring their newly acquired knowledge and delight in using the polysyllabic Greek derivatives that surround it. However, when I have subsequently discussed the subject with some of them, I found that they have not been able to make direct applications to operating problems, even when they have made conscious efforts to do so. They conclude, reluctantly, that the models rarely cast any light on their problems.

COMMENTS

By David J. Jones

I am not an expert on price theory, or even on the determination of prices in a real business situation. However, I shall set down a few observations reflecting some of my own experiences as to the possible usefulness of price models to businessmen. The bulk of my work lies in the field of long-range investment planning, involving, among other things, trying to improve techniques for evaluating investment proposals and their results.

Increasingly, businessmen—and especially those involved in long-range planning—have to improve their awareness of broad economic and social forces affecting the world environment in which business is carried on. It seems to me that a large portion of university economics over the years has rather deliberately focused upon seeking a better understanding of how an "economy" operates within fairly large political entities. By trying to analyze and, where possible, measure overall demand factors and the availability of various resources, general economists seek to gain an insight leading toward more enlightened public policy. Now, I do not think a modern businessman can be indifferent to these endeavors at the national and international level, particularly not in a company such as mine. An effort to keep abreast of developments in economics helps the company to act as a corporate citizen in a more enlightened manner, both in initiating proposals for change and in defending institutions under attack. Further, if, independently of the businessman's will, public policies are proposed and implemented, business must adapt itself to these changes whether for good or for ill, and it helps to have as much foreknowledge as possible.

Now, as I understand it, those particular aspects of economic theory having to do with market and price models were not claimed by their originators to be literal transcriptions of the real world, but merely analytical devices helping an observer of the real world to gain some insight into the workings of the business and political environment. Grossly oversimplified though the models were, they helped in an educational process by permitting analytical examination of a few factors extracted from their context for whatever benefit this might give when a more complex, real-life situation was being grappled with. I will not say that existing price and market models of themselves have been major contributors to determining real economic conduct. They form merely one imperfect analytical device, a crude analogue if you will, which, together with a number of other crude tools, is usually felt to be better than nothing when trying to understand the real world.

The problem of the general economist as a student of and advisor to public bodies and other groups in the field of national economies is considerably different from the problem facing the individual businessman in his daily decisions. Indeed, the distinction between the two kinds of problems, that is, economics and business administration, has led to the growth, especially in this country, of two different professional schools. Admittedly, there are points common to both types of discipline. Perhaps we should be trying to emulate the natural scientists who now tend to consider the spectrum of scientific knowledge to be unbroken, with different branches not compartmented, but phasing one into another.

I would agree that, for business-administration purposes, classical price and market models are of limited usefulness. It is doubtful whether a model approach developed in the universities can do more than arouse in the businessman an awareness of the need to analyze his own problems in depth. I cannot conceive how anyone other than the businessman can provide the refinement and detail of assumptions and projections needed to study a concrete business problem. This is no criticism of economists as such, who have often provided the analytical approach, or at least created in the businessman a feeling of need to develop his own approach.

Insofar as models have an effect on public opinion, a considerable incentive exists for the businessman to keep abreast of developments. In most basic industries, businessmen are called upon to justify their activities to large numbers of people: governments at home and abroad, taxing authorities, unions, and so forth, in addition to stockholders. If these various audiences have been preconditioned as to what is "right" and if their ideas of rightness differ from what is feasible in the real world, a businessman is faced with considerable problems, particularly since his justification of his conduct cannot today be entirely in terms of his own individual direct and immediate interest, but, rather, must be expressed in arguments based on his own terms of rightness. It seems to me that for such purposes as, for example, government regulation, one of the principal defects of classical market models is an assumption that so-called perfect competition is the normal state of affairs, and that any imperfections in a real-life situation are brought about by inefficiency or wickedness of some kind. It would seem to me more realistic to base judgment on the observation that competition in some form is a characteristic of human behavior and that classical, perfect competition is merely a limiting, special case, rarely, if ever, achieved in practice. Similarly, absence of competition in the form of a complete monopoly is a limiting, special case which rarely, if ever, happens in real life. Now, I recognize that distinguished economists in the 1930s began to talk in terms of imperfect competition, workable competition, the theory of the firm, and the like, and this was a step forward. However, further progress seems needed to bring the models closer to real life, particularly by taking account of the industrial structure which governs competition in most lines of activity. Greater realism here would remove some of the failure of communication between businessmen and those who still cling to the models of perfect competition.

All too often, in discussions based on models, markets are conceived of in terms of traders' markets, where participants are buying and selling goods from stock which had been created by some earlier process not discussed. More effort, it seems to me, needs to be devoted to the market problems that arise when an industrial manufacturer sells in competition with other industrialists through a group of intermediaries who, in turn, sell to retailers who, in turn, sell to the final consumer. It would also help to recognize that businessmen have to determine their course of action today considering the long time which must elapse before a new product or process can be worked from the research phase, through design and construction of plant, to manufacture and distribution of the final goods. Obviously this means that the businessman works on guesses about the future, i.e., probabilities, not on market models of the trader type.

Classical models of declining marginal utility, and the like, were developed in an era when most economic activity dealt with necessities or semi-necessities. The psychology of utility was influenced by this. As Western economies increase in their affluence, more and more of the goods and services involved in commerce are not essential, and the behavior of people with respect to them is different from the behavior of people in less-developed societies and from the behavior patterns implicit in the early models.

The classical demand schedule conceptualizes that different amounts of goods can be sold at different prices, according to some fairly smooth curve. Much reasoning rests on this, and it sounds fair enough. The odd thing is that this is almost wholly a conceptual matter. In the modern world, with many nonessentials competing with one another for the customer's dollar, what is known as the customer's caprice is a major business problem. It may be possible to test, on a very limited and only locally relevant scale, the effect on sales of changes in selling price, but how long these test results will remain valid is a problem. As far as long-range investment planning is concerned, the situation today may be entirely different from the situation likely to exist when the factory starts production. Furthermore, in many lines of industry, changes in price cannot, practically, be made frequently or on a large scale, and infrequent price changes give plenty of scope for other factors in the situation to change, and thus to cloud or mask the effects on sales of price change. Thus a businessman may understand that, conceptually, "somewhere out there" is a demand schedule, but he cannot plan on using it in decisions.

Increasing use is being made of operations research, which involves some form of analytical technique based on quantifying assumptions and projections. The use of modern mathematics and computers no doubt will bring some additional enlightenment, but first there will be a transition period, since the businessmen high up enough to make final decisions usually are not familiar with the mathematical notations, or even with the concepts, involved. Furthermore, I know of no mathematical technique which, by itself, improves the quality of some of the key inputs. However, I happen to be optimistic that within a generation or so, improved analytical and computational techniques capable of handling more variables than could earlier methods may give us greater insight, not only into the problems of the businessman, but also, perhaps, into those of the general economists working in the field of public policy, whom I alluded to earlier. I certainly hope so, since I do not, myself, feel that present-day mathematical economics is getting across to the business audience, which is, by its actions, influencing what the economy is, even though the mathematical economists, through their influence on public policy, affect the environment for business.

By *Richard B. Tennant*

Since Professor Oxenfeldt's paper is a good one with which I disagreed on few details, it will not be necessary to attempt a point by point rebuttal. This frees me to make a more general statement of certain ideas of my own which may involve a different perspective on these problems than he has shown, and a quite different opinion of the value of normal models than has developed so far in this discussion.

It seemed to me, in reading this paper, that, while its quality as a whole was extremely good, there was a surprising gap. On the one hand, it demonstrated a deep understanding of the way in which markets actually work, but, on the other, it considered, essentially, the simple models of neoclassical theory. While he discusses the importance of developing new models—and, incidentally, defines them so loosely that almost any systematic method of thinking involves the use of a model—the main comparison that he sought was that of the simple conventional models with the complexity of market behavior.

I think that to gain understanding of this problem we need to go somewhat deeper. We need to study not only models but model building, and not only model building but the economist's other tools and perspectives which may be helpful for business decision making. It is my conviction that the conventional models are of some use, model building is of more use, but of the greatest use are the economist's tools and perspectives.

Let me explain further what I mean. If you take the models of the firm as developed in elementary economics and apply them to a business pricing problem, you will not get very far in solving that problem. On the other hand, the skills which academic economists develop in their academic work are, I believe, of great assistance in solving business problems. I am concerned mainly with this point, but I shall also give an optimistic evaluation of the value of even the simple models.

Why should economics be valuable in the solution of business problems? Let us consider what the business problems are. Business involves the management of people, money, and other physical resources, in a complex pattern of time and space. It deals in choices which involve the allocation of resources, and this is exactly what economics is about. Because business problems are so largely allocation problems, and this is the principal concern of economics, it would be surprising if economics did not bring a useful perspective on business problems.

As we know, and as Professor Oxenfeldt's paper has pointed out very well, business problems are extraordinarily complex. These problems have been dealt with and decisions have been made by businessmen for hundreds of years. Sometimes the results have been disastrous and sometimes they have been very good, but, nevertheless, the decisions have been made, usually without benefit of economic analysis. Usually these judgments have been based upon some analysis, but a principal reliance has been upon judgment and common sense. Now, judgment can assume a whole range of characteristics, ranging from the crudest empiricism to a high level of intuitive insight. It can be both less powerful and more powerful than analytical approaches.

One of the important developments in management over the last few decades has been the growing attempt to apply analytical methods, and so to reduce the area within which general judgment must be applied. The professionalization of managers, the separation of management from ownership, the growth of competent staff, and, in more recent years, the development of new analytical methods in operations research, have all been part of a movement to bring analysis and factual information to bear on management problems.

What is it, then, that economists have to offer to this development? I hold that the principal economic ideas and tools are especially valuable in attacking the decision problems of management. The basic ideas of resource allocation, the trade-offs in resource use or in different kinds of results, the specific formulation of these trade-offs in terms of marginal rates of substitution, the marginal engine, as mentioned, are all directly helpful in management decision making. The concept of abstract forces, the interdependent relationships which define a firm's external environment and internal pressures, offer assistance to the businessman in understanding his problems and in finding solutions to them.

These relatively straightforward ideas and tools are helpful in approaching decision problems. Of course, economists have gone further than these and have been among the principal architects of the newer methods of operations research. Managerial economics, in its concern with the internal problems of the firm, covers much of the scope of operations research. However, for our purpose, in examining the success of ordinary economic models, I do not wish to stress the contribution of the more highly mathematical models of operations research, but the insights and analytical aids that can be secured from straightforward economic reasoning. The economist has habits of thought and points of view which give him a unique ability to be helpful.

I will even argue in opposition to some other opinions expressed here today that the simple models of neoclassical theory are themselves a substantial help in approaching business problems. They are oversimple, they are incomplete—but they also have substantial value.

What is it that the simple models do? First, they identify factors that need to be considered. In the pricing equilibrium of the standard model of the monopolistic firm, the essential determinants of the most profitable price are the elasticity of demand and marginal cost. In fact, if you manipulate the usual conditions for the equality of marginal revenue and marginal cost, you will find that in the standard model, the ratio of price to the marginal contribution is equal to the elasticity of demand. Thus, we are stating not only the identity of certain factors but some interrelationships between them, and both these accomplishments are helpful. It is not obvious that elasticity of demand and marginal cost are the principal determinants of the most profitable price, and it is not obvious what the relationship between them is. The model provides clarity in both of these respects.

I don't want this to be understood as claiming something that I don't mean. This is not a simple-minded way of going about setting prices, and any firm that was to rely purely upon these factors and upon an estimate of their quantities in setting prices would probably not do very well. Pricing is more complicated than this in its dynamic and strategic aspects. But, for what they do, the standard model and these simple conclusions are useful. They are a place to start thinking and they illustrate some of the relationships and elements that are important in an actual pricing decision. Not that you can take the standard model and apply a formula from it to relieve you of the responsibility for further analysis and judgment in practical decision making. What I am claiming is that part of the analytical problem is substantially simplified in a way that would be unlikely in the absence of these models, or of something like them.

Of course, the models are not as good as they could be. Professor Oxenfeldt has been very persuasive in his paper about the need for building better models. Certainly, what we need is not the simple application of our present models on a cookbook basis, but the application of economic analysis to business problems, to build better and more sophisticated models for better purposes. Better models, however, need not always be terribly complex ones. The models we want will depend upon the problems we are trying to solve. Models can be too simple and incomplete, or they can be too ambitious and detailed. The important matter is to tailor them to our analytical requirements. It is in the nature of models that they abstract from reality and simplify reality in order to make problems sufficiently simple to be solved. We proceed to deal with real problems by solving them a piece at a time. It is not a failure of a model to be simple if its simplicity is properly designed for the partial problem solution we are attempting.

In defending the usefulness of models for business purposes, I would even like to raise the question of whether they are not better suited for business problems than they are for purposes of academic research. The regular models of the firm, with their assumptions of profit maximization, are not necessarily good descriptions of the way in which business firms behave, and it may well be that the equilibrium properties derived from these models are not valid as descriptions of what happens in the economy. When, however, we attack business problems, we are ordinarily concerned to maximize profits, or at least to optimize something. With this problem of prescription, our models do not suffer from the assumption of profit maximization, but rather can serve as ways of organizing our ideas in trying to increase profits.

MODELS OF VALUE THEORY
AND ANTITRUST

BY MARK S. MASSEL, MEMBER OF THE SENIOR STAFF, THE BROOKINGS INSTITUTION

Three factors limit the use of the models of neoclassical value theory in the solving of antitrust problems. To begin with, there are substantial differences in the scope of neoclassical theory and antitrust law. Second, the models of value theory fail to take account of a number of important forces in modern markets, forces which are key factors in the analysis of antitrust issues. Third, the tools of analysis of value theory do not satisfy the operational needs of antitrust litigation and negotiation.

Considerable progress has been made in applying empirical economic analysis in antitrust. Legislators, agency heads, lawyers, and judges are employing economic analysis more and more frequently. A number of economists have made considerable contributions to the formulation of policy and to the administration of the antitrust rules.

However, no one has successfully employed the models of value theory in this analysis. The analytical tools which are applied were not forged by the tool makers of value theory. Economic inquiry in antitrust turns on such analytical problems as definition of the market, statistical tabulations and samples, differences in prices paid by various purchasers, exclusive arrangements, vertical integration,

The interpretation and conclusions in this paper are the author's and do not necessarily reflect the views of The Brookings Institution.

and attempts to monopolize—factors which are not prominent in value theory.

Although they deal with similar subjects, the objectives of value theory and antitrust do not mesh. The implicit objective of value theory is to encompass the full workings of a market. The theory centers on a model of pure competition. In contrast, antitrust rests on a narrower basis. It does not embrace all of the elements which influence competition. Rather, it is dedicated to the improvement of a circumscribed group of factors which affect imperfect markets.

While there has been substantial improvement in the application of economic analysis in antitrust, there is considerable need for further advance. Such progress will depend upon closer cooperation between the legal and economic professions. This improvement will not be accomplished by arbitrary applications of value theory in antitrust.

A meaningful analysis of the uses of the models of value theory in antitrust must be based on an understanding of the setting for such application and of the basic premises of value theory. Against this background we can examine the differences in the scope of antitrust and neoclassical theory; factors which influence modern competition but which are not encompassed in value theory; and the reasons why the tools of analysis of value theory fail to meet the operational needs of antitrust. Finally, we can consider what might be done to improve the application of economic analysis in practical antitrust enforcement.

Uses of Economic Analysis

The uses of economic analysis involve somewhat different problems in the formulation of antitrust policy and in litigation. While many aspects of policy are influenced by litigation, there are significant differences in the application of economic analysis for these functions.

Policy making includes the legislative process, the formulation of rules, and the development of judicial precedent and administrative policies. It covers the nature of antitrust violations and the remedies which are applied.

Litigation and negotiation constitute the day-to-day operations of antitrust enforcement; the preparation and trial of cases in the courts and in administrative agencies; the negotiation of consent decrees and orders; and the trial and negotiation of private damage actions. They present different sets of problems to the government agencies and private parties, to plaintiffs and defendants, and to lawyers and judges.

POLICY

Economic inquiry is applied in several ways in the course of policy development. It is employed in examining and evaluating general market conditions and current policies, as well as in the consideration of new antitrust rules. Such use of economic analysis is limited by the dimensions of antitrust and by the confined role of the technician in the general formulation of public policy.

Economic inquiry provides a basis for the consideration of competitive conditions and of trends. It can indicate the extent of concentration of economic power in the economy, in various regions, and in individual markets. It can supply clues to an evaluation of trends of competitive and monopolistic forces.

Economic analysis can be usefully employed in the review of existing policy and of its influences. Such analysis can delineate the interrelations among the various government policies and can indicate inconsistencies. It can throw light on the effects of these policies on the state of competition and on the health of the economy, as well as on the various segments comprising it.

An important aspect of policy review is the consideration of the need for change and the review of new proposals. In the process, economic analysis can formulate various alternative policies that might be cast to meet the public goals. At the same time it can develop predictions of the economic effects of each of the alternatives.

Any evaluation of the role of economic analysis in such policy development must take account of the basic limits imposed by the process of formulating public policy. Policy issues in antitrust are fairly confined. There are no opportunities for revising the entire structure of the laws. Rather, considerations relate to modifications of existing substantive law or changes of procedures. Should the production and distribution of petroleum products be divorced? Should consumer financing by automobile manufacturers be forbidden? Should manufacturers be permitted to set resale prices? How should Federal Trade Commission orders be enforced? Should all mergers which create companies beyond a given size be forbidden?

The history of antitrust, as of other forms of government regulation, reflects a development through the process of accretion. Thus, current antitrust policy is based on well over 40 statutes which have been passed over a period of 70 years, together with an even larger number of amendments. The same process of legislative accretion has provided a complex administrative structure with a pattern of overlaps and inconsistencies in functions which are assigned to some 20 agencies.[1]

Added to this statutory maze is an overlay of judicial and administrative interpretation of legislative policy. Over the same 70 years, thousands of judicial and administrative proceedings, accompanied by a multitude of decrees and orders, have contributed to policy development. A wide variety of judicial opinions guides the courts and administrative agencies. Administrative rulings and negotiations, many of which are never tested in the courts, provide yet another set of guides.

LITIGATION AND NEGOTIATION

Although economic analysis can make an effective contribution to litigation and negotation in antitrust, its opportunities are somewhat

---

[1] It should be noted, parenthetically, that this paper is limited to federal activities. It does not cover the many regulations affecting competition which appear on the books of the 50 states and a number of cities. While state and local policies have serious consequences, they are too varied and complex for this discussion.

limited at present. While there is a developing cooperation between lawyers—who dominate antitrust enforcement—and economists, there remain substantial impediments to further progress. Moreover, the litigation process, which set the background for the administration of our antitrust laws, does not provide an effective procedure for the trial and consideration of economic issues or for the formulation of adequate remedies.

A full-blown program of economic analysis in the administration of antitrust would call for continuing inquiry to determine what markets require attention; what deficiencies can be cured by antitrust remedies; what anticompetitive forces require other types of remedies; and what are the effects of previous antitrust proceedings. Such a review program would enable the agencies to apply the limited resources available for antitrust activity more effectively. At the same time, such a program would help the President and Congress to develop better estimates of the budgetary requirements of effective enforcement.

Currently, litigation procedures are not ideally suited for the trial of competitive issues. The procedures were developed for the adjudication of issues which were considerably less complex than economic analyses of markets. They are constructed to deal with the personal testimony of witnesses regarding fairly direct factual observations rather than with economic inquiry, detailed market studies, statistical material, and informed analysis. Their formal procedures are not well suited for clear delineation of economic issues and evidence. They impose tremendous analytical burdens on judges who are not equipped for the task.

Despite its many limitations, litigation does offer opportunities for the useful application of empirical economic analysis. The determination of what current market problems are important and what prosecutions could produce meaningful remedies is a prime requisite to effective enforcement. Economic inquiry can be employed to develop the theory of many cases as well as the types of remedies that would be effective. The clarification of the economic issues of a case would give the litigants, as well as the judge, a clear view of the nature of the proceeding. Definitive demarcations of the issues would make it possible to fence out much of the extraneous material which clutters so many case records, material which imposes an unmanageable task on the lone judge who must try the case.

During the course of the litigation, economic investigation can be used to develop evidence and to develop clear presentations and interpretations of the evidence. Indeed, the antitrust field presents many opportunities for using economic analysis in the interpretation of precedent; for example, in the determination of what is the relevant market within which competitive effects are to be examined. In defining the market, economic analysis is required to determine which of the past proceedings covered a market situation that is most closely analogous to that of the current case—the basic technique for evaluating precedent.

The limitations on these applications of economic analysis are substantial. Lawyers and economists have not yet learned to coordinate their activities. Their methods of defining and solving problems differ. Differences in the terminologies of the two disciplines make it somewhat difficult for them to communicate. Even the same terms, "price discrimination," for example, do not convey the same meaning to the two professions. Their frames of reference are not the same. Lawyers have an established framework within which to look for solutions. The language they employ is set by statutes and court decisions. Their predictions are settled by the decision of the highest court involved. In contrast, economists operate within a broader and more nebulous framework. There exists no economic high court to determine how words should be used or to determine the accuracy of predictions which, in the final analysis, depend on uncontrolled market forces. Even when a prediction is fulfilled, there is always the bothersome possibility that its accuracy was due to market factors which were overlooked in the analysis.

Active cooperation between the two professions has been limited by a degree of intellectual provincialism enjoyed by some members of each group. Many lawyers want to operate within the bounds of conventional legal procedures and are suspicious of such evidence as statistical data. Some economists insist on using abstract, involved analyses—such as those of the models of value theory—without bothering to translate their analysis into terms which would be useful to the lawyer.

Models of Value Theory

In the light of this background, what can the models of value theory contribute to the solutions of antitrust problems? Do they offer a methodology which can improve policy formulation and litigation? Do they provide an analytical framework which can accommodate the dynamic variables which influence the state of competition under modern conditions? Do they fit markets of imperfect competition, markets which combine competitive and monopolistic forces? For the answers we must turn first to a quick sketch of the basic assumptions which underlie the value-theory models.

The competitive models of value theory envisage markets in which a large number of buyers and sellers compete with each other in the sale and purchase of a single product of uniform specification. No provision is made for differences in quality, reputation, service, or warranties. Accordingly, there is perfect elasticity of demand for the products of any individual seller. Everyone must charge the same price as his competitors in order to continue in business.

In addition, any buyer and seller can freely leave the market and anyone can enter it. Investments and risks do not seriously affect entry or exits, nor do technological factors. The motivations of the competitors are clear. Each is engaged in continuing efforts to maximize his profits, though high profits cannot be made in the light of the cost-price relationships under pure competition.

The pattern of competition is restricted to price and is delineated by a limited number of variables: factor prices, volume, unit cost, and unit price. Prices of productive factors—land, labor, and capital— are market determined and affect each producer in the same way.

Unit costs—defined in marginal terms—are influenced solely by differences in the volume of production. All fixed costs are assigned to the first unit of production. Marginal costs follow a continuous line which fits a rather clear schematic pattern. Similarly, demand is influenced by price only. The volume of sales increases when price is low and decreases when price is high.

Through this schematic arrangement, a simple geometrical pattern describes the effective marginal costs and marginal revenue. Both prices and sales volume are determined by this price-cost-volume relationship.

Because of the effective balance of responses between demand and supply, the markets of value theory produce an efficient working relationship between demand and capacity. The long-run equilibrium which is described in the model avoids underutilization of capacity as well as shortages of productive facilities. Indeed, the existence of excess capacity in the long run indicates that there is an interference with competition. Temporary lack of balance in the short run may be inferred, but it poses no significant hurdles for the price geometry.

The general conditioning factor in these models is the existence of a frictionless economy which maintains an idealized equilibrium with effective balances and counterbalances. While the equilibrium is not conceived as a literal state of affairs at any one time, it constitutes a powerful gravitational force tending to pull all markets into shape.

The models do not encompass the dynamic factors which interfere with the underlying forces. While they describe the ultimate equilibrium, they do not deal with the path which leads to it. Therefore, they tend to concentrate on conceptual poles—competition and monopoly. They do not contemplate degrees of competition. They do not deal with such issues as: how can a market be made more competitive; which of the factors influencing competition are more important; which of the frictions which interfere with the progress toward equilibrium is more significant.

During the past thirty years several suggestive variations of neoclassical value theory have appeared. Attention has been directed to competition among differentiated goods (trademarked items are the outstanding example), to separate demand curves for individual sellers, to the interactions of the price decisions of sellers in a market of few competitors, to the problems of two competitors occupying an entire market, and to the markets which contain only one or a few buyers. The jargon of value theory has been considerably enriched. Such terms as "monopolistic competition," "imperfect competition," "kinked demand curve," "oligopoly," "duopoly," "oligopsony," and "duoposony" have expanded both the vocabulary and the horizons of the theory.

Each of these excursions has reflected a dissatisfaction with the postulates and dimensions of neoclassical value theory. Each has demonstrated notable gaps between value theory and current market conditions, showing some important market variables which are not accommodated by the earlier work. Some of these newer developments have clarified a number of the explicit assumptions in the theory. The geometry has been developed in greater detail. The differences between "pure" and "perfect" competition have been carefully explored.

An important phase of these recent developments has been an effort to analyze the operations of the individual firm. Instead of concentrating on competition in the market, the newer treatment supplies models which portray the supply and demand functions of the firm.

Yet, for use in antitrust the newer models do not differ substantially from the neoclassical. True, elements of product differentiation and selling activity are recognized and the models seek to portray the workings of competition which is not pure. However, they do not bring such variables as selling costs into their geometric analysis. When they proceed to analysis of the market—the basis of most antitrust activity—the conventional geometry dominates the scene. In general, there does not seem to be a substantial distinction among the several variations of basic value theory with respect to their application in antitrust.

Differences in Scope

A most important limitation on the use of the models of value theory in antitrust stems from strategic differences in the scope of the two fields. Value theory is more limited than antitrust in its consideration of noneconomic factors. Antitrust is more limited in its treatment of economic factors. Within the economic sphere, value theory is concerned with perfect competition while antitrust is patterned to improve competitive conditions in imperfect markets.

While neoclassical theory is preoccupied with economic problems only, antitrust policies are founded on a broader mixture of ultimate public goals. Public policies regarding competition are founded on political, social, ethical, and even international objectives. They are tied up with welfare concepts relating to standards of living, to the status of workers, and to the well-being of small business and agriculture. They are influenced by public concern about the political consequences of concentrated economic power. In this respect, antitrust involves broader aims than the single objective of value theory, the most efficient allocation of resources.

On the other hand, antitrust is more limited in the scope of its control over economic forces. There are sharply limited bounds for the antitrust function. Its compass excludes a wide range of governmental activities, some of which exert strategic influences on the state of competition. A judge may order a company to follow specific business practices. In extreme cases he may divorce some of the firm's activities or even split it into several parts. However, he has no opportunity to change the structure of an entire industry. The Federal Trade Commission has even narrower authority except for the application of the antimerger statute. It can order a company to discontinue certain practices. However, it cannot lay down affirmative rules about methods of operation, divorce a company's activities, or order it to give patent licenses.

Of even greater importance is the limited purview of antitrust. Antitrust jurisdiction does not cover a wide range of government activities which influence the competitive matrix in many markets.

It carries no power to lower barriers which fence out foreign competition, such as tariffs, quotas, classification rules, and customs regulations. It imposes no control over the tremendous government purchases—federal, state, and local—which have a substantial bearing on the state of competition affecting many important products and services. Nor can antitrust authority use these purchases to induce new entrants into specific markets. Similarly, antitrust action does not include any power over the substantial federal research and development programs which might influence future market structures. Nor does it touch on the range of tax rules which influence the acquisition of other firms and the "spinning-off" of parts of a company.

In contrast, value theory is concerned with the broad concepts of competition. Its models reflect all of the conditions in a market, though they are not fully described or analyzed. It is not limited to a narrow range of market factors. Conceptually, it deals with final market performance rather than particular forces.

Stemming from these basic differences in scope is a significant distinction in the orientation of value theory and antitrust, one which presents serious operating problems for the application of the models. Whereas value theory is concerned with perfect competition, antitrust is dedicated to improvements in imperfect markets. When the value theory model might indicate basic changes in the total structure of a market, antitrust action is limited.

These differences in scope entail practical consequences. Market conduct which would reflect the absence of perfect competition may constitute a powerful competitive force in an imperfect market. On the other hand, the same conduct may be anticompetitive under other market conditions. Therefore, antitrust requires a more subtle analysis than value theory. Two illustrations demonstrate these differences: exclusive arrangements and price discrimination.

EXCLUSIVE ARRANGEMENTS

A number of antitrust problems have involved exclusive arrangements. A supplier may compel his customers to purchase all of their requirements of a product from him. Or he may force a customer to purchase item B in order to get item A, as in a tied sale. These exclusive arrangements violate the antitrust laws if they tend to lessen competition substantially. In some proceedings such arrangements have been held to be violations merely because they affected a substantial amount of business. In other cases the courts attempt to deal with the probable effect of these practices on competition.

The competitive effects of exclusive arrangements do not fit a set pattern. Some may increase competition. Others may extend or strengthen monopoly influences. In some markets, exclusive contracts may help to induce new competition. A potential supplier may not be willing to make the investment required to break into a new market unless he has some assurance of sales volume. Under such circumstances, an exclusive arrangement may actively promote competition.

On the other hand, existing suppliers may use such exclusive arrangements to tie up all distributors and to prevent the entry of new competitors. Similarly, a handful of manufacturers can employ such practices to control resellers' prices indirectly. Price stability at the retail counter may promote similar protection for manufacturers' prices.

The models of value theory do not seem to be very helpful in gaging the competitive effects of such arrangements. Given the precepts of the theory, all such practices would indicate market imperfections, since their use to induce new entrants would be taken as a clear reflection of barriers to free entry.

PRICE DISCRIMINATION

A prominent antitrust rule forbids price discrimination which may lessen competition substantially. However, such discrimination is permissible if it can be justified by differences in cost or by a reduction which was made to meet the price of a competitor.

In value theory, a difference in prices charged to two customers would not constitute a price discrimination if it reflected in the costs of dealing with them. However, all price differences which are not cost-justified would denote an anticompetitive situation.

The models make no allowance for imperfect markets in which price discrimination would be a competitive force. Nor do they provide a working basis for the analysis of cost differences. The concept of pure competition does not cover sellers who make secret price reductions to some customers in order to obtain additional volume when they would not cut prices across the board. It does not contemplate the possibility that such price cuts might lead to wider and wider circles of price reduction. Indeed, such an influence would be incompatible with a model which precludes excess capacity in a competitive market. Yet, price discrimination depends on excess capacity.

Under certain conditions excess capacity may be a prime stimulant of competition. Many businessmen feel that competition is tougher when their competitors have idle capacity. Underutilization of productive facilities may lead to price cuts—frequently starting with discriminatory reductions—or may prevent price increases.

Overcapacity does not always indicate monopolistic forces. Surplus plants may be influenced by previous market rivalry, by changes in consumer tastes, or by the forces of innovation. Plants may have been built or enlarged because of inaccurate predictions of future demand. Each competitor might have anticipated taking over a larger share of sales than he could obtain because other producers or distributors had the same idea.

Moreover, full utilization of capacity might denote a lack of competition. Unless sales volume is expanding quickly, or sales are at seasonal peaks, the fact that suppliers are producing all they can may be a symptom of strong monopoly forces. A single monopolist may postpone expansion until he has satisfied a high-price segment of the market. The members of a cartel may restrict expansion to avoid "spoiling" the market.

Similarly, excess capacity may reflect a curb on competition. A monopoly, an oligopoly, or a conspiratorial industry may hold prices high enough to make large profits. Their setting of price-points on the demand schedule may require the limiting of market supplies.

It is possible that the teachings of value theory have influenced policy regarding price discrimination. The administration of the Robinson-Patman Act seems to be founded on the assumption that all price discrimination will probably lessen competition. Therefore, economic analysis is rarely employed in the enforcement of the act.

This mechanical application of the law does not seem to vitalize competition. Indeed, there are occasions when the law against price discrimination has supported the effectiveness of actual or tacit price understandings among competitors.

In brief, the models of value theory do not provide a framework for analyzing the effects of price discrimination on competition. They are oriented toward a market which is fully competitive. They provide no basis for stimulating competition in an imperfect market, but require complete reorganization. Hence, they involve a scope of analysis which differs greatly from antitrust.

Shortcomings of Value Theory

The models of value theory fail to take account of a number of significant forces which affect competition in modern markets. Hence, they do not provide an adequate frame of reference for markets in which competitive and monopolistic forces are blended. They overlook many important elements; mainly, the various forms of competition, the behavior and composition of costs, and the influences of diversification and innovation.

FORMS OF COMPETITION

An unsettled set of policy issues in antitrust revolves around the question of what forms of competition should be encouraged. Should antitrust policy be geared to promote price competition only, or should such other types of market rivalry as design, sales promotion, and service be encouraged as well? In evaluating competition in a market, how much attention should be given to nonprice factors?

How can the analysis of price competition accommodate these other factors? How important is consumer information and misrepresentation in the competitive framework?

Market rivalry is, of course, composed of many elements. In addition to price, manufacturers compete with each other in the quality and design of products and of packaging. There is substantial rivalry in service, availability of deliveries, and warranties of quality. Buyers are influenced by such factors as stability of quality, acceptance of returned goods, and promptness in making good on warranties. Availability of products at convenient locations and times has a substantial influence on many types of consumer purchases.

A significant element of market rivalry is sales promotion. This activity takes many forms, such as advertising; the development of an effective sales force; the distribution of samples; and the evolution of attractive product and package design. Not all of this can be completely divorced from production and price. It is frequently difficult to determine the line of demarcation between the costs of production and of sales promotion. Design improvements and expensive packaging may be regarded as sales promotion costs. However, most consumer products do require design and packaging. Hence, many costs combine elements of production and sales promotion. Indeed, the packaging costs of a host of consumer items outweigh the costs of producing the items, themselves.

Neoclassical theory is preoccupied with price competition. It makes no allowance for other forms of competition. It ignores the consumer satisfaction which derives from multiple choices of quality. In fact, a literal application of theory would overlook agreements among competitors to limit these other forms of market rivalry in order to support a price agreement.

Such recent developments in theory as "monopolistic competition," bring out the importance of product differentiation and recognize sales activity. However, these theories do not account for such forces in their geometric analysis of the market. Nor do they provide a firm basis for evaluating the influences of these forces on competition.

One teaching of value theory which is helpful in examining the workings of competition is the importance of adequate consumer information. The theory implies that the consumer's ability to judge quality is a significant factor influencing the effectiveness of competition. Therefore, it suggests that effective competition calls for sufficient consumer information, or, as a minimum, that there must be protection against misinformation. However, this implication does not seem to require more than a common sense understanding of the workings of competition.

COST

The treatment of cost in the models of value theory fails to provide an adequate basis for an understanding of competition in modern markets. The analysis overlooks many significant factors affecting the behavior of costs and it neglects some of the most compelling forces generated by competition in an advanced technology.

The analysis of neoclassical theory starts with given costs schedules. Little attention is paid to what influences costs, except for such broad factors as raw-material prices, wage rates, rent, and the cost of capital. The bearing of competitive pressures on efficiency and on unit costs are ignored.

Value theory concentrates on production cost, ignoring the costs of distribution and of other methods of competition. Since its market model is a place where all buyers and sellers are located, it does not call for an analysis of the costs of the various channels of distribution. Each level of distribution could, of course, be analyzed as a separate market. However, the variety in the channels of distribution for the same items limits the application of this analysis. One manufacturer may sell to whosesalers only; another may sell to wholesalers, chain-stores, and rack-jobbers; a third may sell to franchised distributors. The same producer may follow one line of distribution for one brand and another line for a second brand.

Significant changes which have occurred in the structure of costs have made certain elements of value theory obsolete. The comparatively elementary treatment of marginal costs has been outmoded by changes in cost structures over the past several decades, changes which have made total costs less responsive to fluctuations in volume. Notable increases have taken place in such outlays as those for research and development, supervision and administration, factory offices, materials handling, repairs, and the maintenance of a system of distribution. These expenditures, together with heavy depreciation charges for plant and equipment, do not change with volume of sales or production. Similarly, because of union agreements and advancing costs of hiring, training, and firing production workers, these employees are not hired and fired to meet the requirements of day-to-day production. Therefore, even total outlays for labor do not respond promptly to changes in volume. The sluggish response of total costs reflects, also, such fringe benefits as unemployment insurance, reserves for pensions, supplementary unemployment benefits, provision for severance pay, and medical plans.

With the increased rigidity of total costs, an elementary marginal cost analysis cannot adequately comprehend current cost-price relations. In many markets, if not in most, prices based on short-run marginal costs would produce losses regularly. The analysis of long-run marginal costs would hardly serve as a practicable gage for current prices in a market.

The pattern of cost-price relationships is further complicated by the multiplicity of products produced and sold by almost all substantial firms. When a plant produces hundreds or thousands of items, a significant proportion of total cost must be allocated. As a minimum, overhead costs must be assigned to individual products. Further complications arise when there are joint and by-products costs. The production of a line of items may have a bearing both upon the costs of distribution and on consumer acceptance.

A profound limitation of value theory is its lack of appreciation of the influence of competition on unit costs and efficiency. A low market price stimulates an active search for costs savings. A production method may be improved. A low-cost stamping may be substituted for a machined casting—possibly without reducing quality. Quality inspection may be employed at earlier stages in order to reduce the costs of spoilage.

Affirmative moves may be taken to reduce costs by increasing volume. A price reduction may bring sales—for the market as well as the firm—to such a level that substantial cost reductions can be effected. The larger output may support new automatic machines. It may enable a firm to place large orders for tailor-made materials which reduce machining costs. Longer production runs may minimize unit costs for "setting up" molds or automatic screw machines.

In contrast, monopoly may further the peace and comfort of a company's management. Lacking the pinch of a competitive price and a potential loss, a firm may exert little pressure on efficiency and costs. A monopolist, or a group of comfortable oligopolists, may provide little resistance to wage increases because prices can be increased easily. Costs may be raised by expensive fringe benefits for management.

Cost-price relationships allow a wide variety of marketing combinations for individual firms, alternatives which are reflected in the counter-moves of market rivals. Decisions about products and price combine an appreciable number of variables. A firm can develop many combinations, for example: inexpensive product design, low prices, high volume, and low costs; expensive design, high prices, high sales promotion expenditure, and high volume; low-cost design, high prices, and high sales promotion expenditures.

The cost policies of producers and distributors are tied up with the long-run decisions which call for investment analysis. In their simplest forms, investment decisions must be made in order to organize a new firm, to expand the operations of an existing company, to start the production of a new item, to enter new markets, or to improve production methods. Each move of this type affects the structure of total costs.

Some pricing decisions involve investment risks. For example, when a manufacturer decided to market a ball point pen at $1.95 in the face of an established market price of $15.00, he made a serious investment decision. His market move was postulated on the premise that the increased volume of sales would permit cost savings which would offset the price reduction. His heavy expenditures for automatic machinery, organization, and working capital involved major risks. Consumers might have assumed that the $1.95 pen was shoddy. Further, even if the pen were accepted, there would remain the risk that demand was not elastic enough to meet his volume requirements.

Because of the wide range of product-price-cost alternatives which may be available to the individual firm, the construction of a competitive model which deals with price only may miss some of the more significant elements of market behavior. In fact, such a model would not explain price itself because it overlooks other relevant variables. Therefore, a model of value theory would not be a useful tool to evaluate competitive conditions in most, if not all, current markets.

DIVERSIFICATION AND INTEGRATION

Issues of diversification and integration have produced knotty problems of antitrust policy, problems which are foreign to the value theory models. The issues relate to such questions as the treatment of conglomerate mergers and the divorce of production and distribution of certain products. Unfortunately, the models of value theory are not germane to any of these problems.

Market structures are frequently complicated by variety in the vertical integration of competing firms. One company may mine raw bauxite and produce aluminum awnings. Others may confine their activities to the production of raw materials, or of parts, or of assemblies. Similar differences affect vertical integration in distribution, with some manufacturers reaching down into distributive channels and some distributors reaching up into production. Such integration upsets any static analysis of markets at various stages of distribution.

Some antitrust cases have dealt with the opportunity that integration offers to lever competitors into uncomfortable positions. By charging high prices for raw materials and low prices for finished products, an integrated company which enjoys a practical monopoly in the raw material can secure a preferred position in the market for finished goods.

Similar features are keyed into the antimerger program. How much weight should be given to a supplier's foreclosure of his competitors' sales when he acquires a customer? Conversely, can a customer gain a preferred position over his competitors by purchasing a source of supply?

Diversification may also produce new competitive forces in a market. Substantial outside companies may suddenly break into a market through integration or diversification. Manufacturers of stamped steel products may find themselves in competition with producers of aluminum or plastic items. Other distributors—such as discount stores, rack-jobbers, and vending machine operators—may upset a fairly stable market. Hence, analysis of the effects of diversification and integration calls for detailed empirical analysis rather than reliance on conceptual models.

Similarly, differences in the degree of integration and diversification of competitive rivals place a new emphasis on the importance of the firm. When a competitor enjoys a strategic leverage in one market because of his position in other markets, an analysis which is confined to the market will overlook some of the most significant factors affecting market competition.

Value theory may suggest that these factors constitute market imperfections and that antitrust policy should be dedicated to their removal. However, does such a solution fit the needs of the day? Will "dis-integration" or "dis-diversification" always inject new competitive elements? Is it possible that the diversity in the activities of market rivals can actually increase competition in some markets? Is it likely that some markets will be closed to new entrants unless substantial firms can enter through diversification or integration?

These issues cannot be treated by a flat rule to allow all such structural developments in all markets, or to forbid them. The basic problem is how to discriminate among the maneuvers, to screen out those which stimulate competition from those which hobble it. Value theory does not seem to offer any bases for such analysis since its premises do not fit these developments.

INNOVATION

A related set of antitrust problems—affecting policy and administration—concerns innovation, a function which is practically ignored in the neoclassical models. Technological advances have a strong influence on the competitive patterns of current markets. Does competition compel sellers to adopt innovations in production and distribution methods, or do anticompetitive forces retard change? Does innovation introduce new competitive elements in a market? Does the patent system induce or retard innovation?

Economists have long discussed a theory that innovation provides substantial competition in the long run. It has been suggested that there is no need for concern about antitrust, about company size, and about concentration, and that innovation is the most effective force for stimulating competition and raising standards of living.

The models of value theory do not provide an effective framework for analyzing these policy issues. They assume a static technology and product uniformity. They do not deal with rivalry among end-use items even though they consider the equalization of consumers' marginal utility and the competitive uses of the factors of production.

Tools of Analysis

The models of value theory fail to provide tools of analysis which satisfy the operational needs of either policy formulation or litigation in antitrust. As we have seen, the models do not encompass the various forms of competition, their treatment of cost is oversimplified, and they fail to provide adequate criteria for gaging the effects of those practices—such as price discrimination and exclusive arrangements—whose influence on competition depends on the conditions of the specific market in question. What is equally important is that the models fail to provide the tools of analysis needed to analyze the specific types of problems which arise in policy-making and administration, such as those dealing with concentration, monopolization, and price fixing. Further, the models provide no help in formulating remedial action after a decision that antitrust law has been violated.

CONCENTRATION

Meaningful analyses of the concentration of industry have strategic importance in the formulation of antitrust policy. Long-run changes in the degree of concentration of specific markets can provide valuable clues regarding the general state of competition in the economy. The broad concentration of power in the total economy presents another valuable bench mark. A more specific policy issue is the desirability of setting definite limits to the degree of concentration that will be permitted in a market. Two questions dominate these issues. What policies would be adopted regarding concentration? How can meaningful measurements of concentration be developed?

The models of value theory shed no light on either of these questions. The models avoid the issue by simply requiring large numbers of buyers and sellers. They provide no criteria for taking account of the technology of production and distribution in determining how many firms would be desirable. Nor do they offer a firm analytical basis for defining the relevant markets within which relative shares may be measured and the significance of the data may be judged.

A significant factor governing the evaluation of concentration in a market is the relationship between the requirements of plant scale and total demand. Technology may require plants of such size that the demand will not support a large number of companies. For example, the production of automobiles will not support as many firms as the manufacture of ladies housedresses. A steadily advancing technology, with its requirements of high-speed, automatic equipment and continuing research, has complicated this issue because of the uncertainty of prediction regarding technological development. Despite the generalization that more firms develop more competition, too many competitors may necessitate such small-scale operations that productivity might be reduced radically, with ensuing effects on standards of living—a prominent factor in antitrust policy.

A troublesome element in any measurement of concentration is how to define the relevant market for the analysis. Modern industry provides a wide variety of substitute products made with different materials, employing an assortment of manufacturing processes, at various geographical sections, and distributed through a multitude of channels. Therefore, definition of the market presents the most difficult analytical feature of a number of spectacular antitrust cases and of concentration studies. With its emphasis on standard items, value theory simply avoids this practical problem.

MONOPOLIZATION

The Sherman Act provision about "monopolization" provides many bothersome tasks for economic analysis. The violation covers the methods followed in achieving a monopoly rather than the mere existence of monopoly. Yet, the first step in finding a violation is the decision that a monopoly exists.

As the antitrust law has developed, monopoly does not mean single-firm control of the demand or supply of a market. Rather, it is conceived of as the power of a company to influence prices and volume. Hence, the issue is one of degree. A company may have some influence on prices in a market; it may have the capacity to bring market prices down; at times, it may be the first company to increase prices. However, it may not have enough power to be classed as a monopolist. Therefore, the key question is whether the company's degree of power rates a finding of monopoly.

The models do not offer a practical basis for the diagnosis of a company's power to raise prices. Since they fail to reflect so many variables which influence the pricing of the firm and the market, they do not provide an analytical bench mark for evaluating a firm's market power.

One of the most difficult factors inherent in a finding of monopoly is the definition of the relevant market. As suggested in the discussion regarding the measurement of concentration, the models of value theory are constructed on the assumption that the market has been defined, and avoid the issue. They offer little help in marking out the limits of the relevant market or in estimating the defendant's share.

Value theory does produce a purported clue to the existence of monopoly forces. It starts with the premise that the entrepreneurial objective is to maximize profits and with the assumption that a monopolist will charge the highest price possible. This combination, together with the cost-price assumptions, points to a single gage of monopoly power. High profits reflect monopoly and low profits reflect competition.

Unfortunately, profits are not a reliable indicator of monopoly power. As suggested above, a monopolist may experience high costs and low efficiency rather than high profits. Conversely, if a market has a high rate of innovation, significant differences in the ability of various firms to reduce costs and to adjust to sudden increases in demand may enable one competitor to earn high profits for a limited period, in the face of active competition.

The evaluation of profits, indeed, the analysis of profit maximization, is much more complex than value theory assumes. Accompanying the need for long-run and short-run policy decisions about costs, is a complicated pattern of profit maximization. Many, possibly most, firms attempt to maximize profit over a longer stretch of time than any accounting period may reflect. Long-range investments, combined with the increasing rigidity of many costs, require long-run emphasis on the drive for profits.

Additionally, managerial discretion regarding profit showings makes the evaluation of profits uncertain, at best. Profit statements are influenced by decisions about inventory valuations, the level of inventories, and write-offs. They are affected by the timing of expenditures for repairs, for research and development, for sales promotion, and for long-range improvements which can be charged to current expenses, such as the costs of drilling for oil or building up a sales force.

The difficulties in analyzing profits are compounded by serious problems of accounting in multiproduct firms. When a company sells in several markets, accounting allocations make it exceedingly difficult, if not impossible, to cast up a profit and loss statement for one item in a manner which is consistent with those used for other products and other firms. Allocations of joint costs of production, distribution, and administration pose tremendous analytical problems. Any intercompany comparison of item profits is complicated by differences in the vertical integration of competitors, in production and distribution.

In the light of these conditions the precepts of value theory, regarding profits as a bench mark for degree of competitiveness, seem to bear little relationship to the bulk of industrial activities. Occasionally, high, sustained profits may provide a fair indication of monopolistic conditions. However, the absence of such a showing does not imply vigorous competition. Further, the models do not provide a basis for gaging the level of profits. They merely suggest that sustained high profits reflect less competition—a common-sense conclusion, but not necessarily an accurate one.

MERGERS

One of the most pressing of the current antitrust problems stems from the Celler-Kefauver Antimerger Act. Cases under this act call for a consideration of the relevant market, the nature of the competition before the merger and after, the degree of concentration in the market, and the effect of the merger on sources of supply for buyers and on potential sales of sellers.

The models of value theory do not seem to shed light on these problems. In fact, antitrust problems of this type are confined to markets which do not fit such models. Hence, it seems quite likely that a literal application of value theory would favor an outright prohibition of such mergers if they develop companies which account for more than, say, 5 percent of a market. Yet, such a precept would

not allow for a closer analysis of each specific situation—a requirement in the consideration of competitive problems in an imperfect
market. For, there are instances when the larger combinations might
provide more active competition in a market which is dominated
by larger companies.

Mergers introduce new problems of market definition. Unfortunately, there is no possibility of setting up a uniform classification
of markets which will meet the needs of all antitrust rules. A market
definition used in a monopolization case may well differ from the
concept applied in a merger proceeding. Thus, while aluminum may
be the dimension of the relevant market in a monopolization case,
the market concept might be broadened in an attack on the merger
of an aluminum producer and a major copper company. Therefore,
the concept of the market must be tailored to the antitrust issue at
hand.

Value theory does not seem to offer operational principles for the
construction of market definitions which meet the specific needs of
the various antitrust rules. As suggested above in discussing monopolization, the neoclassical models simply do not deal with the complex
problem.

PRICE FIXING

The antitrust laws prohibit all price agreements, a position which
comports with the models of value theory. However, no one would
contend that an understanding of these models is necessary to determine that price agreements are anticompetitive.

The most important application of the models would be to support
an inference, based upon circumstantial evidence, that collusion
exists. If the models of value theory could demonstrate how competitive prices would have behaved in the relevant market, they
would be of great aid in evaluating such circumstantial evidence.

However, it seems highly unlikely that a market which is under
antitrust scrutiny would contain the numbers of buyers and sellers
which the value theory model requires. Further, no one has been able

to develop the cost and demand schedules required by such a model during the trial of an antitrust issue.

REMEDIES

A substantial deficiency in the application of economic inquiry in antitrust stems from a shortcoming in the procedures followed. In the main, antitrust prosecutions have concentrated on findings that the law has been violated. Comparatively little attention has been given to the development of remedies which would effectively maintain or restore competition. Economic analysis has been used more widely in testing the existence of a violation than in formulating appropriate remedies. There has been a dearth of research regarding the effectiveness of past decrees. Currently, there exists no body of empirical data regarding the types of remedies which might be most effective in any proceeding. Bits and pieces of evidence seem to indicate that some decrees have been effective and that others have been completely ineffective. Despite 70 years experience, there are few guidelines for decrees based on empirical analysis.

In any efforts to develop a body of criteria for constructing remedies, it hardly seems likely that the models of value theory would make a contribution. First, they are not pertinent to an effort to improve competitive forces in an imperfect market. Second, they offer no help in determining how to obtain a competitive condition beyond the common-sense stricture to eliminate impediments to competition.

Theory and Methodology

The value of theory in any discipline depends on its contribution to the development of analytical methodology. A theory which strides to inexorable conclusions, without a rigorous basis for testing its application, may be useful as an intellectual exercise but it cannot serve as a basis for public-policy decisions or for the application of those policies. A theory which supplies answers only through eclectic contemplation, producing solutions which are not testable, may better serve the needs of theology than of research and analysis.

It is possible that the underpinnings of value theory can be tied in with rigorous methodology which would be useful in antitrust. Such a methodology might call for field studies to test the reasonableness of the postulates and to develop new ones which would reflect the conditions of modern markets.

However, it seems likely that such a procedure cannot be applied to value theory. Neoclassical theory seems to depend on a closed system which works through a semimechanical process with no interferences from outside sources or nonconformist competitors. Its symmetry may depend entirely upon this set of conditions. In that event, new postulates may spoil its balanced operations so drastically that it could not maintain its present shape.

At the moment, the value of value theory is that it supplies a conceptual framework which demonstrates the overall advantages of eliminating undue interferences with the operations of the market. In the hands of the early writers, the theory was aimed primarily at government interferences, not private ones. Adam Smith doubted the possibility of removing private interferences through government action. Yet, this is the purpose of antitrust policy. Hence, the uses of its models in antitrust may possibly constitute a perversion of value theory itself.

The use of the models of value theory in antitrust is affected by a basic conceptual difficulty. The basic models discriminate only between the polar concepts of monopoly and competition. They are concerned not with how to make a market more competitive but with what would be a fully competitive operation. They describe a condition rather than the guidelines for attaining it.

Antitrust, on the other hand, involves another problem—how to increase market rivalry. It is directed to improvising improvements, rather than to reconstructing all conditions affecting competition in a market. It deals with specific, narrow issues rather than with all the factors influencing market rivalry: factors of entry, exit, and investment; conditions of the markets for the raw materials consumed in manufacturing the products under study; suppliers of labor and services; rivalry among buyers; and interrelations with other markets. It does not cope with the broad range of governmental activities which affect competition in a market. Therefore, antitrust cannot be the instrumentality for satisfying all of the requisites of the models of value theory.

Unfortunately, the reference points of neoclassical theory do not satisfy the requirements of antitrust. They deal with the overall situation, not with parts. They concentrate on the final destination, not on the road or the roadblocks. Therefore, they fail to provide the operational tools of analysis which might be applied.

The models of value theory have had little discernible effect upon the thinking of either the policy makers or the administrators of antitrust policies. Antitrust is dominated by lawyers who do not enjoy a background in economic theory. Therefore, the application of any tools of analysis is in the hands of those who do not understand neoclassical theory.

It seems likely that the models of value theory will never provide operational tools for antitrust lawyers. They involve long chains of abstract reasoning. They employ many concepts which have no observational counterparts. They tend to oversimplify the variables which influence market rivalry. Few lawyers have the inclination to follow the abstract reasoning or the geometry of marginal cost and revenue curves. Administrators and policy makers do not understand the models, how they operate, or how they can be applied. Since they are engaged in finding practical solutions to limited competitive problems in markets which cannot satisfy the requirements of value theory, the content of its models fails to impress them.

What, then, can be done with economic models in the formulation and application of antitrust policy? Can useful models be developed? Must they follow the patterns of value theory or are there other types which would be more useful because they provide analyses which can be applied in both policy making and litigation?

One possibility would be to relate the uses of models to the methodology of litigation itself. With few exceptions, antitrust litigation depends upon inferences drawn from circumstantial evidence. The plaintiff presents an hypothesis and develops data in support of it. He argues that his evidence is compatible with his hypothesis and is not compatible with others. In opposition, the defendant has several alternatives. He may argue that the plantiff's evidence is compatible with a new hypothesis; he may disprove some of the plaintiff's evidence; he may introduce additional evidence to show that a new hypothesis is more reasonable. In many proceedings, he uses all of these alternatives.

This system of inference—constructing and testing hypotheses—is the heart of antitrust litigation. It calls for the development and testing of models. Does the model fit the data? Would another model prove a better fit?

The construction and testing of hypotheses is a basic element of the methodology of rigorous economic analysis. In fact, it is the basis of scientific method. To this end, economic theory should provide antitrust with an appropriate framework for defining questions and issues, for ascertaining relevant evidence, for developing hypotheses and testing them.

In developing the uses of models through the methodology of hypothesis, based on the conditions of a specific market, economic analysis can make a substantial contribution to the development of antitrust policy and to litigation and negotiation. It would provide tools which are tailored to the operations of the antitrust laws. Since it would be meaningful to the lawyers, it would help to overcome the important barriers which exist between the two professions. In this development, the models of value theory would seem to be a hindrance, not a help.

COMMENTS

By Irston R. Barnes

May I begin by expressing my appreciation and admiration for Mark Massel's incisive demonstration of the two propositions that economic analysis has a vital role to play in antitrust work and that market models of value theory have not been useful tools in solving antitrust problems. As always, in considering economic problems which demand legal answers, Mr. Massel's ambivalence illustrates the advantages of uniting the two disciplines.

In affirming my general concurrence with Mr. Massel's conclusions, my remarks will not be so inclusive as his paper. In line with my somewhat more specialized experience, I shall consider the application of the models of value theory to the selection and trial of antitrust cases. This is the area in which attempts to use value theory have been most vigorously tested in a variety of industries and markets.

I find myself with a curious impression about value theory after a reading of the four principal papers. With the exception of the paper now being discussed, all of the papers reveal a touching loyalty to our academic past. Each author has found value theory of relatively little use in his particular work; yet each suspects that perhaps it is more useful in other areas and that, in any event, it should, or could, be made more useful.

Mr. Massel finds that value theory fails in its antitrust applications through three circumstances: substantial differences in the scope of value theory and antitrust law, a neglect of significant forces in modern markets, and the failure of the value theory analysis to fit the operational needs of antitrust.

I agree, but I should prefer to emphasize the failure of value theory to fit the basic realities of business and market behavior and the inability to obtain objective data to test the concepts of value theory. If value theory could have been tested with objective data, is it likely that economists would have long accepted conclusions that oligopoly must tend toward a stalemate or that product differentiation typically leads to monopolistic results in the economy? In my observation, value theory has operated as a handicapping hypothesis in many antitrust cases, foreclosing inquiry into all facts relevant to an examination and understanding of competition in action. The self-delegated authority with which value theory speaks has too often ensnared the uninitiated, both economists and noneconomists, into uncritical interpretations of economic "laws," into thinking with definitions and classifications, and into accepting untenable conclusions.

The inherent limitations of value theory, summarized by Mr. Massel, should have stood as a clear warning against misapplications of value theory to the real world of business and antitrust. These inadequacies are explored in depth in Professor J. M. Clark's splendid effort to chart a new course in *Competition as a Dynamic Process*. Two inadequacies are fundamental: the equilibrium models of value theory are incapable of coping with the dynamic or growth aspects of the economy, and the oversimplified selection of variables (even if relevant objective data were available) removes the models from the actualities of business conduct. Moreover, as Professor Clark has shown, where the newer models of imperfect competition appear to offer firm conclusions, the answers are, too often, wrong in ascribing monopolistic results to situations which remain actively competitive. Particular weight attaches to Mr. Massel's analysis in the critical realm of cost-price relationships, especially in view of the options available to the firm as between investment or operating costs and current or future costs, and considering the extent to which changes in the structure of costs have deprived marginal costs of critical significance in determining production and price policies. In addition, as Mr. Massel notes, value theory is inadequate in the presence of multiproduct diversification of firms and the extension of sales across widely scattered geographical and functional markets, in the dominance of longrun objectives for the firm that do not fit the assumptions of short-run profit maximization, and in the general use of price as simply one tactic in the broad strategy of competition. It has long been clear that the worlds of business and public policy have been making demands on theory which theory is not prepared to fulfill.

Mr. Massel has examined value theory as a tool in representative types of antitrust litigation. Perhaps the issues may be further clarified if we ask what antitrust wants in the economy, and how value theory has been used in litigation.

Antitrust wants genuine independence in action, not a mere absence of collusion, on the part of business firms. It wants a progressive economy which is growing, adopting improved technologies, and offering innovations and new products to consumers. It wants consumers competent to choose knowledgeably from an adequate range of products. And it wants reasonably full employment, particularly for its labor resources.

In seeking these goals, antitrust is directed, according to the under

standing of an earlier age, against interferences with the market mechanisms, as by collusion or monopolization. It also seeks (inadequately)
to preserve a structural framework for competition and to define a more
satisfactory plane of competition. In its seventy-year history, antitrust
has received relatively little help from economics generally, or from value
theory in particular, in achieving a more effective approach to maintaining
competition. Such a contribution might have been made if economic
theory had addressed itself more comprehensively to identifying the
structural requirements for effective competition in specific industries,
to lowering the barriers for new entrants, and to distinguishing those
patterns of competition which, in particular industries, are inconsistent
with an efficient and progressive economy.

Despite all inadequacies, value theory and its models have frequently
appeared in antitrust proceedings. Qualifying as expert witnesses, economists have used the apparatus of value theory to pronounce judgment
on the competitive or noncompetitive character of industries. They have
testified that substantial (or identical) uniformity of prices is consistent
with independent competitive determination of prices in industries dominated by a few large sellers, and their testimony has been used to persuade examiner or judge that an imputation of collusion would be unreasonable. Other economists, looking at the same facts, have testified
to the opposite effect. They have been prepared to predict confidently
the character of market conduct from the number and relative size
of competitors, and have found encouragement for progress even in
such innovations as newly designed and more eye-catching packaging.
They have quite generally failed to distinguish, for specific industries, the
market structures, the size disparities, or the patterns of competitive
moves which are promotive of competition on efficiency grounds, from
those which encourage or permit the choice of competitive moves which
lead to increasing concentration and more effective discipline of competition by the dominant firms in the industry. Such testimony, which
seeks to give the status of facts to opinions which concern nothing more
than possibilities (or even high probabilities), brings confusion to the
antitrust record and disrepute to economics and economists.

Defenders of price theory's usefulness may think that Mr. Massel
has given scanty consideration to the newer variants of price theory,
especially since so many economists have found profitable employment
interpreting imperfect and monopolistic competition to courts and com-
missions.

These models of value theory have been used by free-wheeling economists to arrive at dubious conclusions from information regarding the structure of markets. They have been chiefly responsible for the recent vogue of the concentration ratio and the correlative legal doctrine of quantitative substantiality. In this numbers game, everyone, including the attorney, fancies himself an expert, qualified to assert (or to deny) that a particular degree of concentration, or a specific change in concentration, is (or is not) indicative of a substantial lessening of competition. Aside from deficiencies in the industry or product categories which concentration ratios purport to describe, market-structure data, standing alone, do not permit reliable inferences to be drawn concerning either present competition or its future prospects. While it must be presumed that in the long run business firms will be responsive to the logic of their market positions, it must also be recognized that, for the businessman, logic is inherent in more than the number and size of his principal competitors. The businessman will also find logic in technologies of production, especially as reflected in long-run costs, in the characteristics of the product (as related to the firm's product mix, its elasticity of purchase, the nature of its uses, its susceptibility to sales promotion, the competence of buyers' evaluations, and a dozen other factors), in the competitive strategies open to the firm and to its competitors, and in the likelihood of new entrants invading the industry. The economist, who, on the basis of a value-theory model and some concentration ratios, attempts to testify to the competitive consequences of a merger, an exclusive arrangement, or a price discrimination, is inviting acute embarrassment if he faces a competent legal adversary.

I should like to emphasize one point which I think Mr. Massel takes for granted. The limitations of value theory are primarily responsible for the overemphasis of price in antitrust proceedings. Value theory says that competitive prices of the same product should be uniform among buyers, flexible, and responsive to costs. If they are not so, then value theory implies that competitive forces are deficient. This result follows, as Mr. Massel has shown, from the fact that value theory does not deal with the nonprice dimensions of the product. Consequently, both in the selection of cases and in their trial, value theory is likely to fail to give a rounded evaluation of the competitive forces at work. This is a probability because antitrust cases commonly arise in industries which exhibit marked disparities in size among firms, with one or a few large firms accounting for the bulk of the market. In these situations, the economist, relying on his value theory and ignoring the smaller firms because they do not fit his model, is likely to conclude that competitive moves will always be stifled because competitors will believe that any competitive moves will be promptly and effectively neutralized. Yet, as Professor Clark has shown, these smaller firms, if competitively strong enough to weather the reactions of their larger rivals, will have incentives to initiate moves which may keep the industry reasonably competitive. Thus it is possible that value theory will brand a market as competitively defective when no alternative market—at least no alternative within the purview of an antitrust proceeding—would be more satisfactory.

Two models frequently invoked by the defense in antitrust matters are the Schumpeter theory of innovation as creative destruction and the Clark theory of workable competition. Each is invoked, with due deference to the deserved reputations of their originators (whose mantles the witnesses sometimes try to wear), to argue that the existing or the prospective state of competition is the type of competition most consistent with a progressive economy. All too often these theories do not justify the assertions made in their names. It was this record of misuse and abuse that caused the Attorney General's National Committee to Study the Antitrust Laws, in examining the concepts of workable competition and of pure and perfect competition, to conclude that " 'workable' or 'effective' competition supplies no formula which can substitute for judgment," and to warn "that economic theories not be applied beyond the limits of their own propositional base." This is, of course, good advice beyond the antitrust field.

While Mr. Massel rightly observes that value theory in itself will not serve to define the relevant market for antitrust proceedings, I do think that the related concept of cross-elasticity of demand makes some contribution. There is, of course, no specific degree of cross-elasticity that unites or divides products in the same or different markets, but where a change in the price of one product brings substantial displacements in significant uses, I should consider this behavior as prima facie evidence that the two products are in the same or related markets. Thus, I could agree with the majority of the Supreme Court in the *du Pont Cellophane Case* [351 U.S. 377 (1956)], that "commodities reasonably interchangeable by consumers for the same purpose" are in the same or closely related markets, even though I could find no evidence of any significant cross-elasticity of demand in the demonstrated capacity of du Pont to alter the price of cellophane in disregard of the prices of the other flexible packaging materials.

The chief disservice of the value theories and their models lies in the tendency of those relying on value theories to dismiss or overlook evidence relevant to the workings of competition, testing the industry or market by the model when, more logically, they should be testing the model against the industry. A correlative disservice arises from attempts to show all the facts, and only those facts, which would make the industry or market seem competitive in accordance with some selected model of value theory. Some of the most inflated of antitrust records, as in the Pillsbury merger case, have come from attempts to use any and every item of business rivalry to paint a picture of active and all-pervasive competition.

A grave deficiency of value theory within its own selected domain is the failure, well illustrated in Mr. Massel's paper, to distinguish the significance, for maintaining price or price-equivalent competition, of the various patterns of competitive tactics and strategies which develop in different industries and markets. While considerations of changing patterns of competition would complicate the geometrical presentations of value theory, it should be possible to consider these matters, along with other environmental factors affecting competitive markets, as Professor Clark has demonstrated.

The probably insuperable difficulties in making value theories fit the real economic world reside, as Messrs. Cassady, Massel, and Oxenfeldt agree, in the steadily developing complexities in the business world— the multiplication of products and diversification of firms into many markets, the strategies of product differentiation and the various patterns of nonprice competition, and the changing character of cost-price relationships, to mention only three. No value theory of practical use will have the simplicity of current models. Nor will one be likely to spring from a unifying deductive insight. More probably, any new theories will come from empirical studies of the kind which Professor Cassady describes.

Neither the strategic position of lawyers in the agencies of enforcement nor the presentation of economic questions in legal settings seems to me the critical reason for the lack of success of value theories in antitrust trials. Lawyers are quite capable of indulging in lengthy abstract reasoning, when they see any profit in it. But like businessmen, they are repelled by the lack of reality in the underlying assumptions, the ease with which economists' conclusions can be upset by specific questions based on the behavior of an industry, and the qualified, conditional character of the statements which value theorists can defend.

Where they are not drawn to prohibit specific activities—arrangements in restraint of trade, or brokerage payments—, the antitrust laws are concerned with judgments regarding the present or future state of competition. As Mr. Massel notes, antitrust trials involve model building, but not with the presently available value theory analysis. One may, therefore, turn the question around and ask whether antitrust enforcement can contribute to the strengthening of economic theory. When the exigencies of the case and the patience of the attorneys permit, the development of a theory of the case and the marshaling of evidence to test and support that theory become a kind of model building directed to showing how to restore or maintain competition. With a little more scientific inquiry and a little less trial expediency, such testing of hypotheses, like the investigations of Professor Cassady, could yield contributions to theories of competition and price. These would not be general-purpose value theories. These would be contributions, first, to developing reliable techniques for the examination of the usages and consequences of competition in any particular industry or market, second, to arriving at some theories relating competition to environmental factors and business practices, and third, to formulating some more general laws of competition. I doubt that these results would ever closely resemble the value theories we have been considering, but I do not doubt that they would prove more useful in guiding business and government agencies in the antitrust field.

By Ewald T. Grether

Mark Massel has compressed a tremendous amount of material, analysis, and opinion and judgment into his paper. We are all indebted to him for adding the ring of legal authority to ideas and conclusions of economists. In the process he has also helped focus thinking sharply on the operational type of analysis involved in actual litigation, in which his experience gives him special competence quite beyond that of professional economists.

I shall hope in my brief statement to accomplish three things, namely: 1) To further emphasize selected aspects of agreement. 2) To enter a caveat, with respect to the interpretation of and nexus with neoclassical economic analysis. 3) To suggest briefly a possible line of development.

Areas of agreement. Received theory, limited to the analysis of price-output variables, is inadequate for the analysis of actual competition, including the basic underlying forces, especially in the areas of concentrated economic power, oligopoly, and large-scale corporate operation. Even the newer models, with their refinements, lead to unrealistic, overly simplified conclusions. Consequently, there is no reasonable way of dealing with such developments as diversification and vertical integration, or with similar institutional factors and changes. The dynamic forces of technological progress and of innovation play remotely outside, without reasonable means of ingress to the closed system.

Mr. Massel makes his most telling points in reference to specific statutory responsibilities placed upon antitrust. His observations would have been even sharper if he had highlighted the evidentiary and analytical differences under various sections of the Sherman, Clayton, Federal Trade Commission, Robinson-Patman, and 1950 Merger Acts. He notes for example, that the very presence of the issues arising out of mergers is clear-cut demonstration that the conditions of simple competition are absent. The only conclusion that one might draw from the simple models of pure competition is that mergers should be disallowed if they involve more than, say, five percent of the market. (In his first draft he used the figure of one percent. It seems to me he was more nearly right the first time!) Exclusive arrangements are in violation "if they tend to lessen competition substantially." But the competitive effects of exclusive arrangements vary with circumstances and conditions. Accepted theory offers no analytical basis for the examination of such arrangements. I should add that it points only to making them per se violations, as some urge. And, finally, there is the labyrinth of price discrimination in which law and economics have become so lost that they may never find each other.

In this general perspective, Mr. Massel calls for, among other things, a special type of or adaptation of economic analysis appropriate to the problems and cases that arise in litigation and enforcement. This is the prime contribution of his paper and deserves very careful consideration and discussion. This special adaptation of economic analysis is in addition to general or aggregative economics which is helpful in the overall review of the economy and in locating trouble spots for antitrust action.

If I interpret Mr. Massel's criticisms and suggestions correctly, he has tucked the baby safely into its crib before throwing out the bath water. Traditional and current economic models are inadequate, but something worthwhile can be accomplished under the banner of economics. The current inadequacies stem not only from such lacks as already depicted but from the inability to make reasonable distinctions of degree. Antitrust should not operate merely in terms of a simple dichotomy of competition and monopoly. It must deal with the more and the less as well as with practicable alternatives. Even more important, analysis and action must focus upon the individual firm separately, or occasionally upon the industry. That is, action is highly particularized; it is concerned with specific situations and special circumstances. Analysis must be sensibly confined in order that reasonable conclusions can be reached. Yet, somehow, it must also fit into a broader framework. The definition of the relevant market is the means of delimiting the field and of confining the analysis. But the determination of relief or remedies must be in relation to larger competitive functioning and, in fact, frequently must escape from economic analysis into a broader orbit.

Apparently, Mr. Massel is stating that it is possible to develop models of analysis that derive from the "methodology of litigation itself" which is essentially a procedure of constructing and testing hypotheses, or if you wish, a form of theory. But this is also "the methodology of rigorous economic analysis" and the basis of scientific method in general. He envisages therefore, that economic theory would provide antitrust with an "appropriate framework for defining questions and issues, for ascertaining relevant evidence, for developing hypotheses, and for testing them . . . based on the conditions of a specific market." Along these lines, economics "would provide tools which are better tailored to the operations of the antitrust laws." The baby in the crib will be reared to do useful things, or, at the very least, to be more useful than his parents.

Now, it is not unusual to adapt economic analysis to special purposes. On the contrary, since economic theory takes only some halting steps toward full reality, the process of adaptation in application is of the essence. But there are some unique factors in this particular type of adaptation. For one thing, it must take place under the firm control and supervision of the member of another discipline—a lawyer. Furthermore, rarely, if at all, can one take more than one step at a time. The constraints of the case, of precedent, and of tradition, are usually strict and confining. It is not surprising, therefore, that budding, young economists often prefer to exercise their maturing talents elsewhere than in antitrust enforcement, or decide to become lawyers, as did Mark Massel.

Unfortunately, we cannot resolve our problem merely by becoming lawyers, although at one time there was a per se prohibition of the use of economists in antitrust enforcements in the Department of Justice.

Something in the nature of economic analysis is required and is being used. In fact, the range and importance of uses is expanding and must continue to expand in response to the inherent necessities of policy-making litigation and judicial determination. The stakes are enormously high for the economy and for individual enterprises. Nowhere else in our society do judges wield power equivalent to their power in a big antitrust case.

Mark Massel has put the spotlight on a very important problem. I doubt, however, if there is or can be a ready-made solution. I can envisage only a slow process of growth in understanding and adaptation of concepts and procedures of analysis. The concepts and tools of economic analysis have invaded the trial briefs and the courtroom and will remain there. But the extent and character of the use of economic analysis will depend to a considerable degree on its contribution; that is, upon its usefulness and relevance.

A *caveat with respect to neoclassical economics*. At one major point, however, I may be in disagreement with Mark Massel. If I read him correctly, he finds little that is useful in what he calls the value models of neoclassical theory. I am inclined to believe that he is not really concerned with neoclassical theory in, say, the Marshallian sense, but with the refinements of price theory of the past thirty to forty years, or less. There may be something of great importance here. Possibly in the process of refining concepts, of drawing harder and sharper lines, and, especially, in seeking more exact measures and indicia, we have moved away from reality instead of towards it. Possibly, our beautiful taxonomies with their simple logic and symbolism may be doing more for the ego of the craftsmen than for basic understanding and wisdom. Admittedly, we cannot operate merely in terms of pure competition or single firm monopoly. Possibly, however, this might be preferable to viewing the economy in terms of numerous, separate, closed-power systems. Possibly, too, some form of open-end behavioral systems analysis might be helpful or useful, but this possibility will not be explored here.

Antitrust cases cannot be decided without broad judgments based upon empirical evidence and argument, including, often, economic evidence and argument. The arguments and the judgments must bear some relationship to the evidence, and, hence, should not be derived from models unrelated to the evidence in the specific situation. The tailored models Mark Massel proposes must therefore be basically different from those of static economic analysis. An important difference will be the gap —narrow or wide, often wide—between the conclusions based upon specific evidence and the judgments as to violation, remedies, and relief. I am inclined to believe that the insights and wisdom derived from the Marshallian type of analysis are more helpful in reaching these final judgments than those derived from the refinements of static analysis. It will be recalled that a concept of biological continuity was basic in Marshall, and, consequently, also an unwillingness to assume clear lines of division, if they do not exist in real life. Furthermore, he probed behind so called competition rather than looking at it directly, and found its meaning in deliberate, free choice, with forethought and foresight, among alternatives. He preferred to speak of "freedom of industry and enterprise" or, more briefly, of "economic freedom," rather than of "competition." He had a strong realistic interest, developed the partial equilibrium and industry analysis, and was strongly oriented toward problems of industrial organization, productivity, and economic development and progress. I suggest that Massel's proposals, instead of running away from or counter to neoclassical economics, have spiritual and perhaps direct lineal kinship with those of Alfred Marshall.

A possible line of development in analysis. Assuming that we agree that 1) static models are inadequate, if not misleading, and that 2) an improved operational type of economic analysis is required, how do we proceed? We can all agree, I am sure, that there is now no generally accepted framework of analysis. I shall make only a few brief comments and suggestions.

In an antitrust case, the firm or firms involved must be viewed in their general and specific environmental settings. Included in the general environment, in our times, must be the rapid advance of applied sciences and technologies which are forcing innovation at all levels of production and marketing, either in cost reduction or in new products and services. These general influences make themselves felt in a highly variable manner throughout our industries and trades. Included, also, must be the basic, general, and specific underlying trends. In all cases, the enterprise or enterprises must be related to their market structures, the most important direct environmental influence, in order to determine the character of these constraints upon decision making. Internal decision making and behavior should be interpreted in relation to market structure and to the goals of the enterprise. The goals are normally multiple instead of merely short-run or long-run profit maximization, often including the maintenance or improvement of relative market position and market share, and sales maximization under minimum profit constraints. Thus, the analysis is "behavioristic," in that the behavior of the enterprise, insofar as is reasonable, is related to its external market structural setting; but it is also behavioristic in that the explicit or implicit rationale of business decisions is involved. In this latter connection the circumstantial evidence to which Massel refers is apt to be important. Unfortunately, however, we lack theories of business decision making, by and for the business enterprise, with which to illuminate this evidence or to aid us in the search for other types of evidence.

In some cases, especially under the Sherman Act, the actualities of past and recent behavior in relation to structure and goals must be established and appraised. But under Clayton Act cases, and especially in mergers, the reasonable probabilities must be forecasted and appraised, instead of the specific actualities. Thus, one is forced into an analysis of dynamic processes and of their play over time, under conditions involving foresight and planning. All major policy areas bearing upon the issue must be examined—product policy, pricing, marketing, organization, sales promotion and marketing, exclusive arrangements, and so on. That is, the basic policies and practices of the firm and/or of the industry should be examined in the dual context of market structure and internal business decision making and practice in relation to antitrust.

Now, all of this probably sounds much more complicated than it is in fact. Actually, this type of analysis is already used to some extent, although the full framework may not be used or exposed. The analysis must be confined within the relevant market and area of effective competition. It should be focused only upon those areas of decision making appropriate to the specific issue. It need not involve performance data except as these illuminate behavior or reflect the constraints of the market environment. It should bring to bear not only the tools of analysis that have been sharpened by E. S. Mason and his numerous and able disciples in the field of so-called industrial organization, but also those that are on the whetstone in schools of business and in the emerging areas of management science and operations research. I do not envisage, however, that courtrooms will become filled in the near future, if ever, with mathematical models, although they may be useful in the preparation of cases. Lawyers and judges have had trouble enough in digesting only a few elementary concepts. The argument and judgments must almost invariably derive from a looser framework than that of a precisely formulated model. But framework we must have, and, in fact, have been developing, to some extent, by case antitrust procedure.

Economists with strong applied interests and knowledge can help tighten the loose structural-behavior analysis that has been evolving. Actually, of course, this tightening has been occurring in a systematic manner on the part of some defendants on antitrust cases. One can well understand how the government might prefer to operate in terms of a relatively simple competition-monopoly framework in order to avoid long complicated economic investigations and arguments. But if the tests derived from static models are as inadequate and misleading, as here opined, then some sort of structural-behavioral analysis, including dynamic time factors, is inescapable.

By Myron W. Watkins

With the first part of Mr. Massel's paper I find myself, like Mr. Barnes, in close agreement. The neoclassical theory of price determination contributed signally to the development and enforcement of antitrust policy in its first half century. But thereafter the role of market model making which assayed use of microeconomic theory to provide a more realistic application of antitrust fell short of the aspirations of its proponents, whether they were sympathetic, hostile, or indifferent to the aims of antitrust. The clash between the teachings of model makers and the legal precepts made for increasing confusion and uncertainty among businessmen and lawyers. Judges, too, shared in the general obfuscation and disillusionment. I venture that the explanation of this is not to be found solely in lawyers' and judges' deficient training in, and familiarity with, economic theory, but, in part, also in an inadequate familiarity among economists with the controlling standards and aims of litigation. In sum, I suggest there is a fundamental incompatibility between the legal, or regulatory, process and the economic analysis process, which stands in the way of economic theory's making its full contribution to legal regulation, in respect alike of policy formulation and of policy application.

Specifically, the essence of law is the provision of rules of general application within prescribed boundaries or spheres. On the other hand, the essence of market model making is abstraction from complex reality to provide a situation sufficiently simple to facilitate analysis of the expected results. The thrust of legal regulation is outward, toward a generalization comprehensive enough to fit and be applicable to the multiple variants of complex reality. The thrust of market model making, indeed, of economic theory generally, is toward narrowing the field of observation and attending solely to a specified, simplified situation. In a society governed by law, which means any civilized society, the process of legal regulation can make little use of, at best can draw only minor benefits from, an exploratory activity which, from its inherent nature, can lead only to *ad hoc* rules.

Every actual market is unique and develops in its own peculiar way. Hence, the complexity of reality. Economic theorists seek to escape the complexity by assumptions that exclude some of the variables. Thereby they may, and often do, facilitate explanation of how the abstract model would work. But this procedure seldom helps one to a comprehension of how a given market in the complex world of reality does work and, hence, whether it conforms to the general rule prescribed by law.

In these circumstances it would be surprising if the construction of market models contributed much to the improvement of antitrust policy or administration. In fact, it is hardly an exaggeration to say that market models are either toys or traps—toys for the economists who construct them, traps for the lawyers and judges who seek to use them. Of course, it may be conceded that the trap is, more often than not, unintentional.

The reason for the futility (or worse) of attempts to use the models in antitrust practice has already been hinted at. The law must deal with concrete situations which are at once unique and inordinately complex. In appraising a specific situation or course of conduct to reach a decision on legality, the law has no alternative to weighing all facets and factors in the complex reality. For illegality invariably turns on intent —whether it is a question of homicide, libel, burglary, or antitrust. The rule of reason admits of no per se offense in any of these spheres. For example, to kill a man is not to commit murder and, contrary to widespread belief, to fix prices or limit output by collusion is not, *ipso facto*, to violate the antitrust laws—witness the Chicago Board of Trade, the National Window Glass Manufacturers' Association, and the Appalachian Coal cases.

Moreover, in the actual development of microeconomic theory the basic premise appears to have been that the structural pattern of a market is very nearly decisive of how it operates. But, while in antitrust enforcement concentration has some significance in conjunction with other factors, for the reasons sketched above, neither it alone nor any other single facet of, or factor in, the whole situation is determinative of the issue. To make it so would be unrealistic as well as disruptive of Western traditions of government under law. The law can dispense with economic theory, but it cannot dispense with common sense, in short, with "seeing things whole" and judging them "in the round."

If I may be permitted a reference to a personal experience, I believe it might be helpful in resolving the problem these papers discuss. Thirty-four years ago this spring, or thereabouts, I was privileged to receive a long (four-page) holograph letter from Oliver Wendell Holmes. He was commenting on one of my early articles, "The Economic Philosophy of Antitrust Legislation" (in *The Annals* of the American Academy). One of the principal themes of that paper was the inherently, incontinently, and ineradicably speculative character of business enterprise. He agreed not only upon the fact but also upon its profound significance. He recalled that one of his Boston friends, a textile manufacturer, had once observed that if he could only anticipate whether polka dots or stripes would be in fashion the next season the whole trade would be in his hands and his fortune would be made. The learned judge observed that *experentia docet*, and suggested his friend might strengthen his forecasts by consulting his wife, who could probably provide a new angle for his consideration, an angle he might otherwise neglect. I take it that here Justice Holmes was implicitly reaffirming and suggesting an extension of his famous aphorism, "The life of the law is experience, not logic."

In conclusion, I suggest that a paraphrase of this aphorism might well deserve consideration in framing a consensus for these papers. Specifically: The optimum administration of a business enterprise system depends on application of norms based on common sense derived from experience, not on application of cut and dried formulae derived from artful hypotheses.

THE USES OF PRICE THEORY

BY KENNETH E. BOULDING, PROFESSOR OF
ECONOMICS, THE UNIVERSITY OF MICHIGAN

The student and, still more, the layman who encounter the rather forbidding mass of literature known as price theory may well wonder what it is all for. In particular, for what task does the acquisition of this particular mass of knowledge fit the student? Most people who actually set prices seem to get along very well without it and, although the people who regulate prices often tend to refer to it, there is an uneasy suspicion that even in this occupation, price theory has created more confusion than enlightenment.

The cynic might argue, of course, that the main function of price theory is to pass examinations in price thory. It is true that if we examine the evolutionary process of mutation and selection by which the curricula of educational institutions are determined, we find that an important factor in the survival of any body of knowledge in a curriculum is its regurgitability. Price theory is magnificently regurgitable. A student can learn it and a teacher can find out quite easily by examination whether the student has, in fact, learned it. As the only physical product of formal education is examination papers, it is not surprising that items in the curriculum which are particularly useful in producing elegant specimens of this product tend to survive.

Not being a cynic, however, I shall argue that price theory arose out of a perfectly legitimate human curiosity about important elements in social life. Adam Smith was certainly not its only possible begetter, but he has good claims to being considered the legitimate father. Perhaps, however, we should regard Adam Smith as a maternal uncle or grandfather and cite Ricardo as the major culprit in our paternity case, for I think it can be argued that price theory today, with all its diagrammatic and mathematical and even conceptual embellishments, still remains in skeleton, and even largely in substance, what Ricardo made it. Ricardo, after all, was a successful stockbroker who presumably never gave an examination in his life. So that even though regurgitability may be an important factor in the academic survival of price theory it had little part to play in the mutation that gave rise to it.

When I was a young assistant lecturer at the University of Edinboro, I taught economics as the history of economic thought. As a result of this, I suspect that the main thing which the student learned and which he carried away from his academic experience was that Adam Smith was confused. I doubt, furthermore, if the student ever resolved Adam Smith's confusion in his own mind. In price theory, however, I think that Adam Smith probably was confused and that it took Ricardo to straighten him out. The confusion in Adam Smith's theory arises because he tried to solve two very different problems by means of the same theoretical framework. One is the problem of the determinants of the structure of relative prices. This has become the main problem of price theory, as usually understood, and this problem Adam Smith tried to solve by the so-called labor embodied theory. The second problem is quite different. This was the problem of the general price level, which Adam Smith interpreted as how to devise a standard of value in long-term contracts which would survive changes of the price level. This was a labor commanded theory which was, in effect, an attempt to write a labor clause into long-term contracts, very much like a gold clause. These two problems have really little to do with each other except under exceptional circumstances (which Ricardo, incidentally, fully understood), where the monetary unit is itself a commodity and hence the price level reflects the relative value of the monetary commodity.

In the development of economic thought the problem of the price level was gradually turned over to the monetary theorists, whereas the problem of the structure of relative prices became the central problem of price theory. Price theory then identified the central problem of economics as that of exchange and, even more particularly, as that of the ratio of exchange. A price, of course, is merely a special case of the ratio of exchange in which one of the things exchanged is money. In price theory money tends almost to disappear as an independent item; it becomes what Walras called a *numeraire*, that is, one commodity which is selected arbitrarily as a "measure of value." The focus of interest is not on absolute prices expressed in monetary terms, but on the relative prices of commodities in terms of each other. Thus, the problem of price theory is not so much, why is butter 80 cents a pound?, so much as, why can a pound of butter be exchanged for six pounds of bread? As every student who has completed the elementary course knows, we could have changes in the absolute level of prices, theoretically at least, without any change in the relative price structure, though in actual historical experience that never occurs. In price theory, then, it is the relative structure which interests us. If we are given a set of prices in terms of any *numeraire*, a simple arithmetical operation will enable us to deduce the ratio of exchange between any two commodities. If elephants are $2,000 apiece, and coal is $20 a ton, an elephant can presumably be exchanged directly or indirectly for 100 tons of coal.

The great question which faces the price theorist, therefore, is whether the structure of relative prices, which I call the price set, is arbitrary. If we substitute one set of prices for another set of prices does this make any difference and, if so, to what does it make a difference? Price theory can largely be interpreted as an attempt to find the answer to this question. We can put the question in another way. Is there any set of prices, divergence from which gets us into trouble? We can further ask, what kind of trouble do we get into? And we can ask a still further question as to whether the kind of trouble we get into enables us to get out of it, that is, produces the kind of behavior which changes the price set in the direction of what we might call of the "least trouble set." This is, of course, what economists have meant by equilibrium.

Ricardo defined the equilibrium price set as, essentially, that at which commodities exchange in the ratio of the discounted labor embodied in them. The labor theory of value is still a reasonably crude explanation of relative prices, at least suitable for a twelve-year-old. If a child asks us why an automobile is worth ten thousand loaves of bread, the rough answer is that the production of an automobile takes ten thousand times more labor or resources, in general, than a loaf of bread. Ricardo's labor theory is, of course, quite sophisticated. Ricardo realized that if the price set corresponded simply to the absolute amounts of labor embodied in different commodities then this would not be an equilibrium set because at this set of prices the production of commodities in which the labor had been embodied recently would be more profitable than the production of commodities in which labor had been embodied some time ago. Hence, resources would move into the former and away from the latter, the price of the former would fall and that of the latter would rise, until the profitability in both lines of production were the same, subject, of course, to possible immobility or different nonmonetary rewards. I would argue that this essentially is Marx's theory of relative prices as expounded in the third volume of *Capital*, for Marx had to abandon the simple labor embodied theory of relative prices for exactly the same reason that Ricardo abandoned it. I would argue, furthermore, that this is not essentially different from the equilibrium price theory of Marshall or even of Walras.

We can get around the problem of the nonmeasurability of the quantity of labor embodied by the concept of alternative cost. If a twelve-year-old comes back a year or two later and asks us the same question as to why the automobile is worth ten thousand loaves of bread, the answer we give him then is that if we give up the production of one automobile eventually with the resources released we can produce ten thousand loaves of bread. This may sound less plausible to him than the earlier explanation in view of the well-known difficulty of beating automobile factories into plowshares, and we can talk about depreciation, replacement, labor transfer and reeducation. We can perhaps persuade him that in the long run, wherein Keynes suggested we are all safely dead, the resources are perfectly mobile and the concept of alternative cost makes sense. The discounted labor theory, however, remains at least a moderately good explanation of why alternative costs are what they are, for if with the resources released by not producing an automobile, we can produce ten thousand loaves of bread, this is surely because it takes ten thousand times more of something to produce an automobile than it takes to produce a loaf of bread, and even though defining that something as discounted labor is not wholly satisfactory, in view of the difficulties of definition and measurement, it is at least crudely acceptable. The ultimate resource, after all, is human time, energy, or perhaps information output, and it does matter *when* this ultimate resource is applied. If it is applied earlier, the product must be priced higher than if the same amount were to be applied later, because if this were not so, as both Ricardo and Marx saw very clearly, rates of profit in different occupations would be different, and hence, capital would flow away from occupations with low profit, the products of which were underpriced because of their long periods of production, toward occupations of high profit with products that were overpriced because of the short periods of production. A relative price structure which corresponded to undiscounted labor embodied, therefore, would produce a distribution of profits in different occupations which would cause a shift of capital toward, and hence a fall in the price of the product, in those with short periods of production and a corresponding shift of capital away from, and the rise in the price of the product, of those occupations with long periods of production.

All of this is very elementary and I fear that my sophisticated reader may be bored. The interesting thing, however, is that we seemed to have developed a large amount of price theory without even mentioning the state of the market, and without mentioning monopoly, oligopoly, and imperfect competition, or even perfect competition. The only assumption which seems to be made here is the absolute mobility of resources, and especially of capital, from occupations of lower return to occupations of higher return. The next modification of the basic Ricardian model, a modification, incidentially, which was already familiar to Adam Smith, is that made by Cairnes, and is the concept of noncompeting groups. All this means is that we may have a price set in which there are differences in the return to capital or to labor in different occupations, but that this price set is nevertheless an equilibrium set, in the sense that it persists and that the dynamics of the system tends to reproduce it rather than to destroy it, simply because of the impossibility of shifting resources from occupations of low return to those of high return. Under conditions of immobility, then, the concept of an equilibrium price set becomes not a point in the vector space but a whole set of points, at any one of which the system is an equilibrium. The set, however, is a bounded set, that is, there are some points outside it; for unless the immobility of resources is absolute, there will be some relative price structure which will overcome the immobility and which will cause resources to move from the less profitable to the more profitable occupations. This, of course, will bring the relative price structure back again into the equilibrium set, or, more exactly, into the set of equilibrium sets. Even now, however, we have not really encountered any states of the market. Monopoly is, of course, a state of immobility. It is only because the monopolist is able to prevent resources from moving into his occupation that he is able to extract a price which gives him a return larger than that of the resources around him. There is still no mention, however, of the state of the market. For all we know, the monopolist may be facing an almost perfectly elastic demand curve, or he may be facing an inelastic one. Now, of course, if he is a profit-maximizer, as we hope, being good economists, he will presumably always push his price into that region of the demand curve where the marginal revenue is positive and, therefore, the demand curve in the Marshallian sense is relatively elastic. What makes him a monopolist, however, is not the elasticity of his demand curve, but the fact that he is able to prevent other resources from entering his occupation. It is the immobility of resources that makes monopoly, whether this is artificial or natural, not the state of the market.

We might almost conclude from the above that the theory of the states of the market was almost irrelevant from the point of view of price theory. It must be confessed, indeed, that price theory got along very well without it for a long time. The theory of the states of the market, indeed, does not develop much before 1930. In Marshall, for instance, the theory of monopoly is a somewhat isolated appendix to the whole structure of his price theory, and although it is clear from a good many references in *Industry and Trade* that Marshall understood very well the nature of the problem of imperfect competition in the real world, he never managed to integrate the phenomenon into the general framework of his price theory. By the end of the 1920s, however, something was in the air. The curious controversy, mostly in the *Economic Journal*, which began with the famous "empty boxes" article by the Economic Historian, J. H. Clapham [1] in 1922 and culminated in Sraffa's [2] extraordinary article of 1926, paved the way for the minor revolution which was represented by the works of Joan Robinson [3] and Edward H. Chamberlin.[4] The name of Roy Harrod at Oxford should probably be added to complete the historical record, though his contributions at that time were mostly in the form of lectures. With Triffin's [5] extension of the imperfect competition notions into the region of general equilibrium theory in 1940, we may say I think that the brief "classical"

---

[1] J. H. Clapham, "Of Empty Economic Boxes," *Economic Journal*, 32 (1932), 305–14.

[2] Pierr Sraffa, "The Laws of Returns under Competitive Conditions, *Economic Journal* 36 (1936), 535–50.

[3] Joan Robinson, *The Economics of Imperfect Competition* (London, Macmillan, 1933),

[4] E. H. Chamberlin, *The Theory of Monopolistic Competition* (1st Ed., Cambridge, Mass., Harvard University Press, 1933).

[5] Robert Triffin, *Monopolistic Competition and General Equilibrium Theory* (Cambridge, Mass., Harvard University Press, 1940).

period of imperfect competition theory came to an end. And I think one can say, in all honesty, there has been very little progress since.

It is hard for the student of today to recapture the sense of excitement which pervaded economics in the 1930s. Marshall's synthesis, like that of Mill before him, had dominated the scene for forty years, in spite of occasional rumblings from the American institutionalists and a few European radicals. In the 1930s, however, this serene but perhaps rather static chrysalis cracked, and out of it apparently came two butterflies: the progressive unfoldings of the Keynesian revolution, on the one hand, and the theory of imperfect competition, on the other. Both of these were clearly in the same genetic line as the Marshallian system, that is, they were not mere movements of protest but were in the main stream of development of economic thought. Moreover, they both seem to clear up two things which were eminently unsatisfactory in the Marshallian economics and with which it had been unable to deal. These were on the one hand, the problem of unemployment, and on the other the obvious nonexistence of perfect competition. When a body of theory cannot account for an important social phenomenon and when it seems to involve assumptions which clearly violate the mass of social reality, it is obviously slated for some drastic revision. In the 1930s it looked as though both of these defects were being taken care of, the first by the Keynesian Macroeconomics and the second by the Robinson-Chamberlin Microeconomics. At the time it looked as if these two butterflies were almost coequal. The liberation of economics from the assumption of perfect competition, which seemed so hopelessly unrealistic in the twentieth century, whatever it might have been in the nineteenth, seemed to stand on a level with the removal from economics of its inability to explain the intractable nature of vast unemployment.

Looking back, now, with the wisdom of twenty-five years' experience, the Keynesian economics, especially combined as it was with the development of national income statistics and a substantial improvement in the whole information system of the economy, looms a good deal larger than what seems, in this perspective, to be a rather textbookish reorientation of price theory, to account for the various phenomena of imperfect competition and the different states of the market. We can sense the difference, I think, in terms of the relative impact on economic policy. It is not too much to say that the Keynesian revolution has produced an enormous impact on economic policy in all noncommunist countries. Views which were seen as the ripe expression of economic wisdom in 1930, in regard, for instance, to the responsibility of national governments for maintaining full employment or even in regard to such a sacred institution as the national debt, would now be considered the exclusive property of the lunatic right wing. Virtually every noncommunist government now regards the maintenance of domestic full employment as a perfectly legitimate objective of its activities.

By contrast, the theory of imperfect competition and the states of the market has produced little. It has not clarified in any great degree the problems of antitrust legislation or law enforcement; indeed, it can be argued that the whole impact of the theory, especially of oligopoly, has been to create a degree of legal confusion which must be almost unprecedented. The antitrust laws were framed on the simple-minded assumption that competition, presumably perfect, was good and that monopoly was bad, and, furthermore, that conspiracy was bad even when it wasn't monopoly. Into this Victorian melodrama of good guys and bad guys, the economist has released a lot of doubtful characters with hybrid, or at least foreign-sounding names, whose roles are so difficult to perceive, that nobody is quite sure which side to be on, and the distinction between good and bad has become almost obliterated. This is a situation intolerable in law, however elegant it may be in the classroom. In restrospect, therefore, the theory of the states of the market seems like a much less impressive achievement than it did in the decade of its birth.

In the light of these considerations, it is not unreasonable to inquire what was the real contribution of the theory of imperfect competition to price theory, or, more generally, what was its contribution to anything. The answer may turn out to be rather surprising. I am prepared to argue that the contribution made by the theory of imperfect competition to price theory was fairly small, though not insignificant, if by price theory we mean the theory of an equilibrium structure of relative prices, in the sense which I have used it, earlier. Beyond this, however, I shall argue that the contribution of the theory of the states of the market to the theory of organization, to the theory of relationships of organizations, and even to such things as international relations, is very substantial, and that what may be regarded as a minor, though elegant, addition to price theory, turns out to be the foundation of a whole general theory of social organization and interaction, which was certainly not what its authors intended. The history of thought, however, is full of such interesting ironies.

Let us turn first, then, to the problem of the significance of the states of the market for price theory, and let us ask, is there any reason to suppose that a change in the condition of the market will affect the equilibrium structure of relative prices. We have already noted the propositions that monopoly power rests on the ability to control the mobility of resources and that the existence of monopoly simply expanded the notion of an equilibrium point in price space to that of an equilibrium range or set. These propositions are familiar to the classical and neoclassical economics and have little to do with the states of the market. There are two ways, however, in which the state of the market as reflected, for instance, in the nature of the demand function facing an individual firm or price setter, can influence the relevant price structure. One is through the development of a larger number of firms in a particular segment of the economy as a result of imperfect markets, with the consequence that each firm operates with excess capacity and an average cost above the minimum. Prices in this sector of the economy will then have to be higher than they otherwise would be, simply because of the imperfection of the market. This is not a monopoly phenomenon in the old sense of the word, because in this case there is no ability to restrict the mobility of resources—in fact, it is precisely because resources are mobile in this particular sector that the phenomenon occurs at all. That is, we have not, here, the phenomenon of monopoly power permitting a price structure which gives the monopolist an unusually high income because of his ability to prevent potential competitors from entering the field. It is rather that the existence of the imperfect markets encourages more resources to enter the field, with the result of increase in the price at which these resources are normally profitable, because of certain inefficiency in the operation of the individual firm. There is no modification here of the fundamental principle that the relative price structure must correspond to alternative costs. What has happened is that imperfection in the market has changed the structure of alternative cost. The modification, however, is likely to be a fairly small one. Creeping up the average cost curve to the point to where it is touched by an imperfectly elastic demand curve is a relatively small adjustment, compared with the kind of shifts which are constantly taking place under the impact of technological change in the whole height of the average cost curve itself.

The second contribution of the theory of the states of the market to the theory of relative prices is the elucidation of certain phenomena associated with price wars, on the one hand, or with price leadership, on the other. The price war may be thought to be a purely temporary phenomenon unworthy of entry into the sanctuary of equilibrium theory. However, it is of some interest to note that under conditions of perfect oligopoly there is some tendency for price wars to break out, and then we are apt to have rather curious fluctuations around some equilibrium, with prices falling in the price war and then rising again in what I suppose we ought to call a price peace, in which a happy state of collusion, gentlemanliness, or just plain political organization prevails. In the blessed long run, of course, price wars have to be paid for or the economic sector will not be occupied. Average price must equal average cost. The threat of price war, however, may be an interesting variant on monopoly power and on the ability to control mobility. Here, again, one doubts that the modification of the equilibrium theory is more than the second order of magnitude. It is nice to have both the theory of price wars and the theory of price leadership, from the point of view of the theory of equilibrium relative prices; however, it is doubtful whether this makes more than a minor modification.

From the point of view of the theory of organizational behavior, and of what might be described as the theory of interaction, the contribution of the theory of states of the market is more substantial. No doubt the theory of the firm is all in Cournot, in 1834, and it is reasonably explicit in Walras. It may therefore just be English insularity and American lateness which creates an illusion that the theory of the firm did not begin until 1930. It must be admitted, however, that from Adam Smith to Marshall, the English tradition did very well without it. In Marshall the only real theory of the firm is that of the monopolist struggling with his nests of rectangular hyperbolas, and this, as I have said earlier, is strictly an appendix. In the English classical tradition the firm is a loose combination of resources brought together on the spur of the moment by the opportunity of profit, an opportunity created not by organization but by the simple structure of relative prices. Whenever the market price is greater than some cost price or supply price resources would flow together in loose protoplasmic conglomerations to make the profitable commodities, and when the market price is less than the supply price, the occupation becomes unprofitable and the aggregated resources, likewise, simply disband and flow to more profitable places. It is to the credit of the theorists of the 1930s—and to the names previously mentioned the name of Jacob Viner [6] should now clearly be added—that they introduced the firm as an explicit agent in the formation of prices and clearly derived the supply curve of commodities from the cost curves of firms. In one sense this is simply a clarification—almost an adornment—of what had been implicit in the classical vision. In another sense, however, it represents a shift in the focus of interest which is continuing to bear fruit. If the Keynesian revolution is a

[6] J. Viner, "Cost Curves and Supply Curves," *Zeitschrift für Nationalökonomie*, 3 (1931), 23–45.

kind of Copernican revolution, shifting the emphasis from the individual to the system as a whole, the other revolution which did not have a name, and which I am almost tempted to call the behavioral revolution, focused attention on the behavior of the individual and thus opened the way to a much more behavioral science, not only in economics but, I think, in all fields of social life. I would not claim that the theory of imperfect competition or of the states of the market is more than a single element, and perhaps not a very important element, in this truly revolutionary shift. It is, however, clearly a part of it and, if today we have behavioral economics which studies the actual behavior of households and of firms, if we have behavioral political science which studies the decision-making processes in political organization, if we have decision theory, game theory, and organization theory, even though this all clearly cannot be attributed to the theory of imperfect competition, nevertheless, that theory is an important and an early part of the behavioral revolution. Any behavioral theory of any kind of organization whatever must involve, first of all, the identification of the essential variables of the organization in somewhat abstract form. It must involve a description of the functional relationships among these variables, and it must be able to describe some kind of boundary between possible and impossible combinations of these variables. Having defined the possible set of positions of the organism or organization, it must then develop some system of ordering, by which one of these positions may be selected as the behavior of the organism under review. All these concepts emerge first in the marginal analysis of the firm and household.

We must then go further and look at the interaction of organizations. The behavior of any one organization is conditioned by its environment, and its environment consists of other organizations, at least in large part. A theory of the behavior of the individual organization, therefore, leads rapidly into a theory of the system of interaction, and of that whole interrelationship among organizations which constitutes ecological equilibrium, on the one hand, and evolutionary development, on the other. This, however, is precisely what the theory of imperfect competition and the states of the market did for economics. The theory of the firm as developed in the 1930s is open to severe criticism. It has, nevertheless, all the elements of a successful theory of organization. It defines essential variables, such as prices and quantities of commodity. It clarifies the necessary relations among these variables, and distinguishes certain boundaries, such as cost curves and demand curves, which separate possible sets from impossible sets. It also postulates a simple principle of selection, namely, profit maximization, by which behavior, that is, the selection of the actual position among all the various possible ones, is carried out. Profit maximization as a principle of selection, again, is open to severe criticism, but it is at least a useful first approximation and it is clearly an example of the more general principle. Furthermore, in the theory of the interrelation of firms, under perfect competition, imperfect competition, and oligopoly, we have a simple model of how the behavior pattern gives rise to a whole ecological system.

We may claim, of course, that both the behavior and the interaction theories are hopelessly oversimplified. Economists have neglected the information problem almost entirely, in that they have assumed that firms knew things that they could not possibly know. I have argued myself, elsewhere, that this is one of the gravest weaknesses of imperfect competition theory: that economists did not realize that by substituting a demand function for a single variable—the price—under perfect competition, they open the Pandora's Box of questions about information which they have obstinately refused to face. This criticism is still, I believe, a just one. Nevertheless, it must also be admitted that the essential structure of the kind of theory that we must have is already there, especially in E. H. Chamberlin, even though in a very much simplified form.

I shall cite two illustrations of the way in which the theory of the states of the market generates general social theory. One is the principle sometimes known as Hotelling's Law. Hotelling [7] showed

[7] H. Hotelling, "Stability in Competition," *Economic Journal* 39 (1929), 41–57.

that under some circumstances the best place for a new firm to settle, under conditions of imperfect competition, was practically next door to an old firm. He jumped immediately, and I think legitimately, to the conclusion that this explained a great many phenomena which I would describe as "adjacencies," in all sorts of social space. It explains, for instance, why automobiles are so much alike, and even why Methodists and Baptists are so much alike, and even why Jehovah's Witnesses are not very much like Methodists or Baptists. Here are propositions which come directly out of the theory of imperfect competition, and which have extraordinarily wide applicability to general social systems.

My second example is that of Dr. Morton Kaplan's attempt to develop a theory of international systems.[8] Here we find a political scientist struggling with the problem of the typology of international systems without any benefit, as far as I know, of the theory of imperfect competition, yet he offers, at the end, a set of classifications which correspond almost exactly to the familiar categories of the economist. It is clear from this example that the theory of the states of the market has generated a taxonomy of "states" which is of great generality, and which applies to the relationships of nations, perhaps even to the relations of things like ideological structures, churches, labor unions, and so on, as well as to the relationship of firms. Economics has always had a certain advantage over the other social sciences in that its subject matter permitted fairly easy abstraction and quantification, thanks to the almost universal, if sometimes rubbery, measuring rod of money. With a measuring rod one can take the measure of an organization, or at least of those aspects of which are measurable, and having taken this measure where the system is measurable, one can understand it better where it is not. It is not sur-

[8] Morton A. Kaplan, *System and Process in International Politics* (New York, Wiley, 1957).

The balance of power system with many similar actors corresponds roughly to perfect competition; with few actors highly differentiated, to monopolistic competition. The loose bipolar system is oligopoly with some price leadership, the tight bipolar system is duopoly; the universal international system is a cartel, and the hierarchical international system is a monopoly.

prising, therefore, that sociological theory, for instance, in Parsons and Homans, often seems to be a generalization of the economist's theory of exchange. Economics, simply because of its measuring rod, has some claim to being regarded as the hard skeleton of the social sciences. In this broad perspective, therefore, the theory of the states of the market may be seen as perhaps a more important contribution to general social science than it is to technical price theory. If I have diminished its glory in one aspect, therefore, I have been happy to increase it in another.

In conclusion one might ask briefly, and hesitantly: "Where do we go from here?" I am prepared to argue that the great deficiency of the theory of the states of the market, and the reason why it has caused more confusion than enlightenment in actual public policy, is that it is not the kind of equilibrium theory which leads itself to dynamic extension and generalization. I have nothing against equilibrium theory, especially when it leads to comparative statics. The great hiatus in economics, however, is a real link between price theory of any kind and the theory of economic development, which, rightly, I think, has occupied the center of the stage in the last few years. This is important for public policy also, if only because economic development is such an overwhelmingly important goal of public policy, not only in poor countries but also in rich. Price theory, however, has said very little about this, although one can piece together, from odd sources, something that looks like a relation between the price structure and economic development. We are all familiar, for instance, with the proposition, beloved of labor economists, that high money wages encourage labor-saving improvements and hence contribute to economic development. We find also in economists as diverse as Joseph A. Schumpeter and T. W. Schultz a certain praise of monopoly on the grounds that it gives rise to technological improvement, and a certain feeling that from the point of view of rapid economic development, at any rate, there is some optimum degree of imperfection in the market and, certainly, some optimum degree of immobility of resources. I have elsewhere developed the notion that because there is a tendency for any existing price structure to become self-justifying, in terms of the shifts in both demand and supply which occur as a result of a given price structure, there is something to be said, from the point of view of economic development, of anticipating today an equilibrium price structure of, say, a generation hence, on the grounds that such a price set will stimulate both demand and supply in directions which are desirable.[9] The proposition that high money wages favored labor-saving improvements is essentially a corrolary of this general proposition. It is clear that what we have here is a set of scattered observations which have never, to my knowledge, been integrated into a systematic body of theory. This is not only strange, but deplorable, for the relation of prices to growth is surely one of the most important questions which can be asked for price theory. From the point of view of public policy we want to know, after all, how to distort the price structure wisely. We particularly want to know what are the results of distorting the price structure, from the point of view of economic development.

If there is not even any general price theory on this subject we can hardly expect to find any theory of the impact of states of the market on economic development. Nevertheless, I suspect that this is the core of the whole policy problem. It is precisely because of the absence of a theory of this kind that the whole antitrust enterprise has become almost a logical absurdity. It is, however, beyond the scope of this paper to write such a theory and probably, indeed, beyond the scope of this author. I will merely point to the need for its existence and hope that some day the pointer will be followed.

[9] K. E. Boulding and Pritam Singh, "The Role of the Price Structure in Economic Development," American Economic Review, 52 (May, 1962), 28.

COMMENTS

By Edward H. Chamberlin

The main theme of Professor Boulding's paper seems to be that classical economics got along very well without a state-of-the-market theory; and that this theory, which according to him, does not develop much before 1930, has accomplished very little. He thinks its contribution to price theory was "fairly small," and that its contribution to the theory of organizations and the relationships of organizations, although more substantial, was not "what its authors intended." Near the middle of the paper it is "open to severe criticism," and there is more of the same. To be sure, there is also a "restoration to glory," and there are "butterflies." But, I am reminded of the weather forecast in an issue of the Harvard *Crimson* years ago, actually put out by the *Lampoon* after the latter had stolen all the legitimate *Crimsons* and substituted their own productions. The forecast was "storm brewing." Unfortunately, I must leave out many matters of first importance, and must cut what I have to say to the bone, supplementing, I hope, by a few references.

In price theory, the classical school seems to have got along without a state-of-the-market theory because they held that prices were relative to costs. In fact, we find thrown together in this admittedly "crude" picture, perhaps Smith, and certainly Ricardo, Marx, Mill (I assume), Cairnes, Marshall, and even Walras. Although this is described as "very elementary," it is an indigestible lump for me. Perhaps I should go back and take *Economics* A again! Monopoly, in all this theory, which seems so clearly a matter of the state of the market, is first reduced to "immobility" and then made to disappear by a sleight-of-hand. The stage is set for the post-1930 theory of the state of the market, which not only is described as thin in quality, but seems to be of limited duration as well. Its brief "classical period" came to an end in 1940, and there has been "very little progress" since. I'm sure we will all agree that Professor Boulding has been doing some admirable things in these recent years, but one thing he has certainly not done, is to read much in the literature of "state-of-the-market" theory. If his conclusion was reached back in 1940, perhaps one cannot blame him too much.

It happens that I have tried from about the middle 1930s to keep some record of material written on the subject. In 1940, when Boulding's interest flagged, the bibliography for *Monopolistic Competition* (appearing in the back of the book) contained about 200 items. In the next 8 years 500 more had brought it to 700; the figure for the next 8 years was 800, bringing the total in 1956 to 1500. Frankly, I haven't been able to read more than a part of it myself. But since the literature of the subject seems to have been growing at the explosive rate of more than double in each period of roughly 8 years, 1956 will have to be the end, so far as my own compilations go. So much for quantity. Time will not allow analysis of quality in the more recent period, but I think that, with a better understanding of the subject, quality has been higher than in what Boulding has called the classical, or pre-1940, period. I might add that he is not the only one to think that the subject died a long time ago. But such does not seem to be the case.

I should like to refer to an article of mine in the *Quarterly Journal of Economics* for November, 1961, "The Origin and Early Development of Monopolistic Competition Theory." As is now widely known, I have insisted for a long time that the theories of Joan Robinson and myself, although treating in limited degree similar problems, were quite different from each other: in purpose, in content, and in conclusions. I believe this has become increasingly recognized, and it is rarer than it used to be to find us emerging together, as in Boulding's paper, like twins from the alleged common intellectual ancestry. The series of articles mentioned by Boulding as "paving the way" for both, is correct for Mrs. Robinson and literally nonexistent for myself. In my own case, the road was unpaved, and it remained so right up until 1933, for the road on which Mrs. Robinson traveled happened to be one passing through another territory, and headed for another destination.

Mrs. Robinson told me, during a long conversation we had at Talloires in 1951, that she had two purposes in mind in writing her book: 1) to "debunk" certain propositions in welfare economics, and 2) to show that laborers were exploited, and I was delighted to find her saying it shortly afterwards in print, in "J. K. Galbraith, American Capitalism: The Concept of Countervailing Power," *Economic Journal* (Dec. 1952), p. 925, thereby giving me the right to refer to it. She was surprised at my telling her that I had had no objective whatever in writing my own, except to give a truer account of how the economic system worked; one objective of the theorist (among others) which had been brought into sharper relief for me by recent work with Professor Fred M. Taylor at Michigan. Perhaps that is why policy conclusions hardly emerge at all. I hold, with Sir Dennis Robertson, that (before talking about policy) "Let's get the analysis straight first." I should perhaps comment in passing that on the two issues which urged Mrs. Robinson on, the indicated conclusions of *Monopolistic Competition* are actually at the opposite pole from hers [see *Towards A More General Theory of Value* (New York, Oxford University Press, 1957), Essay 16]. This ought to be deeply disturbing to those (and it seems clear that Boulding is one of them) who still thinks the two theories are one, except for issues in semantics.

I have been speaking more generally than I intended, and must now mention a few specific topics, with a sentence or two for each.

Boulding unmistakably condemns state-of-the-market theory on the ground that it has created unprecedented "confusion" in the antitrust field. But would anyone (and would he himself) want to go back to the "simple-minded assumption" on which "the antitrust laws were framed," that good and bad equal perfect competition and monopoly respectively? Perhaps confusion (for a time) is a necessary price of improvement.

Of the two "fairly small" ways in which "imperfect competition" can influence the relevant price structure: the second, price wars and price leadership, seems to me to antedate the theories in question by decades, and I see no reason why they should be dragged in at all, although they both fit easily enough into state-of-the-market theory. Incidentally, it seems to me that oligopoly theory does more to explain why price wars do *not* break out more often, than why they do.

The other influence on price structure is "excess capacity," and subject is far too complicated to get into at all, here. The term has several meanings, and not often the one which Boulding seems to have in mind, *viz.*, simply production to the left of the minimum point on the cost curve. My own meaning is not this, and Mrs. Robinson does not even use the term, so it is hard to say what she would mean by it, if anything, and whether she would even entertain the idea. Most discussion of the problem has been on a much more difficult and involved level. Mr. Harrod, although he once accepted the idea, recanted in 1952, and warned all and sundry against it. I have rebutted his position at length (*Towards A More General Theory of Value*, Essay 14), and can only say here that I am very happy to have Boulding's support, if indeed I do have it. The issues go far beyond anything he has said in his paper.

But are these two the only ways in which price structure is affected by monopolistic competition? Since the demand curves facing firms must be of all degrees of elasticity, and (as I see it) oligopolistic forces are fairly widespread, not relatively small at all; then, like other surpluses, they are a problem. I am at a loss to understand why it should be denied that they affect the relative price structure. It should be further noted that nonprice competition in terms of product and advertising are not even mentioned.

Professor Boulding mentions "Hotelling's Problem" (of products moving towards each other in social space), with rather sweeping approval. But Hotelling's theoretical explanation of the phenomenon was refuted as early as 1933, in *Monopolistic Competition*, Appendix C, has been widely acknowledged, and is a part of the literature. (See also *Towards A More General Theory of Value*, pp. 125–29, on the "end problem" and further aspects). In fact, the refutation is so easy that one can without a qualm put *QED* at the end. Products are grouped together in what Boulding wants to call adjacencies for a variety of good reasons, but Hotelling's is not one of them.

Dynamics. We are told that the "great deficiency of the theory" is that it does not "lend itself to dynamic extension and generalization." Yet Schumpeter, a pioneer in Development, who, in spite of valiant efforts, had a hard time with the theory in its static form, became enthusiastic about it in the last years of his life precisely because he thought it opened up new and fruitful extensions into dynamic theory, "the competition which really counts" (*Ibid.*, Essay 10). Indeed there are many who hold that the theory makes sense only as one of dynamics, and it is easy to see how the argument would be especially convincing with regard to advertising and the nonprice area.

Finally, is one really expected to take seriously the statement that "the theory of the firm is all in Cournot in 1834?" Indeed the theory of the firm, particularly with respect to the relationships between firms, has expanded until Cournot's simple hypothesis, important as it was as a beginning, seems now a mere historical curiosity.

Let me close on a more hopeful note. Professor Boulding has told us of a "Pandora's Box" which has been opened, and I agree. But let us not hide the contents or rule them out. The contents must be fully explored and developed, and their implications for economic and for general social theory must be laid before us.

By John M. Clark

First, as to terminology, I shall use the term "imperfect competition" to cover the group of theories that includes oligopoly, or the competition of the few, competition of differentiated products ("monopolistic competition," in Chamberlin's vocabulary) and combinations of these conditions. Next, I am glad to find myself in concurrence with much of what Professor Boulding says, though with divergent views on a few points. As to the effect and usefulness of imperfect-competition theory and its models, while I have long held the view Boulding expresses, that they are of less basic importance than the Keynesian economics, which stands as a major revolution, I am pleasantly surprised to find myself defending them, with obviously necessary qualifications, against Boulding's limited estimate of their effect, especially in the antitrust field. Their impact has contributed some clarification, not exclusively confusion. They are not final truths about the actual market, but they are significant pioneering in neglected aspects of it. And now, some three decades after they took a dominant place in price theory—decades in which much inductive evidence has accumulated—the time should be ripe for further developments. This process might be easier if theorists could acquire the habit of regarding their models as expressing, more or less typically, not things that must happen, but things worth looking for as probable results of important determinants: things which may happen or may not, when the determining conditions are made more numerous, in the approach to greater realism.

Boulding speaks of the "classical" period of imperfect-competition theory as having come to an end in 1940, with little progress since, though he finds the present full of potentialities in broader fields, stemming from imperfect-competition theory but not comprised within it. Does this, perhaps, hinge on whether the conventional idea of the scope of price theory is broadened in response to these developments, at least by taking them into its premises? I have had some doubts whether my own recent attempted broadening of the treatment of competition would be accepted as within the boundaries of "economic theory." But there seemed to be room for expansion.

My chief dissent from Boulding's paper is on a matter of rather ancient history, and might be disposed of by recording my firm conviction that Adam Smith did not treat the relative prices of commodities as determined by the labor embodied in them. He distinguished this problem from that of the measure of "real value" when the price level changes over time, to the extent of treating them in different chapters of the *Wealth of Nations*—the latter in chapter V and the former in chapters VI and VII. The measure of real value he found in labor embodied or labor commanded, which he too casually mentioned in the same breath, as if they were interchangeable for this purpose. The determinants of relative prices he summed up by saying that the "natural price" of anything covers the "component parts of price"—wages, rent, and profits—at their natural levels. He was quite explicit that it was only in a (hypothetical) primitive society, prior to appropriation of land and accumulation of capital, that these determinants were reduced to the labor required, for example, to kill a deer or a beaver.

Ricardo made as much as he could of embodied labor as a determinant of ratios of exchange, and disposed of rent as "not a part of price," but he had to make room for profits, as Marx did, also, in the notes that became the basis for the posthumous third volume of *Capital*. Marx's earlier view persisted in the exploitation theory of profits and in the loaded question: "Why do products not exchange at their values?" But these are not the questions we are here to discuss.

The attempt to define the uses of theory to the theorist certainly invites the cynical comment which finds a major use in the regurgitation of the theory on examination papers. To this I might add the well-nigh invincible advantage for this purpose—and for the textbooks that subserve it—of relationships that can be expressed in two-dimensional diagrams, preferably leading to an equilibrium expressed in the intersection of two lines. Any theorist would tell you that these diagrams are oversimplifications, presumably serviceable as first approximations toward understanding the more complex relations of reality. But for this purpose, they are exposed to misleading uses or interpretations. They are inherently limited to one independent variable, or at most, two, and many more are needed for more realistic explanation. Further, there is a positive temptation to "reify" the diagram; to picture a business enterprise as existing and functioning in a world consisting of intersecting curves on paper, and to picture an experimental policy decision, with all its complexity and uncertainty, as motion along one of these curves, whose precision on paper belies the impossibility of knowing them precisely in the actual world.

Mathematical functions can increase the number of determinants, but they involve other difficulties, for which we have not time in this discussion. To illustrate the pitfalls of reifying: in imperfect-competition theory, the supply functions, formerly in general use, are almost universally replaced by cost functions. This is proper in this setting, but theorists seldom explain why they make this shift, and sometimes they have continued to use supply functions where these were misleading and cost functions should have been used.

Professor Boulding speaks of the conception of perfect competition as having prevailed in the nineteenth century to such an extent that its occasional absence called for explanation. It is true that Cournot's treatise and Marshall's mathematical appendix dealt with it; but I am still sure that the fully developed theory of perfect competition, defining all the necessary conditions, was not embedded in the prevalent thinking of economists prior to, let us say, World War I and was not, as one speaker has suggested, the animating idea of the antitrust law of 1890, or of the legislation of 1914. When this model has been explicitly elaborated, elaboration has been to show that actuality is different. F. H. Knight so used it, defining the conditions of a profitless society, as an incident to his theory of profits.[1] And my hypothesis is that the real embedding of this theory in the prevalent thinking stemmed from the theory of imperfect competition, being emphasized by the imperfect-competition theorists as a means of defining the nature and extent of the change they were making. Prior to this, the failure of actual markets to reproduce the results expected from competition was regarded as merely one instance of the general fact that actual behavior never reproduces theories precisely, and the failure to do so seemed to require no theoretical analysis. In the light of imperfect-competition theory, the discrepancies had causes which did require analysis of a theoretical sort. When the requirements of perfect competition were thus fully and precisely defined, it was revealed not only as nonexistent, but impossible, and, I would add undesirable in the light of the requirements of dynamic progress. This full definition of its requirements ended its use, as a picture of general conditions. It became an analytical point of comparison; and was used by some as a normative standard, guaranteed to yield an unfavorable judgment of actual conditions. This normative use, I would contend, is misleading, for reasons that would take too long to elaborate here.

When the antitrust laws were framed, the evils of "cutthroat," "predatory," and "unfair" competition were widely understood. They played a decisive role in the great leading cases of 1911, and in the formative legislation of 1914. In appraising the relation between the antitrust laws and imperfect-competition theory, the first thing to keep clearly in mind is that these laws attack actions, while the theories describe conditions. The laws did not make conditions of imperfect competition illegal—not even the condition of monopoly. They attacked actions of monopolization and agreements in restraint of competition.

[1] F. H. Knight, *Risk, Uncertainty and Profits* (Boston, Houghton Mifflin; Cambridge, Riverside Press, 1921) pp. 76–86.

When imperfect-competition theory exhibited some degree of the evils associated with monopoly, as inherent in these hybrid or intermediate conditions, apart from monopolizing intent or directly anticompetitive actions, this naturally led to a desire on the part of the antitrust authorities to attack these evils, under laws not explicitly designed with them in mind. The legal attack required the identification of actions of an anticompetitive sort, and this led to reading such actions into the market behavior of imperfect competition, though the law might not have forbidden such market behavior in itself.

For example, the model of pure oligopoly conceives price competition as being stalemated because firms expect any competitive moves to be so promptly and completely met as to leave the initiator no chance for a competitive gain in volume of business. This suggests an attack on identity of prices (which, in a different setting, is a feature of "perfect competition"). And since there is no law against meeting a competitor's price, the doctrine of "conscious parallelism" was evolved as a legal weapon, inferring collusive action from the circumstantial evidence of the observed behavior. If this had been unqualifiedly adopted, it would not only have obviated the need of furnishing direct evidence of collusion; it could have led to absurd and anticompetitive results, outlawing competitive meeting of rivals' prices, along with collusive actions aimed at stalemating price competition.

In the basing-point cases, it was argued that freight absorption (which rated as price discrimination) was used as an instrument to bring about identity of delivered prices. But the court's order in the cement case hinged on concerted procedures implementing this process and making the identity of prices more uniform and precise than independent action of competitors would have done. Freight absorption was not forbidden as a means of meeting competitors' prices, but they had to be the verified prices that competitors were actually charging at specific destinations, not the prices which it was calculated the competitors would charge over a whole market area if they added calculated freight to a base price, inferred from a limited number of observed delivered prices. Thus, the scope of freight absorption was drastically limited, while identical sealed bids were, in effect, deprived of the status of a meeting of competitors' prices. On the other hand, room was left for recognition that some freight absorption is useful competitively, and the unfortunate effects of an absolute prohibition were avoided.

As to discrimination between particularly customers, it is recognized that this may or may not seriously injure their competition with one another. However it may be one way in which an oligopoly stalemate among sellers may be jolted loose, by competitive price reductions which might not be instantly met and neutralized. Thus, admittedly imperfect competition might be substituted for the stalemate of universal price identity. The upshot is some uncertainty, such as always accompanies the extension of case law into fresh areas of problems; but it does not appear as sheer confusion. "There is method in't," consistent with the method of oligopoly theory. The introduction of categories more discriminating than "good" competition and "bad" monopoly or conspiracy is a gain, not a loss.[2]

One such category, which the antitrust laws have apparently (and properly) left out of their scope, is the "element of monopoly" which the theory finds inherent in product differentiation. This is not, in itself, the sort of thing at which the law is aimed, unless collusive or monopolizing behavior is found in connection with it. As to the restriction of scale of production and accompanying increased costs which are inferred under the tangency theorem, these appear to be results that may follow from short-sighted policy on the firm's part, but are, by and large, quite unlikely. And I agree with Boulding that even where they happen, they are "a relatively small adjustment, compared with the kind of shifts which are constantly taking place under the impact of technological change . . ." Other effects of product differentiation appear much more important, both for good and ill.

But space permits to deal with only a few of the challenging questions raised by Boulding's highly individual and stimulating paper. One such question suggests a revision of a bit of verse on a somewhat similar theme which I wrote over ten years ago:

> Some theorists are made to squirm
> By questions asked about the firm.
> Will modern corporate creations
> Evolve organic motivations?

[2] As to conspiracy, in my dictionary, evil or illegal purpose is part of the definition of the term. Concerted action may be used to promote effective competition—as by simplifying a confusion of package sizes—as well as to restrain it.

TOWARD THE CONSTRUCTION OF
MORE USEFUL MODELS

BY WILLIAM J. BAUMOL, PROFESSOR OF ECONOMICS,
PRINCETON UNIVERSITY

These papers have been largely oriented toward questions of methodology. There is always something unsatisfying about methodological discussions. One feels, somehow, that one has not gotten down to the real business to be accomplished—that one is only talking about doing things rather than doing them. Nevertheless, it is important to stop occasionally and take stock, to look around and see what has been accomplished, and to consider where one goes next. Although in the very nature of research it does not always go where one intends it to, or even expects it to, sometimes a bit of planning and exchange of ideas about planning can be extremely helpful.

The bulk of these papers have been concerned with nonmathematical models, with models which were with us and constituted the mass of the literature until the late 1930s. It is my opinion, however, and I am sure that this is partly prejudice resulting from the nature of my own work, that a discussion of models, which avoids any consideration of mathematical models, is truly a performance of Hamlet with the Prince of Denmark absent. In what follows I shall, therefore, be unable to restrain myself from making frequent allusions to models which are highly mathematical in nature and to the general work of the operations researcher, which is so intimately connected with recent developments in economic analysis. Indeed, I feel that much of the criticism which has either explicitly or implicitly been levied against models so far has resulted from the decision to restrict the discussion largely to literary and simple geometrical models. The increased respectability with which the economic theorist has recently been viewed, both by the pure mathematician and the most practical of businessmen, is partly, at least, connected with the developments in mathematical model building.

In sum, I believe we have come much further and accomplished a great deal more than the discussion of this conference has suggested. In this paper I shall indicate why I believe this to be so and shall then turn to what I expect to see in the near future—what developments and major changes are likely to affect the work of the model builder.

Models: Definition and Classification

First of all, it is incumbent on me to give my definition of a model. I do not believe that there are any absolutely valid definitions and, as has earlier been indicated, many of us hold fairly divergent views as to what constitutes common usage for this term. My definition, therefore, is merely offered for purposes of communication—to indicate what I mean when I use the term and not to suggest that others must use it to connote the same thing. Many of you will remember those fascinating machines which were concocted from the fertile imagination of the cartoonist, Rube Goldberg—a device, for example, to get one up on time in the morning, consisting of the most marvelous conglomeration of miscellaneous paraphernalia—a bucket of water, a parakeet, an alarm clock, a baseball bat, and a variety of other items. As the sun rose it would lead the sleeper to turn around in his bed to face away from the sun, thus a string tied to his toe would become taut. This would wake the parakeet who would then jump off his perch. That, in turn, would release a spring, and so on through a long variety of mechanisms until finally some tripping device overturned the bucket of water, pouring it upon the head of the sleeper. Such a machine, to me, is a perfect prototype of an economic model. It contains two of the major features of a model. It is unrealistic and it is a mechanism which works—it does something. We are able to start by pressing button A, and can then watch a whole chain of interactions and their workings and finally see the end result, effect B. More explicitly, I visualize a model as a scaled-down version of the huge machine which constitutes the working of the economy as a whole, or even of some portion of it in which we are interested. But this scaled-down version is also a working model. That is, it can function. It can produce results and it can be used to enable us to find out what happens when we press different buttons, and when we tinker with different parts. It is, in effect, a device which enables us to see what happens when we conduct a variety of experiments—a device which enables us to get the answers to questions like, what would happen if we did so-and-so instead of such-and-such?

It is also important to distinguish between two types of models which constitute a hierarchy. The first class is made up of the abstract models which have employed the attentions of the economic theorists; the second class consists of the far more specialized models which must be and have been used by these who are more interested in either application or description of the detailed workings of the economy. It is important to distinguish between the two types of models because, in general, neither can accomplish the functions which are the special task of the other. It is therefore easy, but entirely misdirected, to criticize a model of one of these types because it cannot accomplish what is desired of a model of the other sort.

The Theorist's Desire for Generality

First, let us consider the more general models which constitute the main interest of the pure theorist. By his very nature the theorist is interested in producing analyses which will be applicable to a wide variety of situations. His desire is to achieve a high degree of generality and he designs his models accordingly. But, in order to make his models generally applicable, he must abstract from the differentiating details which characterize particular situations and particular problems. He must ignore the personality of the president of one company and the preconceptions of the board of directors of another. He must abstract from the differences between the competitive situation of food retailing in Philadelphia and that in Los Angeles. All this is very natural and clearly desirable. And yet, in the course of this abstraction and generalization, he pays a heavy price because he is likely to assume away all trace of personality and character in the individual firm. He is apt to leave it a hollow and uninteresting shell. For often it is the differences between firms, and not their similarities, which make them interesting. In short, the more general a model, the more empty it is likely to be, and the theorist must decide at which point he stops the process of generalization because it is no longer worth the price. In this process we are likely to emerge with constructs which, though they serve the theorist's purpose very well, are already far too abstract to meet the needs of the applied mathematician or even of the investigator who is trying to shed light on the details of some institutional description. Models like the marginal cost equals marginal revenue construct or the Edgeworth box diagram simply do not correspond closely to any actual situation, and taken literally and by themselves they are of only limited applicability. At this point I think we would do well to take seriously the statement of a number of theorists that they were primarily trying to develop tools, because this is how I believe these models can best be viewed. They are not ends in themselves; they are merely means which the analyst of applied problems must take and adapt for his immediate purposes.

Models Designed for Application

Thus we come to the second category of models, those which are specially tailored and adapted to the individual situation and the individual problem which is to be investigated. We are interested in the pricing of the rifles of a particular company, or the product line of a particular department store, or the advertising decisions of one soap manufacturer. We can no longer be satisfied with the general models which are presented to us by the theorist. Now we must come to grips with the details of the particular situation and problem at hand. We must develop a very special model, one which probably has never been used before and which may never be used again. It must correctly represent the circumstances which are relevant to the problem.

There is a point which is especially significant here. Models, in their very nature, are oversimplifications. Their whole power rests in their simplicity. This means that in representing reality they exhibit only its most salient and most immediately relevant features. In other words, in constructing a particularized model, one should consider as many of the relevant phenomena as one can list and then decide on the basis of the purpose of the investigation, which of those to omit from consideration. In a study of the pricing policies of a hardware retailer, the wholesale price must surely be an important ingredient in the analysis, whereas the availability of storage space, while it might affect sales and hence influence pricing indirectly, will ordinarily be ignored in the model. On the other hand, a study of the inventory problem for this same firm will have to place heavy emphasis on the availability of warehousing space, and current wholesaler price may be considered a largely transient and peripherally relevant phenomenon. It follows, then, that not only will different particularized models be required for each different subject studied, but even for a given subject, we may have to contruct different models when we consider different problems.

As I have stated, I believe much confusion and unnecessary hostility has been generated by failure to differentiate between the two types of model, which we may refer to as the general and the particular. I have somewhere stated that I have never, in any of my business work, used a single model taken from economic theory but that, paradoxically, I have never undertaken a single application in which I could have gotten along without one. What I mean, of course, is that the general models, because of their generality, were totally inapplicable as they stood. But they and the theorems which were developed about them served as prototypes for the constructs necessary to handle the job at hand. Thus, in every application these general models were helpful to me but they were never usable as they stood.

From this follows a result even more paradoxical—that economic theory is now, in many cases, proving to give more satisfactory results to the businessman than it does to the theorist. The reason, of course, is that the economic models, in their operations research form, which have been designed to handle particular business problems, have in many cases been eminently successful in coping with those very well-defined and very limited problems. Because these models were so specific in design and purpose, they were able to handle the situations well and they also sometimes turned out to be rich in empirical content. Thus, the businessman faced with very specific decisions was given specific forms of assistance. The theorist, on the other hand, finds himself in a more ambiguous position. Unlike the businessman, he is not simply trying to solve day-to-day problems. He wants more than this. In effect, from his models, he wants to have his generality and to use them, too. He desires his models to be widely, if not universally, applicable and at the same time he wants them to be rich in empirical content. Unfortunately, these two goals are in direct conflict. The result has been great dissatisfaction with what he has produced, and the economist is always apologizing either because of the excessive specificity of his results or, more often, because of their lack of specific content. My feeling is that he really need not apologize—that once he recognizes the limited purpose of a general model he can get along with his work with a perfectly clear conscience, knowing that he cannot expect of his results something which they are not designed to achieve.

Economic Models and Operations Research

I have several times referred to operations research models as economic models. Perhaps this requires a little justification. I visualize the relation between the operations researcher and the economist as being somewhat analogous to that between the engineer and the physicist. The one applies the ideas produced by the other. But, both in the case of the operations researcher and the engineer, the application requires more than the knowledge of the theory—it requires a considerable degree of artistry, a degree of intuition and good judgment—things which can never be learned by a pure study of the abstract analysis. Operations research, to me, is, then, applied mathematical economics. If the economic theory is good theory it should be extremely helpful to the operations researcher. Indeed, the assistance should work both ways. The experience of the operations researcher in applying the work of the economic theorist may often suggest ideas and improved approaches to the work of constructing pure theory. But operations research, at least in its dealings with business rather than military problems, is clearly concerned with the subject matter of the economist. If business decisions are not of interest to the economist, then what is? Thus, I am not a little surprised when people appear to deny that operations research and economics are intimately related. The very close interrelationship of the two literatures and the considerable overlapping of its practitioners, are really hardly surprising.

We who are well aware of the limitations and oversimplifications of our economic models may be a bit astonished at the apparent success that these models or their derivatives have had in coping with specific business problems. It is easy to suspect that the normally hard-headed businessman has been smitten with a temporary attack of feeble-mindedness in accepting the use of such obviously imperfect constructs. But those of us who have spent most of our time in the shelter of the academy have forgotten one major luxury which is available to us and which is not offered to the businessman or to any other responsible decision maker. We always have the right to say that the evidence is insufficient for any conclusion to be drawn, and on these grounds to abandon any particular analysis or to postpone judgment on any particular problem. The one option that is not open to the decision maker is the decision to avoid deciding altogether. He must always make up his mind on the best of available evidence, imperfect though that evidence may be. Of course, its very imperfection may color the nature of the decision he makes. It may dictate that he employ much more caution than he otherwise would.

If our models, despite their limited validity and their relative poverty of detail, enable him to handle his problems somewhat more effectively, enable him to make his decisions somewhat more systematically and with a somewhat higher payoff probability, then they will have served their purpose—they will have been successful, from his point of view.

One of the characteristic features of most business problems is their great degree of complexity—the vast number of alternatives which are available to management, the degree and complication of the interdependencies in decision patterns, the bewildering variety of relevant phenomena. All of these mean that the businessman must be crying for a simplifying technique—one which is capable of reducing complexity to manageable proportions—and this is precisely what the mathematical economic model is designed to do. Mathematics can help to transform complexity and chaos into an orderly system. The design of the model, if done well, should introduce simplicity in a way which minimizes the distortion of reality. The result is a tool which, though imperfect, is precisely of the variety which is needed by the businessman. And I firmly believe that we have only scratched the surface—that the application of our models to business purposes has only just begun, that, particularly as computers become more powerful and more readily available, demand for the man trained in the use and construction of this sort of model will increase to levels never seen before and hardly anticipated.

Out of this flourishing of direct application will also come, I believe, a better understanding of how these models can be helpful in explaining the functioning of the economy, and the varying levels of abstraction which will be necessary to adapt them for this purpose.

Relationship Between Theory and Data

So far, I have dealt with prospects for the application of economic models to business. I would like to turn now to the future of economic models in pure economic research. Here, there is a major point which I would like to emphasize and which will be the focus for the remainder of this paper. In many ways economics is a peculiarly fortunate discipline. Despite our reservations, its reputation outside the field for having a rather advanced, subtle, and sophisticated body of theory is not entirely undeserved. In any field, it has been my experience that practitioners have always been most highly impressed with what they do not know and what they have not accomplished, and economics is certainly no exception. Nor is it wrong that this should be so. Our theory still has tremendous weaknesses, still has only dealt with a very small proportion of the problem areas of the subject, and has dealt with them in a very limited way. And yet, compared with many other disciplines, our theory is nevertheless in an advanced state and provides a powerful mechanism for many purposes. This, as I have just said, is widely conceded outside our field. On the other hand, in some of the other behavioral disciplines, the impression exists that our models, while analytically or theoretically rich, are extremely poor empirically, and that the economist is particularly impoverished in his fund of data.

I would argue that this is in fact not the case—that the economist is in an advantageous position not only in the wealth of his theory but also in the mass of empirical information which is available to him. Vast quantities of statistics are continuously ground out by government agencies, by private firms, and by research groups throughout the world. Sometimes this flow of information appears to have attained the proportions of a deluge.

It is a complete misunderstanding of the economist's problem to say that lack of data is one of his main difficulties. Not only are quantitative materials readily available, there are in addition, institutional studies of a wide variety of types and subjects, many of them of extremely high quality. Our profession includes many persons skilled in empirical research. The economist's traditional relationship with the statistician is probably closer than that of the practitioner of any other discipline. The particular weakness of economics, then, is neither in its theory nor in its data. Rather, its unique disadvantage lies in the complete separation of the two. I can think of no other field of study with a well-developed body of theory which is so completely removed from the available empirical information, or of a field in which information gathering is so frequently divorced from the theory.

Of course, it is easy to say that theory should base itself more firmly on empirical grounds and that data collection should be more directly oriented to the needs of theory. This is the type of vote in favor of virtue which is totally useless to anyone, and such exhortations, by themselves, are likely to prove as barren as the attempt to produce interdisciplinary cross-fertilization by simply placing the practitioners of the various subjects in close proximity. Interdisciplinary cooperation will surely produce few results until the disciplines have reached a stage of advancement where they can easily be helpful to one another. And similarly, in economics, empirical and theoretical work will only come together when they are both ready.

However, I do believe that that time is now at hand. Indeed, in a few cases, or at least in an isolated sector of our work, some important efforts have already been made. Much of the work of the econometricians has been directed toward that end and much of it has been illuminating. But despite these efforts, at present the bulk of our theoretical and empirical work goes on in isolation.

Some Tasks for the Theorist

Before indicating the grounds for my limited optimism, it may be appropriate to make a few observations indicating some general things which can be done both by theorists and data gatherers to adapt themselves to one another's needs. First let us consider what can be done by the theorist. The main thing he must recognize, in light of what has already been said, is that his most general models are usually not in a form which can be helpful to the empirical worker. He must be prepared to sacrifice some degree of generality in order to provide the richness and concreteness which can be used by the empiricist.

Second, the theorist must specify much more clearly in his own mind, in his discussion, and above all, in the construction of his analysis the objectives which he is seeking to pursue. I believe this is one of the major reasons that Keynesian analysis has proved more tractable than other portions of economic theory, from the point of view of the empiricist. Keynesian theory takes off toward a concrete objective. It asserts that unemployment is a problem and asks what variables can be taken to influence its level and how they can be manipulated to reduce this undesirable phenomenon to a minimum. The significant point here is not that Keynes had taken on an applied or "practical" problem but that the object of his investigation was concrete and relatively well defined. This sort of predetermination of the specific nature of the problem to be studied is, in my opinion, an almost indispensable requirement for building models which will be useful to the empiricist. In such an analysis it is relatively easy to arrive at rational decisions as to which data are relevant and which irrelevant, which variables are important and which unimportant. In the case of the Keynesian analysis, the level of investment and its determinants, such as the rate of interest, were, on these grounds, rightly or wrongly, judged to be an indispensable part of the employment-determination mechanism while the degree of monopoly was not. The result was that the theory hypothesized a number of fairly well-defined relationships involving a specific set of variables about which information could be collected and whose parameters it was possible to attempt to estimate.

Much of the writing of pure value theory has refused to accept so confining an objective. Its goal has been to explain, in some ultimate sense, the behavior of wide classes of units and their decision-making processes. As a result, the number of explicit hypotheses that emerged were few, the number of explicit functions equally small, and the field, instead of providing specific directions and requests to the empiricist, offered him merely a hunting license and said: "Why don't you go out and see whether things work out the way we have said they do?" Naturally, with instructions so vague, the relationship of the empirical findings to the theory have proved quite tenuous.

Another important, though obvious, admonition to the theorist is that he should formulate his models in terms of variables which can be measured. Unfortunately, this is an option which is not always available to him. Concepts, like changes in taste and technological progress, will always play an important role in economics and they cannot be entirely abstracted from. Yet, it is desirable that a conscious attempt should be made, wherever possible, to cast our models in this way and I suspect it is rare that this attempt is explicitly made, except when the empiricist is constructing a special model for his own purposes. Indeed, it is probably for this reason that a number of well-known theorists who have recently participated in empirical work told me that they found it necessary either to recast substantially the currently available models or to develop completely new ones better adapted to the data. That is, they found the existing models to be in a form which was just not usable.

And Some Tasks for the Empiricist

But it is not only the theorist who must change his ways. The empiricist, too, must adopt new attitudes and new approaches. Too often I think he begins with the question, "What can the theory do for me?" rather than with "What can I do for the theory?" This, of course, is starting off on the wrong foot.

Empirical studies also frequently suffer from a vagueness of purpose and a generality of subject matter. There is a close analogy here with an incident concerning one of my students. In discussing the subject of his term paper with me, he asked me whether I had any objection to his writing about Turkey. I assured him that I had no prejudices against the Turks or the Hungarians or the Senegalese, and that the important question was not whether he would write about Turkey but what it was in the Turkish economy that he was going to discuss. "Turkey" is surely too vague and general a topic for a student's paper. And yet we are willing to proceed in the same way ourselves. Industry study after industry study seems to be produced in precisely that spirit. We set out to study the furniture industry or the automobile industry or the mouth-organ industry without beginning with a clear set of hypotheses which our study is designed either to support or reject. Let me make myself very clear on this point. I have no objection to industry studies conducted in this spirit. They may serve a purpose of their own which is commendable and desirable. I argue, merely, that these will never prove a means to produce a closer union between empirics and theoretics. For this purpose it will be necessary for the empirical researcher to formulate a set of hypotheses closely related to the theory which he is studying and to predesign his study so that it will prove an effective and efficient instrument for the testing of these hypotheses. Until this is done the theorist will find the empirical materials to be so vague and so diffused as to offer him very little or no help at all.

This also has a related implication for the specific procedures used by those who employ the interview method to gather their data. I have rarely seen studies of this sort conducted with an explicit hypothesis in mind. More generally, the interviewer begins with the idea that his subjects will tell him how operations proceed in the field which is being studied. I am not suggesting that the interviewers are naïve and that they do not know the pitfalls involved in answers which are neither frank nor knowledgeable. Indeed, the sophistication of these investigators is often remarkable. My objection is not that these persons are insufficiently wise but that they are insufficiently specific for the needs of the theorist, and, indeed, that their interviews are not designed to deal with the theorist's problems.

This leads to a final and probably subsidiary point about the technique of testing hypotheses by interview methods. Because interviews are, necessarily, to some extent rambling and unstructured, it is easy for the interviewer to fall victim to the temptation of believing that the interview has confirmed his preconceptions. Since his data are necessarily vague and ambiguous he can read them any way he wishes, at least within wide limits, and so the usefulness of an interview test of hypothesis comes under a cloud. I suspect it would be helpful as a device for avoiding such biases to undertake some degree of pre-commitment. That is, it would be desirable for the interviewer to specify before he begins his interviews what alternative types of evidence he would not be surprised to find. He should indicate both the type of evidence which would lead him to reject his hypothesis and that which should add to his faith in it. Moreover, in specifying these two types of outcome, he must make sure that both are plausible—that it is not out of the question that evidence either in favor of, or against, his hypothesis will emerge from the interview. Perhaps such a procedure will occasionally prove too stultifying and yet it will, I think, sometimes be worthwhile, in order to guarantee the objectivity and the efficacy of the interview technique as a means for the testing of hypotheses.

Studies Involving Both Theory and Fact

Let me turn finally to some examples wherein empirical and theoretical research have been combined—examples which constitute the basis for my guarded optimism. An important application of this sort is provided by the so-called business game. Systematic work in this area has recently been conducted by Shubik, Stern, and a number of other investigators, and in some cases they have turned up remarkable results. Many of these investigations have been directly applied to some of the theoretical models of oligopoly analysis. One case, which was specially interesting, involved the so-called problem of the prisoners' dilemma. This is a standard game-theoretic model. Briefly, the situation is the following: two prisoners who are suspected of a crime are arrested and questioned separately. Each prisoner knows that if neither he nor his fellow culprit confesses they will both go free. If one confesses and the other does not, the one who has remained silent will be heavily punished while the one who "squeals" will be let off with a minor penalty. Finally, if they both confess they will be punished almost as heavily as if one had remained silent. This case at first appears rather far removed from the problems of economic theory, but it is really at the heart of the mechanism of competition. The whole point is that behavior is totally different when people can get together and act in confidence that all others will behave in the same way than if they make their decisions in complete independence. The individual farmer knows very well that he would make more money if he could restrict his crop in confidence that every other farmer would also do so. But he knows that this is unlikely and that therefore he must produce as much as he can. The result, of course, is lower farm prices for everyone, and either the benefits of competition or the need for farm supports are the necessary consequences (depending on the point of view). The analogy with our two prisoners should be clear. If they could collude we know that both of them would find it advantageous not to give any information to the police. But in the absence of the opportunity for collusion each may find it advantageous and desirable to tell everything he knows and the result may be to their mutual disadvantage. Preliminary business-game experiments along these lines suggest that this is precisely the sort of behavior that one can expect in practice—that people placed in a situation analogous with the prisoners' dilemma seem to have very little confidence in their partners in crime. There is still, of course, much to be done along these lines, but, certainly, these results are highly suggestive.

Another illustration combining empirical work with theory involves one of my own studies. Recently, I recognized an empirical situation which seemed to offer great promise for direct testing of the Cournot oligopoly model. It will be recalled that the Cournot model suggests that oligopolists have explicit or implicit reaction curves. Each firm's reaction curve is a specific function which tells how that firm will respond to the decisions of its competitors. In the Cournot model these reaction curves are used to describe a sequence of developments over time, in which the first firm responds to the second, the second to the first, then the first to the second, and so on, ad infinitum. That is, the first firm charges such-and-such a price, the second firm then responds by charging some other price which leads the first firm to modify its price, and so on. In reexamining these models, I realized that the advertised prices of retail supermarkets offer a fine opportunity for the investigation of this sort of model. As we know, supermarket grocery chains rely on pre-weekend sales for the bulk of their business. As a result, many quote special prices that are decided upon for this part of the week, and are publicized in one or a few advertisements which appear in newspapers about the middle of the week. This process involves a fixed minimum reaction period; one week; information on advertised prices which is available to all competitors; and records which are available for many years back. A preliminary study attempting to fit reaction curves statistically to these data provided some interesting and promising results. However, people who are well versed in the practices of the industry were quite skeptical, not without considerable justification. They felt that the procedures which were employed involved too many pitfalls and that the basic model was a naïve and an excessively simple representation of the facts of the case. Nevertheless, I hope to go on with this investigation, and by more careful formulation and closer attention to some of the statistical traps, to produce more acceptable results. Indeed, discussion with some empirical investigators, during the course of the conference at which this paper was first given, quickly generated a degree of enthusiasm on both our parts, and has offered suggestions for improvement of the basic model which should be very helpful. A number of additional variables which should be included in the analysis were suggested and it emerged from the discussions that this decision problem must be considered one involving simultaneous relationships. The list of items to be advertised, the amount of space to be devoted to each item in the advertisement, and the prices of these items are not determined independently. And while competitive advertised prices are no doubt an important, and perhaps the most important, single variable influencing these decisions, other elements, such as supply prices, seasonal influences, and the like, are apt to play a significant role. There is, of course, no reason why subsequent work on this study should not take these other elements into account and thereby produce a much more sophisticated piece of work.

However, to me, the significant thing is not the specific study. Rather, two auxiliary phenomena require emphasis. One is the existence of specific problems which offer particularly felicitous opportunities for the testing and further development of the theory. I believe such opportunities are increasingly being sought out and will yield a rich harvest of results. The second point to be noticed is the speed with which the empiricist and the theorist in this case were able, at least, apparently, to get somewhere when each formulated his questions in the form appropriate for the other.

I think it is clear that we are both going to have to learn to talk to one another more effectively so that each of us can communicate information specifying exactly what he needs from the other. I believe more and more of us are now willing to make the attempt and I believe that more and more such attempts are going to be made.

In sum, I do look for some progress in this the weakest area of economic analysis—the interarea between data and theory. I would not be surprised if here were to emerge some of the most exciting developments in our discipline in the next few years.

INTERPRETATIONS AND CONCLUSIONS

BY ALFRED R. OXENFELDT, PROFESSOR OF
MARKETING, THE GRADUATE SCHOOL OF BUSINESS,
COLUMBIA UNIVERSITY, AND

RICHARD B. TENNANT, ECONOMIST,
MC KINSEY & COMPANY, INC.

This paper represents a novel experiment; we hope that some will consider it "noble." Since the conference raised many interesting issues and stirred up illuminating discussion, but did not "settle" anything, a device was sought that would capitalize on the considerable work and thought that went into the conference. The device selected was to ask two persons actively associated with the conference, who were deeply interested in its subject, and who represented opposing viewpoints, to hammer out a common view. It was expected that the authors would add to what was contained in the papers and discussion at Arden House. They were told explicitly that a consensus of sentiment expressed at the conference was not sought. They were asked to draw upon whatever sources and resources were available to them—main papers, formal discussants' papers, published works, and discussions, among other things. In particular, they were asked to reflect upon what they had learned and to add whatever they knew or believed from their personal experience and from the discussions that took place between them in the course of preparing this paper. The end product was to be a paper that represented their best current thinking, which presumably had been enriched by participation in the Arden House conference. It was hoped, that they would be able to prepare a common report rather than feel obligated to write two divergent reports.

For those who may want to participate in such a noble experiment in the future, a brief account of the way the paper was prepared may be helpful. The authors read the papers presented at the conference and then met several times to discuss what they might do. Frequently they found themselves stating what they felt had "come out of the conference." After considering several different ways of handling their assignment, they decided to cover each of the areas assigned to the authors of the four main papers and to introduce those four sections in a separate section, dealing with the nature and use of models in general. The section on models is both a summary and an introduction to the other sections of the paper.

Initially, each section was the responsibility of one of the authors. Prior to the writing of most sections, the authors discussed the subject until it began to take some shape and the line of thinking emerged. After a draft was prepared, there were repeated discussions and successive revisions. In the process, the original division of authorship was lost and an essentially joint document emerged.

On the Nature and Uses of Models in Economics

The first Columbia Conference was concerned with a specific set of analytical models: the standard market models of price theory. There are, however, many other kinds of models useful in analytical work, and it is the purpose of this section to discuss the nature of these models in general, as well as to describe the character, content, and properties of the market models in particular. This wider discussion is desirable not only to put the market models in perspective, but also because it may be better to use other types of models than to attempt to improve the market models themselves in circumstances where the latter are unsatisfactory.

WHY MODELS?

In the simplest dictionary definition, a model is a facsimile or reproduction of some aspects of something else. Such facsimiles may include a simple verbal analogy, a scale model of a plant, or a mathematical statement of a production process. That such varied types of model can be useful problem-solving tools reflects fundamental characteristics of the processes of creative thought and the physical universe.

The processes of creative thought. Recent research [1] into the ways in which people think and solve problems leads to several conclusions.

1. In order to think about any external phenomenon, the brain must have some internal representation to work with. This "image" may be visual or auditory in nature, or may have quite different characteristics.

2. Much of the mental activity in creative thought is unconscious. Unconscious incubation precedes the flash of illumination, or the "aha!" reaction, with which a thinker achieves insight.

3. A key element in problem solving or understanding is the mental set, or way of looking at the problem. Problem solving can be conceived of as a search in which possible solutions are first identified and then judged satisfactory or not. In all but trivial problems the number of possible solutions is extremely large, and a random search (as, for example, in solving a set of simultaneous equations simply by trying random numbers) would be excessively time consuming. However, creative problem solvers have processes of selection, called "heuristics," based on their experience, which enable them to restrict search to possible solutions possessing high probability of being satisfactory and, hence, to move much more rapidly to a solution. The use of heuristics and the changes in mental set as one heuristic is replaced by another constitute the strategy and tactics of problem solving.

[1] See, for example, A. Newell, J. C. Shaw, and H. A. Simon, *The Processes of Creative Thinking* (Santa Monica, RAND Corporation P-1320, 1959).

4. Logic is used at many stages of the creative process but does not dominate it. Only routine or trivial problems can be solved by logical processes alone. In more difficult problems, logic requires direction by the internal imagery, unconscious incubation, and mental sets mentioned above. When so directed, logical reasoning is effective, and indeed indispensable, in bringing half-formed ideas to explicit statement, in working out implications of partial solutions, in demonstrating proofs of solutions, and in communicating findings to others.

These characteristics of creative thought indicate that models of some kind are essential to creative thought and that models of different kinds, satisfying different purposes, may be helpful at different stages of the problem-solving process. Internal imagery itself implies a model of the outside world and, to this extent, at least, thought is inseparable from models. Various types of models, such as an analogy or metaphor, a more formal representation of one property of the problem by another in the model (as when money flows are represented by hydraulic flows), or even a simple check list, may provide perspective and help the problem solver to look at his problem in a new way. Finally, complex mathematical or other models may be helpful in stating interrelations, working out implications, and, in general, extending the power of logic in those parts of the creative process that belong to it.

The physical universe. Not only the characteristics of creative thought but also the nature of the physical universe require the use of models in problem solving. The world is so complex relative to the limitations of the human mind that some simplification or abstraction from reality must be made, if there is to be any hope of understanding it. And once we have abstracted from reality, we are investigating properties of a model of reality and only hopefully, properties of the real world.

Two levels of abstraction are involved, that of relevance and that of simplification. Any study, because it is limited by its purpose, looks at only part of the universe. For example, the bacterial count on a coin is part of the reality of a transaction in which that coin is used. But it would not normally be relevant to the economic issues of the transaction. Ordinarily, studies in economics, like studies in all other disciplines, consider problems limited in scope. Both in framing the problem and in marshalling evidence, they abstract from the irrelevant matters that are all mixed in together in the real world.

The elimination of irrelevant matters is, however, only the first stage of abstraction. In many fields, but especially in the social sciences, there is usually a further need to simplify, narrow in scope, and isolate problems, not because other matters are irrelevant, but in order to secure a problem small enough to solve. The real problem is converted to a problem in a model. The assumptions of *ceteris paribus*, so characteristic of economic theory of all types, are the mark of a decision to exclude certain phenomena and issues from study. They are excluded not because they are of no interest but in order to concentrate attention on strategic variables that are subject to control or simply in order to reduce a problem to manageable size. Analytical convenience and adequate application to reality are often opposed.

KINDS OF MODELS

The variety of intellectual purposes served by models and the different balances that can be struck between analytical power and fidelity to reality have resulted in the development of many kinds of models which may be classified in a number of different ways.

One obvious difference among models is in what might be termed their "formality." Models cover a wide spectrum, from informal verbal analogies, which may provide insight or aid communication, to formal scientific models, possibly taking a mathematical form. Between these extremes one might find casual models like check lists, which attempt to itemize all of the forces at work, to less casual lists, which group these forces and indicate their relative weight.

Another classification depends on the way in which the model reproduces the real world.[2]

1. Iconic models, such as a globe or photograph, look like the real object they reproduce. They convey information about it and may also help the viewer to see the reality from a new perspective.

2. Analogue models, such as a thermometer (where length indicates temperature) or a graph of quantitative relationships, represent one property by another. They may provide a clear description of important relationships, facilitate the analysis of changes in particular variables, or assist the problem solver to approach his problem from a new direction or from fresh perspectives.

3. Symbolic models, such as a set of differential equations or a linear programming matrix, express selected relationships of reality in mathematical or logical symbols. They make possible the concise statement of the aspects of reality selected for study and are particularly suited to tracing the effects of changes in selected variables and to the analysis of interrelationships among them.

Several other characteristics might be used to classify models. Some models seem to stress description while others emphasize explanation —though all models involve elements of both. For example, the models employed in cost theory have a substantially higher descriptive component than those of monopolistic competition. Similarly, models of airplanes in wind tunnels, while they serve important explanatory functions, are more descriptive of reality than engineers' drawings. Similarly, some industry studies are so written that they represent models of the industry (eliminating much of the historical, institutional, and anecdotal material industry studies usually contain); these would represent more highly descriptive models than, say, the market models of oligopoly in general. Symbolic models of an industry, in contrast, generally contain little description, are highly abstract, are confined to variables that are quantifiable—at least conceptually—and are usually designed to provide explanations by

[2] C. W. Churchman, R. L. Ackoff, and E. L. Arnoff, *Introduction to Operations Research* (New York, Wiley, 1957), pp. 157–62.

the display and analysis of functional relationships. It should be noted, however, that all models, of any kind, are abstract to some degree.

These model classifications are by no means complete, and still other classes could probably be identified. To some extent, such classification helps to illuminate the nature and uses of models. More important, the variety in classification suggests that other types of models might be invented to meet the continually changing needs of scientific and other problem solving.

In terms of these varied criteria, it is interesting to classify the standard market models of pricing theory. They are highly formal models, usually presented in analogue, graphical form, though the symbolic form is also used. They are highly abstract and are concerned far more with explanation than with description. They are logical in character and primarily serve the purposes of logical analysis. However, the deep indoctrination of economists with these models undoubtedly affects the nonlogical as well as the logical aspects of their work. The mental set with which economists approach problems of industrial structure and behavior and public policy are heavily influenced by their knowledge of and commitment to these models. In this there lies both benefit and danger. The models may assist in problem solving or serve as blinders.

THE STANDARD MODELS OF THE FIRM,
THEIR NATURE AND CONTENT

The conference was concerned with a special set of models of the firm in various market states. These may be taken to be models completed by the end of the 1930s and still in use today. We do not include such later mathematical formulations as linear programming, inventory models, or game-theoretic, oligopoly models.

The content of these models can be described in terms of a selected set of variables and concepts, assumptions and propositions concerning these, and a framework of relationships among the variables and concepts. In what follows, we shall consider these models as a whole, including the variables, concepts, propositions, and framework, without distinguishing those parts which were in the literature long before the models were complete. We are not concerned with the history of economic doctrines but only the utility of a specific set of tools.

Variables and concepts. Variables in the models include prices and quantities of outputs, prices and quantities of inputs, and a few other variables such as total revenue derived from, and expressible in terms of, these variables.

The principal concepts are as follows: 1) the demand schedule for outputs; 2) the supply schedule for inputs; 3) cost in various meanings of which opportunity cost is the most fundamental. Other important cost concepts include sunk, fixed, and variable; 4) marginal concepts such as marginal cost, marginal physical product, marginal revenue, marginal rates of substitution; 5) elasticity; 6) profit; 7) the entrepreneur; 8) short run; 9) long run; 10) scale of operations.

Assumptions and propositions. The following assumptions and propositions concerning the concepts and variables are essential parts of the content of the models: 1) The universe is static. Tomorrow will be like today. Time is not considered except as its passage is necessary to allow shifts to occur from one equilibrium to another. 2) The firm seeks maximum short-run profits. 3) The firm is merely a computing point without financial needs. 4) The quantity produced equals the quantity sold. There is no inventory. 5) The firm sells directly to customers for its products and buys directly from suppliers for its inputs. There are no distribution channels. 6) The quantity demanded is a continuous downward sloping function of price for the market as a whole. 7) Nonprice variables either do not affect market demand or do not change. 8) The quantity of inputs supplied is a continuous function of price for the market as a whole and is usually upward sloping although downward sloping exceptions may also be explored. 9) In conditions of perfect competition, the demand curve for outputs of the firm, and the supply curve for inputs to the firm are perfectly elastic. In monopoly conditions, the firm faces downward sloping demand functions and may face non-horizontal supply functions. 10) Whatever the demand and supply functions may be, they are known by the entrepreneur for a range of input or output quantities. 11) If some input factor is limited in quantity to the firm, other input factors show diminishing marginal products as they are increased beyond some point. There is some such point where this will be true. As an arithmetical consequence, marginal cost increases with output beyond this point of input employment. 12) Marginal cost is known by the entrepreneur for a range of quantities. 13) Two significant relationships are purely mathematical in nature: marginal cost equals average cost at its minimum, and the ratio of price to the excess of price over marginal revenue equals the elasticity of demand.

A framework of relationships. Based on these assumptions and propositions, the standard models of the firm establish equilibrium conditions involving a complex set of relationships between supply and demand conditions, quantities of input and output, cost, revenues, and profits. Significant characteristics of this framework are as follows: 1) In searching for the most profitable price, output, and scale of plant, the firm balances cost and revenue conditions so that marginal revenue equals marginal cost. 2) Permanent survival requires that price equal or exceed average total cost. 3) If the firm produces more than one product, it does so in such quantities that their marginal revenues are in the same ratios as their marginal costs. 4) Input factors in the production of any product are employed in such proportions that the marginal costs of acquiring them are in the same ratio as their marginal products. 5) In perfect competition, the scale and output of the individual firm are limited by rising marginal costs. In monopolistic conditions, rising marginal costs may be a factor but, if not, output and scale are limited by declining marginal revenue. 6) In perfect competition, the equilibrium conditions listed above take a special form so that the pattern of outputs and of inputs is optimal not only for the firm but for the economy. In monopolistic conditions, maximized profits for the firm do not imply that the total allocation pattern is optimal.

Functions of the standard models. When the nature of the standard market models is set down as in the preceding sections, a number of obvious implications arise concerning the kinds of uses that might be made of them and dangers that may exist.

1. Direct application. The models discuss criteria for maximum profit in the firm and implications concerning the allocation patterns that result. On the surface, it might seem that they could be directly applied to the making of optimal profit-maximizing price and output decisions or to the establishment of public policy. It is clear from the very nature of the models, however, that these approaches involve serious dangers. As we have seen, the level of abstraction in the models is high and one should not be surprised if elements in the real world, not included in the model assumptions, indicated different sorts of decisions, both for the profit-seeking entrepreneur and for the judge of public policy. For example, companies with secure markets will often hold prices below the level that marginal costs and the elasticity of demand would suggest, and do so quite properly, in view of the dynamics of competition or the political climate. Similarly, antitrust controversies in which price identity is taken as evidence both of active competition and of its absence imply that at least one side has applied a model that does not include all relevant variables.

Not only are the models extremely simple in their assumption structure, but some of the assumptions are clearly contrary to fact and, thus, further impair the utility of the models as guides to profit or public policy. Businessmen ordinarily do not have the information concerning demand or cost conditions assumed for them, and profit maximization is not as clear an objective in the real world as in the models.

2. Analytical aids. Models find their proper, and quite reliable, application when used to organize thinking as one aspect of more

comprehensive studies of industrial behavior, of business decision problems, or in certain areas of public policy. Although over-simplified, the standard models do provide concepts and tools to use in thinking about many practical problems.

Models of price theory increase our ability to understand complex interactions of multiple factors; they also provide insights into the nature of allocation patterns and the balancing of opposed considerations. These problems dealt with in the model also exist in the real world. And though the problems are much more complicated in the real world, an understanding of the balances and interrelations found in the models can be helpful as a starting point. The marginal concepts are useful in analyzing opposed pressures on output and price. The models draw specific attention to cost conditions, demand characteristics, and barriers to entry for their effects on industry structure and behavior. They illuminate some parts of the processes by which prices are adapted to cost and demand characteristics. The insights offered by the models have proved enormously superior to those of unaided intuition.

These general types of assistance to our reasoning ability about firms and industries have great practical importance, even though it is hazardous to use the models in a direct, predictive way. To the extent that the market models illuminate the nature and effects of market forces, they are capable of wide application. It is difficult to imagine any business decision, antitrust problem, or industry study that does not require an understanding of the forces operating in the industry in which the problem occurs and the interrelationships among those forces.

It must be stressed, however, that the use of the standard models for any purpose does involve serious pitfalls for the unwary or the incompetent. While the models act as useful organizers of thinking and provide ways to look at decision problems or public policy problems, they may also act as inflexible frameworks, preventing the user from considering variables or relationships not included in them.

The models must be used with skill. They are powerful tools in the hands of a competent economist, but seldom productive in the hands of an amateur.

Directions for improvement. These limitations of the models suggest certain potential directions of improvement. More adequate models might take into account some of the important matters assumed away at present. The pressure of financial needs and problems of distribution channels might be included. More attention could be given to the nonprice aspects of demand. More realistic decision rules might replace the assumed marginal adjustment of which few businessmen are conscious. Other aspects of business decisions besides the adjustment of price-output levels might be included. The consequences of ignorance and lack of knowledge might be explored. The dynamic problems of adaptation through time and of uncertainty should be incorporated into the model if they can be.

Unfortunately, all of these directions for improving the market models encounter substantial difficulties. Marketing, financial, and dynamic problems often are so rooted in circumstances peculiar to specific firms and industries that they do not fit well in a general model of the firm. Some of the factors that are fairly general do not lend themselves to the kinds of graphic or symbolic analyses out of which the present models are built. Even while these circumstances explain why progress with existing general models has been so limited, they also suggest that the commitment of economists to present model types is unfortunate, and that progress may be achieved through the exploration of other less elegant types.

The difficulties noted do, however, suggest how the standard models of the firm should be used. In solving particular problems, whether for business operations or for public policy, the general models must be modified, through substantial additional analysis, to create specially tailored models for particular circumstances. The market models as they stand are extremely general in their characteristics and are not very powerful when "applied" in this form. They are best regarded as general machine-tools of the economist that are to be used to produce special-purpose tools. From the general market models one can construct specialized and more complex models to meet particular needs. Used as analytical tools for further model building, rather than as finished products, market models of the firm have their greatest value.

Market Models and Industry Studies

Empirical studies of industries, markets, and individual companies are undertaken with various ends in view and there is a consequent variation in the usefulness of the market models. In some types of industry study market models make a negligible contribution, while in others they are of great value.

VARIED OBJECTIVES OF INDUSTRY STUDIES

We may distinguish the following important classes of industry study (omitting those undertaken in the interests of corporate or personal publicity, personal scandal mongering, or social protest).

1. Noneconomic scholarly inquiry. Many students of industry seek other kinds of knowledge than those of primary concern to the economist. Economic histories of industries often concentrate on historical, biographical and technological matters or upon sociological change. And even when concerned with economics, they often stress matters of development rather than the kinds of issues with which the market models deal. This is not a criticism of these other kinds of inquiry; there are many directions for legitimate scientific inquiry. Those under present discussion do not ordinarily derive much aid from the market models, though even here, opportunities for assistance probably are being overlooked.

2. Market measurement. Empirical studies that seek to measure the size or growth of markets or to predict future sales deal with only a portion of an industry's economic activity. Hence, they are likely to make little use of the market models that serve mainly to provide a unified analytical explanation of a wide range of economic activities.

3. Studies of market institutions. Some market investigations have as their purpose an explanation of the emergence, functioning, and consequences of specific market institutions. Although such studies may derive some help from marginal analytical tools, they are unlikely to find the integrating function of the market models of much assistance.

4. Testing or illustrating theory. Some industry studies have the goal of testing the validity of the market models and others, more optimistic, try to show how the market models apply. The latter objective is good pedagogy and the former is in the direct line of scientific method, but neither testifies to the utility of the market models. If empirical investigation shows a good correspondence with the models, this is evidence of their "accuracy." However, it is not a measure of the usefulness of these models that they are available for test.

5. Explanatory studies of industry structure and behavior. Other industry studies attempt to discover why an industry is built the way it is, why it behaves the way it does, and where dynamic forces are taking it. Such analytical studies can be undertaken for a variety of reasons: (a) They may be designed to suggest new directions for a general economic theory of the firm or to build a specific model of a particular industry in the interests of scientific illumination. (b) They may be designed to throw light on business problems. Such environmental studies give the business executive superior general perspective, and if they identify forces at work, successfully assist in identifying the problems, opportunities, and constraints that he faces. (c) Such studies can also contribute to public policy. By providing understanding of the forces affecting structure and behavior, an industry study can help define measures and objectives of performance, can help detect opportunities for reform in the light of feasible alternatives, and can reveal the real constraints and limitations that the world imposes on ideal policy objectives.

Studies of the type defined in number 5 are those which come closest to the interests of the economist as distinct from the economic historian or the marketing specialist. And it is in just these kinds of studies that we find the greatest contribution of the market models.

CONTRIBUTIONS OF THE MARKET MODELS

The market models may contribute to an analytical and explanatory study of an industry in the following different ways: 1) By providing a way of looking at the industry and its problems. 2) By identifying key variables and relationships. 3) By identifying issues of performance and problems. 4) By the tools of marginal analysis which, here as elsewhere, provide the cutting edge of economic reasoning.

A *way of looking at the industry*. The market models of the firm portray the firm as adapting to environmental pressures in its search for maximum profits. All firms in the industry together are subject to economic constraints, and the individual firm is further subject to the constraints imposed upon it by the behavior of competitors.

This concept of the adaptation of firm and industry to environmental pressures and the allied idea of a balance of opposed forces are helpful in trying to explain industry structure and behavior. An industry's structure is ordinarily rooted in characteristics of the economic environment, including its own technology. The behavior of a firm reflects some of these same factors as well as the pressures of its competitors, which in turn partly reflect their number and sizes. These explanatory elements in an industry study directly parallel the concerns of the market models, and it is doubtful that we would clearly understand the interaction of these factors without the models.

Industry studies of earlier days tended to be heavily historical, biographical, and technological in their content. Many are worthwhile contributions to economic history, and it is possible, with the insights now provided by the market models, to see in them a substantial explanation for industry structure and behavior. However, it is rare for one of the older industry studies to give as explicit a

treatment of the effects of economic forces on structure and behavior as we can now achieve on the basis of a more explicit model-
guided investigation.

Of course, the balance of forces struck in the market models typically results in a stable equilibrium. While we are interested in
stable elements of equilibrium where they exist, we are often more
interested in the processes of dynamic change and in the out-of-
balance forces that promise further changes in the future. These are
matters that lie quite outside the standard market models. The
models provide no direct help in this direction.

Key variables and relationships. In addition to providing the general concepts of adaptation to environment and of the resulting
equilibrium, the market models identify a limited number of related
variables in the environment as being of key significance. While
some of these variables and relationships would probably be considered in any industry study, it is doubtful that they would be
identified as quickly, clearly, and comprehensively without the help
of the models.

1. Demand characteristics for the product. The market models
present the demand curve as a principal influence on the firm and
the elasticity with respect to price as its most significant characteristic. These are matters with which any broad industry study must
be concerned, although they may not be central, in some cases. The
elasticity of demand for the individual firm and for the total industry are different, a fact that has important implications for real
industries and that helps to explain the kinds of competition that
are worthwhile and the gains to be secured through collusion. Also,
the concept of demand contained in the models is rigorous and avoids
the ambiguity and errors that result from loose and nontechnical
definitions.

Of course, the study of any real industry must be concerned with
other characteristics of demand than price elasticity. Sensitivity to
other influences, such as advertising, promotion, distribution efforts,
new products, and the level and rate of growth are all characteristics

that need examination and that are not generally found in the models. Other practical matters, such as the degree of communication and price and sales reporting that exist in any market, are implicit in estimating price elasticity, and the models may be said to raise questions about them indirectly.

2. The supply of inputs. Another major environmental influence in the models is the character of the supply of inputs. In many presentations, input supplies are taken as given and are merely subsumed in the cost curves. In monopsony models, however, input purchases are given explicit treatment, and attention is thereby directed to the price elasticity of supply.

The supplies of inputs have important economic effect in various ways, and the market models illumine them and identify supply considerations as a key variable in many industry studies. The market models may help to explain long-term variations in relative factor prices (including wages) and thereby account for the factor mix within the firm. The standard models provide at least an initial interpretation of shifts in relative factor prices.

3. Technology and costs. The third pivotal environmental factor incorporated in the market models is the production function, which describes the transformation of inputs into outputs and, together with input prices, determines cost curves. The cost relationships postulated in standard models are extremely simplified, but they draw attention to the relationship between total cost and marginal cost and to the scale of output at which marginal cost turns sharply upward. The latter determines whether the firm must remain small enough to accord with conditions of approximately perfect competition or whether it may, for technical reasons, grow large enough to encounter market limits and, consequently, operate in some kind of monopolistic structure.

The relationship between total costs and marginal costs, in reality as well as in the model, determines the pressures for increased volume, the dangers of price wars, and the incentives to collusion or nonaggressive competition. These relationships are clearly presented in the market models and might be overlooked by investigators who did not employ these models.

In general, treatment of costs in the market models helps us to understand and describe actual cost structures in an industry study. The important relationships between total and marginal cost point up strategic matters to be investigated in almost every industry study. We might look at these things even if we did not have the market models available, but it is doubtful that we would come to these matters so quickly and directly.

Performance and objectives. The market models of the firm present conclusions about the effects of environmental conditions on industry structure, on the nature of competition and, through these, on profit results. Industry studies may build a comparable bridge between observed environmental conditions and the consequent results. The economic theorist, the businessman, and the antitrust specialist all are aided by studies which establish empirical generalizations about industry structure, industrial practices and performance.

Explaining performance. The market models direct attention to technology, cost, and market characteristics as determining the number and sizes of firms in an industry and as erecting possible barriers to the entry of new competition. The number of firms, the cost structure, and demand characteristics, in turn, are interpreted in the models as affecting the nature of competition. The models differentiate a number of possible competitive situations ranging from violent price wars to complete collusion. Finally, the models suggest the kinds of profit results to be expected, according to the severity of competition.

These concerns in the models are paralleled in explanatory industry studies. These, too, require an investigation into the size and number of competitors and the limits on competitive entry. In actual markets there is, of course, great variation in the size of firm that an industry's technology permits or requires, and barriers to entry are equally varied in kind and magnitude. The models help empirical investigation by drawing attention to these problems and by suggesting alternative patterns.

Similarly, the characteristics of competitive behavior are an essential part of most industry studies, and these can often be traced to the effects of industry structure, market characteristics, and cost relationships. Most actual industries show some mixture of competition and cooperative elements, and industry studies are ordinarily designed to explore this issue. The scope of an industry study of competition includes the matters considered in the models, and the models are helpful in suggesting some, though not all, of the elements necessary for an explanation.

Finally, industry studies are concerned with the profit record and with an attempt to explain it. It is highly likely that among the reasons for a particular profit experience found in an industry study, the factors and interrelationships of factors presented in the market models will be included.

Issues of performance. The analytical patterns of the market models draw attention to a number of aspects of performance of primary interest to economic theorists, businessmen, and makers of public policy. Barriers to entry are relevant to the businessman's tasks and to the commercial opportunities that public policy seeks to protect. The mix of competition and cooperation relates to the businessman's optimum policies and to the government's concern with competitive standards. The profit levels attained are a primary concern of businessmen and a possible indication to the policy maker of effective performance or exploitation. Criteria of performance, of course, are related to possible remedies. The businessman may be searching for profit improvement and the policy maker, for expansion of competition as a method of economic control.

These issues of performance raised by the market models are paralleled by the concerns of most economic industry studies. These too, in any specific industry situation, may be concerned not only to explain structure, behavior, and profits, but to interpret them in terms of the problems they set for businessmen or for public policy. In evaluating performance as well as explaining it, industry studies draw assistance from the market models. Although neither the explanatory variables, the interrelationships among them, nor the indexes of performance include all that are of possible interest, they provide a minimum list and an explanatory framework that has proved of substantial assistance to investigators engaged in industry studies.

LIMITATIONS OF THE MODELS

Although the preceding sections indicate many ways in which market models are helpful in industry studies, they also suggest that these models, by reason of their extreme simplicity and generality, go only part of the way. Firms and industries in real life are made up of people, and have a specific organization and an historical past. The firm has market concerns that are not reflected in the models, has financial needs that are not covered, and is seldom in such a stable condition that a static equilibrium theory can give a reasonably full explanation of the forces at work.

Hence, a competent industry study has to take into account a good many things in addition to those treated in the market models. The static economic constraints are only a part of the influences to which the firm and industry have to adapt. The pattern of historical development is an essential factor, since things that happened in the past often control what can be done in the present. Organizational and personal influences on behavior must be regarded as well as the pressures of demand, supply, and technology.

Not only must industry studies consider factors other than those included in the market models, but they must consider them with a substantially different purpose. Where the focus of the market models is on static equilibrium conditions, industry studies try to explain why things are the way they are, and, more importantly, what changes can be expected. For many purposes of business management, or for the better adjustment of public policy, it is even more important to know what are the out-of-equilibrium conditions which may force changes in the future than it is to know why things came to be as they are.

In another important aspect, however, industry studies of the analytical types we are here discussing have strong elements in common with the market models. Not only do they derive help from those models, but they themselves essentially are models of a more detailed and specialized type. To the extent that industry studies try to answer the questions that the models raise concerning structure and behavior, and to the extent that they find successful answers to these questions, they have created new models specific to that industry. Even the fullest industry study is selective and abstract. It may look at many more factors than the market models but it does not look at them all. It selects for analytical purposes, and when it selects to answer the kinds of questions suggested above it has established an analytical framework of the same general type. Analytical industry studies, while they draw assistance from the market models, themselves constitute perhaps the best way that improved models can be built.

Market Models and the Businessman

The job of the business manager is largely one of resource allocation and hence is highly relevant to economics. He must direct the use of men, money, materials, equipment, and other resources in a complex pattern of time and space. He must continually make decisions about investment, product mix, prices, inventories, and the balance of activities in planning, purchasing, production, and marketing. He makes these decisions on the basis of his own knowledge, analysis, and judgment and on the advice he receives from internal staff or outside consultants.

The market models may assist the businessman by contributing to his own thinking or by improving the advice he receives. In either case the contributions of the models are of two general types: those giving the businessman a better understanding of his industrial environment and those helping him make better specific decisions.

UNDERSTANDING THE ENVIRONMENT

Day-to-day operating decisions, as well as long-range planning and corporate strategy, must take account of what the general economy and industry climate make possible. Insight into these environmental conditions can greatly improve the operating decisions of executives and the counsel of advisors. As shown earlier, the market models are helpful in analyzing industrial situations, and improved understanding of a company's industrial environment is one of the most important types of assistance that the models may provide.

Certain types of industry study are especially useful to the businessman. Any study of an industry is likely to bring together data that a manager will find helpful. But, an analytical economic study making use of the market models is likely to raise, and may answer, questions of basic significance to management.

Among the critical questions raised in such a study are: 1) What explains the number of firms in the industry and their size distribution? 2) What explains the existing degree of competition and cooperation between firms? 3) What forces that promise future change can be identified?

Successful answers to such questions, focusing on forces at work in the industry, can help the executive by giving him superior general perspective, by identifying important problems requiring his attention, and by indicating opportunities for, and constraints on, business action offered and imposed by the environment.

Not every industry study provides such help and not all business executives are in need of it. Skilled and experienced executives generally know their industry and its pressures better than anyone else. Frequently, they possess perspectives on the economic forces operating in their industry that would be illuminating to the economist. Often, that is not the case. Businesmen and business consultants new to an industry or to a specific problem area often find that economic studies of their industry help them quickly to identify and understand what would otherwise be unfamiliar problems.

Moreover, even an experienced executive may gain insight into his firm's capabilities and opportunities from economic studies of his industry, for they generally emphasize different factors and interrelationships than the executive does. Such studies offer a different perspective and, together with the executive's own view, tend to deepen his understanding. Most executives are not required by their job responsibilities to consider all of the significant questions about their industrial environment that a competent economic study will raise.

There is ample evidence that many experienced business executives find economic studies of their industry helpful. They say so, and they pay to have such studies made. The basic advantage is one of improved perspective, an orderly arrangement of information about the industry that gives known facts a new meaning, and a stripping away of the detail in which many executives become entangled.

As discussed in Section 2, industry studies can be strengthened substantially by the application of the market models. It is in their use in industry studies that the market models probably offer their most significant aid to business executives.

HELP WITH SPECIFIC BUSINESS DECISIONS

In addition to these indirect types of help through industry studies, the market models may improve business decisions by providing general analytical tools, an analytical approach, or specific decision rules. The first two uses of models offer the greatest promise. The third may do more harm than good.

General tools. An important analytical tool is the marginal concept which underlies the market models. The marginal cost or revenue of an action identifies clearly the effect of that action in a way that averaged or arbitrary costs and revenue measures do not. By thus expressing the implications of alternative courses of action in a conceptually clear manner, marginal analysis provides a useful tool for businessmen.

Marginal analysis is, of course, not the sole property of the market models of economics. The concept of the derivative is its mathematical equivalent which is used in many fields. And the margin was used in economics long before the market models. However, the whole range of marginal concepts has received full development in the market models and is clearly expressed there, in relationship to some important business decisions. This clear expression represents a significant contribution of the market models to business-decision making.

Marginal analysis is, in fact, increasingly used in making business decisions. Accounting and financial executives have incorporated substantial elements of incremental thinking in their work. Line executives may or may not use these tools creatively, but many appear quite open to staff or consulting analyses that use them. The spread of corporate staffs, the increasing sophistication in business education, and the continuing professionalization of management guarantee a growing use throughout industry of these simple and effective analytical tools.

An analytical approach. The market models also provide an illuminating way of looking at the firm situation and a place to start thinking about its problems. They picture the firm as balanced between the opposing pressures of its input and output markets and of its technical capabilities, and show its decisions as involving compromises between opposed forces of costs and revenues. Even though the models are very general and do not describe any firm accurately, they do permit a skilled business analyst to structure the economic factors operating in his situation in a way that adds clarity. Moreover, the models may suggest a more specific model with greater relevance to the particular factual situation. The market models suggest that business decisions might be approached by arraying the consequences of alternatives under the headings of changes in marginal costs and marginal revenues. They further suggest some of the more important ways in which marginal costs and revenues may be influenced by various courses of business action. In these ways they can help businessmen and their advisors to analyze and resolve business problems.

Specific decision rules. Although the help derived from the market models, in the form of general tools and analytical approaches, is significant, many users demand more of the models and regard them as establishing explicit decision rules. The reasons for this are plain.

It is characteristic of the market models that they provide a specific determinate equilibrium that maximizes profits for the firm. If one believes that the models describe reality accurately or interprets reality as conforming to them, he will derive explicit decision rules from them and regard many practical decision problems as solved. It is quite possible, for example, to turn the analytical relationship of marginal revenue, price, and the elasticity of demand into a decision rule, and simply to set prices at a level that establishes the proper relationship between the marginal contribution which can be measured and an estimate of the elasticity. Clearly, such behavior would be misguided. Business decisions made in this manner would be more likely to lead to harm than good. The models are extremely general, they are without empirical content, and they do not provide conclusions on any specific business decision.

In this respect the market models differ from the operations research models that have been developed to resolve particular business-decision problems. An inventory model, or a linear programming warehouse-location model, is designed to provide numerical answers, and either permanent decision rules or a short cut to analyzing future problems of the same sort. In contrast, the market models illuminate problems but do not solve them. They help to structure analysis but they are not a set of algorithms that lead to specific numerical results.

Managers and advisors. The misuse of models to derive decision rules is especially likely when executives themselves attempt to apply them. Such attempts are rare for reasons developed below, but we have seen a number of executives fall into this trap.

Businessmen do not usually make good economists any more than economists usually make good businessmen. There are different habits of mind in the two groups as well as different levels of professional training, and both affect the way in which models will be used, or whether they will be used at all.

Because of their remoteness from particular decisions of the real world and their character as abstract intellectual constructs, the market models do not meet the practical businessman's needs. They suit the economist's preference for precise statement and incisive reasoning, but executives are often indifferent to, or repelled by, the theoretical elegance that the economist finds attractive. As a result, most businessmen make no use whatever of the market models.

When, on occasion, the business executive sufficiently overcomes his impatience with theory to make explicit use of the models, he often is still looking for immediate practical results and has a correspondingly strong motive to see practical decision rules in them, if possible. He may use the models to make predictions, or as ready-made tools for decision making. It is rare in the authors' experience for businessmen, or business students for that matter, to master price theory and use it effectively. As a result, although the market models have a significant potential contribution to make to better business-decision making, this potential is not often realized by business managers in their own use of these tools.

The tendency of businessmen to misuse the market models raises a direct question as to how much of the benefit of economic analysis is to be derived from the executive's own thinking and how much from the assistance of professional advisors. Certainly an increase in economic sophistication of executives is desirable. A wider spreading of marginal concepts and better understanding of the meaning of cost is to be hoped for. On the other hand, the use of scientific models in problem solving requires professional competence if it is to be well done.

American business management has to deal with all manner of scientific and engineering disciplines in its product and process development and in managing its own complex affairs. However, executives have not been forced to become scientists in order to develop new products, or operations research specialists in order to secure the benefits of that discipline. Neither is it necessary that businessmen become economists. They can benefit by economic advice, and the growing body of corporate economists and economic consultants indicates that they recognize the need for such advice. Economic literacy is desirable in business executives, as it is in all citizens, but parts of the field are best left to competent professionals. The manipulation of market models probably is one of these.

THE NEED FOR FURTHER MODELS

The extreme generality of the market models and the difficulties that businessmen find in their use suggests that other types of models are required if the needs of the businessmen are to be fully served. This conclusion is further supported by the great diversity of detailed decisions that executives are required to make.

Even among pricing decisions, there are several distinct types that involve different, critically important variables. Among the most important classes of price decision are the following: 1) model line pricing problems; 2) producer-reseller pricing problems; 3) life-cycle pricing; 4) price versus non-price sales promotion decisions; 5) price decisions for different time dimensions; 6) price discounts and discriminatory pricing.

In these decisions, the independent variables and constraints vary greatly. Presumably, the intellectual tools that would assist one in understanding them also differ considerably.

The diversity of detailed decisions suggests that, as a minimum, special-purpose models could be developed. These might be direct descendants of the traditional market models that have been extended to introduce additional variables, or modified to take account of some particular time dimension or for some other purpose. Alternately, quite different types of models could be developed.

At one extreme, businessmen may find helpful, in their own thinking, remote models like simple analogies. For instance, some price setters gain considerable insight from viewing a line of models as a team, particularly a football team. Intermediate models might include such things as check lists, i.e., complete enumerations of factors or variables in a decision, or lists with the variables grouped or assigned quantitative importance. Finally, at the other extreme, mathematical models may contribute to better decisions.

Some may object to so broad a definition of the term "model," but if defined as an intellectual construct that in some degree reproduces reality and assists the user in understanding it, then some analogies clearly qualify. Unfortunately for some pricing problems, we may not be able to progress much beyond models of this form for some time. Far better a good analogy than a poor statistical-estimating equation.

Models helpful to the businessman may be secured outside price theory. Illumination may be gained from the models developed in sociology, anthropology and other social sciences, even as some of those fields have been enriched by economic theory. Political science has concerns with international power relationships highly analogous to oligopoly and might, conceivably, offer businessmen more powerful models than does price theory. It is important to seek out those related subjects treated by other social science disciplines to learn what help they offer business executives.

It should be emphasized that there may be no single, best type of model for the businessman. Not only are decisions varied, but even the same decision may benefit from being reached in different ways. For instance, in setting a product line, there is no need to be restricted to a single model. The team analogy may be helpful, and so, also, may be an understanding of the theoretical models which deal with business costs. Mastery of the marginal principle can be of considerable aid. The more models available, the greater the total illumination for anyone who knows how to use them and refuses to be abused by them.

Finally, it may be helpful both to the businessman and to the development of economics to discover what models business executives currently employ. As indicated earlier, modern psychology teaches that the human mind must structure the elements in a problem, in order to achieve understanding. The structure may be inefficient or downright wrong, but it does, nevertheless, enable the perceiver to organize the information he possesses and to cope with the problem in some way. Some model is used wherever there is a conscious decision, even though the model itself need not be conscious. In constructing special-purpose models for business application, the best place to start might be with the business executive, himself. Once the different models that executives employ to make specific price decisions have been made explicit, economic theorists may build upon the best of them to increase their power and vigor.

Businessmen will welcome illumination in almost any form that is offered. Those who would help them would do well to experiment with different forms of models. Conceivably, the models for price making used by businessmen are more effective and illuminating than those developed by economic theorists. To test that hypothesis might well occupy the efforts of some economists who would otherwise strengthen their addiction to existing models, to which so many businessmen appear allergic.

Market Models and Antitrust

The makers, administrators, and enforcers of antitrust policy may secure help from the market models indirectly, through the better understanding of the economic forces at work in particular industries, and directly, in the analysis of particular issues.

UNDERSTANDING INDUSTRY FORCES

As frequently stated, the major contribution of the market models in all applications comes from their assistance in understanding the economic forces operating in industry. Such an understanding is prerequisite for the diagnosis and correction of objectionable industrial conditions, even as it is for business decisions, market investigations, and economic theory.

To understand industries and markets, of course, requires far more than mastery of the market models. By the collection of data and the close study of individual cases, plus the application of what they have learned from industry history as well as from the models, many economists have developed a high level of understanding of industrial arrangements and of their consequences. Economists have been active in describing and analyzing data about industrial operations and have amassed a considerable body of case histories that assist them in understanding other situations. It is therefore to be expected that economists would be employed, both by prosecution and defense, in antitrust actions, and by congressional committees and administrative agencies when new legislation is under consideration—even if they do not make much explicit use of the market models.

How much of the economists' knowledge of industry economics can be traced to the models and how much to other aspects of training and experience is a question to which there can be no complete answer. The conclusion reached earlier was that the market models contribute substantially to industry investigations.

DIRECT APPLICATIONS TO ANTITRUST

In addition to the general illumination of industry economics, market models have sometimes been applied to a number of specific issues in antitrust policy formulation and enforcement. There are others to which it appears that application might be worthwhile. Among the most important actual and possible uses are the following.

They might help frame antitrust legislation by helping to determine what conditions and practices are objectionable; determine the relative importance of the objectionable conditions; determine which objectionable conditions can be corrected; indicate the measures that might be taken to correct objectionable conditions; and forecast the outcome of the corrective measures.

They might help determine which cases to prosecute under prevailing law by helping to assess the magnitude of the social and individual injury resulting from existing arrangements; determine whether a feasible remedy exists.

They might, finally, assist in litigation involving alleged violations by helping to develop a theory of the case or alternative theories; select data to implement the selected theory; and prescribe the remedy to be requested in a specific case.

It is obvious that all these purposes to which the market models might be applied would be served by an understanding of the forces at work in particular industries. To the extent that the market models contribute to such understanding, they are applicable to antitrust problems. There remains, however, a question of whether the models make an explicit and direct contribution to the antitrust problems listed. The remainder of this section is concerned with this question.

The conclusions reached are as follows. 1) The market models are not applicable to many antitrust problems and are usually not applied. 2) Many direct applications of the model actually made are inappropriate or ineffective. 3) In some cases the market models provide real assistance. 4) There is pressing need for the development of improved models for antitrust purposes.

Market models inapplicable. Whether we are concerned with the formulation of antitrust policy or with its implementation, we are dealing with the real world, and we require a searching empirical analysis of prevailing conditions and practices. It is necessary to know thoroughly the conditions that prevail—something the models cannot reveal, for they necessarily lack factual content. Whatever the models may contribute to an understanding of facts, they are not a substitute for them. And, consequently, we cannot derive direct conclusions for antitrust policy from the market models alone.

Not only are the market models lacking in factual content but, as explained earlier, they are also partial and incomplete, for they omit such factors as nonprice sales stimulants, middlemen, and the like. Moreover, only a small portion of the issues germane to antitrust policy are included within the models. It is not surprising, therefore, that they have had a minor role in policy development and execution.

Existing antitrust legislation is directed against objectionable conditions and practices that were uncovered without aid from the market models of price theory. Furthermore, the basic concerns of antitrust have been different from those of price theory. The motivations underlying the antitrust laws were mainly those of "fairness" rather than economic efficiency, though the latter was explicitly recognized. The implicit value judgment, that small firms should be protected, even at some economic cost, was not based upon economic reasoning, although it does raise issues that the market models illuminate.

Not only has antitrust policy been based, historically, on other grounds than have the market models, but also, it is difficult to see any substantial, direct contribution that the models could make to policy formation.

No reliable standards for appraising either market structure or behavior can be derived from the market models. For example, one cannot reach valid conclusions on the following questions simply from the models themselves. Is an industry with four firms more objectionable than one with seven? Is a very high rate of profits for a few large firms in an industry where small firms are making very low rates of return "objectionable"? Is such a situation more or less objectionable than one in which all firms are making an attractive, not very high, rate of return? Is an industry that spends 30 percent of its sales dollar on sales efforts of one kind or another more objectionable than one that spends half as much? Under what circumstances, if any, should sales efforts be banned altogether?

Such measures of performance as can be derived from the market models are not generally accepted and should not be. The degree of excess capacity (almost an undefinable concept and even more unmeasurable in concrete cases), the ratio of marginal revenue to marginal cost, the level of profits after taking account of normal profits and opportunity costs, ease of entry, product differentiation, and consumer and seller "knowledge," are not even very good, let alone the best, indicators of industrial malfunction. (This represents both our view and the current consensus of those specializing in antitrust problems.)

The market models are no more effective in implementing antitrust policy than they are in framing it. In selecting cases for prosecution or in perfecting litigation, there is substantial distance between the concerns of the models and the concerns of law. There is, regrettably, a difference between what is "good for the economy" and what is "good law." Circumstances that violate the law—even a "good" law—might serve the public in purely economic ways.

When regulatory agencies find more alleged violations than they have resources to prosecute, they must do several things. First, they must select the alleged violations that might be the most serious. That is, they must decide where to look for violations to which they should devote their limited resources. Ordinarily these will represent classes of violations. Second, they must select individual cases for prosecution, perhaps on grounds of being sure of winning, to establish a valuable precedent, or to eliminate a situation that does serious damage.

While this latter aspect of damage is closer to the concerns of the market models, there is still a substantial difference between economic and legal concerns. In bringing suit against antitrust violators, a regulatory agency is concerned to extend protection to individuals who may be injured, as well as to safeguard social welfare. The market models contribute little to the assessment of damage to individual firms in specific cases; they are far more useful in analyzing the social welfare effects of industrial arrangements than in analyzing their effects on individual firms. To assess injury requires definition of injury, concepts and models to help detect it, and measures of magnitude. Price theory and price theories have paid little attention to such problems. Their attention has been focused on industry-wide and social effects.

Neither are the market models well suited, by their basic nature, to help identify departures from legality. They deal with economic efficiency and social welfare as economists define them, without regard to how Congress and the courts define them. Consequently, they have dubious relevance to matters of legality, as well as to the extent of the injury resulting from illegal acts or circumstances. Departures from existing legal standards are discovered mainly by detective work, rather than by economic analysis.

The market models are usually not applicable to the problems of proof and evidence involved in establishing antitrust violation. When a case revolves around practice rather than industry structure, the theory of the case generally is noneconomic. It typically involves a matching of alternative explanations for business decisions, the prosecution finding the decisions motivated by the desire to gain or exploit market power and the defense holding that the decisions are simply the customary and reasonable business actions of prudent men. The market models of price theory do not figure much in such legal theories.

Even the selection of data for legal purposes derives little assistance from the market models. Most of the basic forces identified by the market models, while important to understanding, are difficult to quantify for purposes of legal proof. How great are the barriers to entry? How great are "economic profits"? How much excess capacity exists? How great is the difference that customers perceive among alternate brands of the same product? The number of firms can indeed be measured, but even this datum involves agreement on the boundaries of the market. What is the effect on existing firms of the threat of potential competitors, including possible vertical integration by customers? While these are all important matters in understanding competitive behavior, they are extremely difficult to measure and, accordingly, do not provide a useful guide to data selection for litigation.

In most cases, the market models are too simplified and abstract to be helpful in antitrust work. In some cases, however, they are too complex, and simpler notions turn out to be more helpful. A frequent issue in antitrust suits is the definition of the relevant market. The prosecution usually seeks to justify a very narrow definition so that the defendant company occupies a large proportion of that market. Conversely, the defense typically seeks to establish that it competes with an extremely broad sector of United States industry and is, therefore, a highly competitive firm. (In some merger cases, however, the positions have been reversed, with the defense arguing for a narrow definition so that two products would not be considered in the same market.) In the development of arguments seeking to establish either wide or narrow bounds to the market, there is reliance on data about substitutability and price interdependence that employs quite simple notions. If one deals with a matter of degree, such as cross-elasticity of demand, it is not to be expected that a model could assist much in determining just where the bounds should be drawn.

Finally, at every stage of the process of public policy, from legislation through case selection to litigation and enforcement, politics and the pressure of special interest can play an important part, and one beyond the reach of the models. Political feasibility sets strict limits to the utility of any policy conclusions arrived at by use of the models.

Inappropriate or ineffective use of models. In most antitrust problems, the market models fail to make a direct, positive contribution because, taken alone, they are irrelevant or incomplete, and hence are not used. In some cases, however, they have had a net injurious effect because they are used when inappropriate, or are badly used.

The yardsticks that have been advanced to measure the social efficiency of an industry, like Lerner's *Index of Monopoly Power*, are not valid measures and, fortunately, are not generally considered valid.

The opposition of many economists, and of policy makers influenced by economists, to large-scale enterprise and to concentrated industrial structures has been based, to a significant degree, on conclusions about market behavior and economic results drawn from models which are either contrary to fact or contain only some of the facts. The preference for, and misunderstanding of, price competition in actual markets reflects thinking in terms of models in which price competition is the only kind of competition given substantial analysis.

Writers of economics texts have frequently gone beyond the proper use of models in prescribing and forecasting the consequences of legislation.

Much active but inconclusive controversy about such matters as resale-price maintenance, mergers, vertical integration, conglomeration, and exclusive dealing, appears to reflect excessive reliance on market models.

In general, use of direct deductions from the models to draw conclusions concerning objectionable conditions and desirable remedies, or to forecast the effects of industrial reform, is improper. Conclusions drawn may prove to be directly opposite to the truth. For example, a prohibition on advertising might raise, rather than lower, unit costs as more expensive forms of sales promotion are substituted. Any statement about industry structure, behavior, or performance, to be valid, must rest upon a detailed study of the industrial situations where they occur.

The models do provide real assistance. Although the isolated use of the models to draw policy conclusions seems inappropriate and dangerous, the models can help in the analysis of specific industrial circumstances and specific practices for purposes of public policy. The market models direct attention to relevant factors and to needed information. Used with skill, they usually help investigators to understand and forecast the consequences of existing and projected conditions.

The major contribution of the market models to antitrust takes the form of rigorous definitions and concepts. They provide a clear definition of the term, "competition," (though there are problems in translating the clear definition of competition in economic terms into an equally clear legal definition). They draw attention to the difference between the initial impact of regulation and its ultimate effect and, in general, emphasize indirect effects rather than superficial and direct effects. Finally, the existing models provide a basis for building better models, when these are needed. We know of no better broad concepts that will assist in the identification of objectionable industrial situations or in forecasting the effects of potential remedial measures.

The need for new models for antitrust. Earlier portions of this section indicated that the existing market models are of some significance for public policy, that their direct application to antitrust issues has many pitfalls, and that some obvious applications are inappropriate. It should be emphasized, however, that regardless of deficiencies, some models are required for effective antitrust policy, and that if the existing market models are deficient, one must use them until they can be replaced by better ones. Still, new and more powerful models must be sought for antitrust applications.

Models of specific industrial arrangements and practices might be developed for the purpose of indicating what might be gained or lost by altering each of them. In that way, decisions about priorities and the costs that would be justified to correct them might become more valid. Since the effects of given industrial arrangements are indirect and are obscured by the effects of other circumstances, direct observation alone cannot indicate consequences reliably. Better models than those we now have, leading to empirical generalizations, may improve our ability to predict the effects of changes in structure or practice.

CONCLUSIONS

For antitrust, just as for other practical applications, the existing market models seem to have substantial virtues but also seem to entail substantial risks and to fall far short of what is needed. Many unfilled needs have been identified, and these represent challenges to economists to manufacture products that will fill these demands. If such products are ever manufactured, they are likely to be built, in large part, out of the existing market models of price theory. Very probably they will represent special-purpose models designed for antitrust applications, and they may even be specialized as to whether they are intended to identify objectionable conditions and practices, to identify feasible remedies for defective situations, to select data to implement theories of the case in antitrust litigation, and so on. A general purpose kit of models may serve the needs of the teacher but they are only modest aids at best to persons concerned with action problems in the field of antitrust.

Market models render their greatest service to antitrust by facilitating rigorous analysis of the functioning and performance of individual industries in markets at specific times and in designated circumstances. There is no quick easy route to policy by superficial conclusions drawn from any set of models.

Market Models and the Needs of Economic Theory

As a science, economics aims to increase our knowledge about the behavior of human beings and their institutions in what some authors have called "the ordinary business of life," and what others, with clearer eyes and narrower interests, have called "the allocation of scarce resources." This knowledge is sought for practical purposes. As Marshall remarked, economics is a fruit-bearing rather than a light-yielding science.

Yet economics is also concerned to yield light, and economic theory is pursued to satisfy legitimate human curiosity, as well as to provide ultimate practical benefits. The joy of the hunt and the pleasures of discovery are important rewards for the economic theorist. Man wants to understand his world even when he cannot do anything to change it.

This section concerns the contributions the market models make or might make to satisfy the objectives of economic theory. The discussion covers the areas of legitimate scientific curiosity, contributions of the market models, and possible lines of fruitful development for the models.

AREAS OF CURIOSITY

If the proper aim of theory is to satisfy legitimate curiosity, what types of curiosity should price theory attempt to satisfy? As Professor Boulding stated, price theory is concerned primarily with the structure of relative prices and the consequences of changes in them. This concern extends considerably beyond the immediate characteristics of the set of relative prices. It includes such matters as: 1) the level of profits as an income source, as well as the price of a not-very-well-defined factor of production; 2) the number and sizes of firms in an industry; 3) the behavior of related market institutions, and particularly of the firms of different types that are the effective actors in different kinds of markets.

In more general terms, economic theory seeks to satisfy curiosity about the allocation of resources in a market economy and about the nature, number, characteristics, and behavior of the institutions that operate in different kinds of markets. To our understanding of all these matters, price theory, in general, and the market models, in particular, provide some contribution.

CONTRIBUTIONS OF THE MARKET MODELS

The contributions of the market models fall into two major classes: those to our understanding of relative prices and those to our understanding of market institutions.

Understanding relative prices. In evaluating the contributions of the market models to price theory, it is useful to consider what we would have in their absence. Much of our general theory of prices was already well developed long before the market models appeared. And, as Professor Boulding has demonstrated, simple demand and supply analysis does a great deal to illuminate problems of the relative price structure. Analysis in terms of demand and supply functions has a long history, and substantial increases in economic understanding were achieved by this means.

Nevertheless, it appears that the market models provide a substantial incremental contribution to value theory. Consideration of the pull and haul of supply and demand does give a rough understanding of certain gross effects but it is not effective for analysis on a finer level of detail and it is not satisfactory for clear understanding. Either price or quantity can be the independent variable in a supply or demand function, as Professor J. M. Clark pointed out, and there is no real basis for deciding which is the case, until we analyze the behavior of the decision-making unit in the market, i.e., the individual firm. It is just such needs that the market models help to fill.

A further major contribution of the models is to make explicit the extreme nature of the assumptions on which supply and demand analysis was based. In classifying and describing different types of markets, the market models have brought the requirements for perfect competition clearly into focus. They have not only indicated the restricted conditions under which supply and demand analysis would be valid, but have also contributed significantly to our understanding of how supply and demand forces work under conditions other than the perfectly competitive.

The contributions of the market models to price theory may sometimes be undervalued because supply and demand analysis prior to the emergence of the market models appeared to give a more satisfactory explanation of market behavior than it actually did give. Our understanding at the time did not measure up to our feelings of satisfied curiosity. Since the market models took away as much apparent understanding as they contributed, some critics have regarded the net contribution as small. The models should, however, be given credit for the full increase in our actual understanding, not merely the change in our subjectively felt understanding.

Closely related to this matter is a complaint, sometimes raised against the market models, which appears, in fact, to be a testimony to their strength. The varied, factual situations to which the market models are adaptable and the different balances of competitive pressure that they can envisage mean that they do not give a clear guide to public policy. Departures from perfect competition are not unambiguously desirable or undesirable, and it is sometimes held that the models have led to confusion in public policy rather than to clarification. While this is uncomfortable and unsatisfactory from the point of view of public policy, it is the result of an increase in theoretical understanding. The world is, in fact, diverse, and circumstances do alter cases. If these models lead to confusion in public policy, it is a confusion in action brought about by greater accuracy in thought. Simple-minded approaches to public issues are the most comfortable, but this does not testify to the quality of the underlying analysis. Furthermore, from the point of view of application, as well as that of theory, it is important to recognize problems even when a solution is not at hand.

Quite possibly, if one were to explain the gross shifts in relative prices over, say, the last fifty years, he could do about as well with the simple supply and demand analysis, as developed by John Stuart Mill, as with the later market models. However, that earlier explanation would omit consideration of differences in economic efficiency, the speed of adjustment of supply to demand, variations in incomes to entrepreneurship, and the extent to which the shift in output took place by changes in the number of firms or variations in the output of established firms. The market models provide a better understanding of these aspects of shifts in relative prices.

For the analysis of moderate short-term changes in relative prices, the additional contribution to understanding provided by the market models seems even greater. Traditional price theory did not, for example, explain, or even suggest, the possibility that changes in market structure might be an independent cause of shifts in relative prices.

Understanding market institutions. The contribution of the market models to an understanding of market institutions is still more substantial than the contributions to the understanding of relative prices. Before the market models, there was no real theory of the firm or industry, and, though economists were by no means ignorant of such subjects, it was the market models that put their understanding into systematic form.

The market models contribute important understanding in several different ways, as follows.

They clarify the interrelationship between individual firms and entire industries. They explain, through the analysis of individual firm responses to changes in product and factor prices, variations in the supply conditions in the total market. Although our understanding of these relationships is by no means complete, the market models have brought substantial enlightenment.

The market models have provided a framework for looking at a firm as an entity and for examining its internal and external behavior. It must be granted that the framework is limited to a small number of variables and a relatively limited pattern of relationships among them. Whatever its deficiencies, however, it is the only substantial economic framework we have for dealing with these problems.

The market models illuminate many aspects of firm and industry behavior, for which traditional price theory offered no explanation. As discussed in connection with relative prices, the market models throw light on such matters as variations in levels of profits, the number and sizes of firms in an industry, and levels of excess capacity.

LIMITATIONS AND NEEDS

Although the market models have provided a significant increase in our understanding of price-firm behavior, they do not provide a sufficient level of understanding, any more than they provide a satisfactory guide to public policy or business decisions. On a high level of generality, they help us understand some relationships, but they do not clarify some important aspects of economic behavior, and they do not lead us to adequate understanding of any specific firm or industry. The many situations and things we cannot explain are a measure of the theoretical work still undone.

Dynamic relationships, distribution channel problems, and financial problems are excluded from the models by assumption, and the models are silent on such questions. Nonprice competition is not adequately treated, although some conditions of oligopoly price equilibrium provide an obvious incentive for the use of such methods. Moreover, while the firm as seen by the market models is an entity, it is an entity of a peculiar sort—a computing point. Actual firms have many other aspects, and even their strictly defined economic behavior may be strongly affected by the past history of events, personal attitudes of executives, organization structure, and political and sociological elements in the relationships of the people who, together, compose the firm's personnel.

In view of all these special, and even noneconomic, influences upon the economic behavior of the firm, there is reason to doubt how satisfactory any purely economic model can be in providing an understanding of firm and market behavior. Certainly models of the extremely limited and general nature of the market models cannot hope to provide satisfactory understanding of any specific firm or industry. What is necessary, as a minimum, is to create specialized models for particular firms or classes of firms, sacrificing generality of application for increased understanding. As we have argued before, such specialized models are important for the purposes of the businessman and of public policy, and they appear no less necessary to the successful attainment of the ends of theory.

The nature of these special models and the elements they should include will depend on the problems we decide to attack. But if full understanding of the economics of particular firms or industries is desired, it is clearly necessary to bring into the models dynamic, financial, and nonprice considerations. Whether historical, personal, organizational, political, or sociological factors need to be included is an open question. But from the point of view of economic theory, the best counsel would be to include such elements only if absolutely necessary.

This preference for keeping noneconomic elements to a minimum arises from the fact that we are dealing with a linked problem of incomplete economic understanding and possible indeterminacy in the economic system. One of the positive contributions of the market models was to increase our awareness of ignorance and our perception of possible indeterminacy. The next stage of theoretical development will, we hope, reduce our ignorance and enable us to see the extent of the actual indeterminacy.

If we had an industry which, in fact, satisfied all the assumptions of perfect competition, the model would give us complete understanding of its economic behavior, and the equilibrium of the firm would be completely determinate. The businessman, under such circumstances, would have no choice but to maximize profit at the intersection of marginal cost, average cost, and price, because in no other way could he survive. When, however, we turn to the models of monopolistic conditions, the equlibrium is determinate only if the firm maximizes profits, and this is only an assumption of convenience used in our models. It is not a requirement of the structure of any monopolistic market. Furthermore, if we relax the assumption of perfect information, we are likely to find that the entrepreneur is faced with such a complex situation, and knows so little about it, that even if he decides to maximize profits, he has no sure way of attaining his objective. For both these reasons, we may suspect that the equilibrium of the firm is determinate only within a very broad range. This impression of indeterminacy, however, depends partly on our ignorance, and the development of better-tailored economic models should both reduce ignorance and indicate the extent to which genuine indeterminacy remains in purely economic relationships. Once we have got as full an explanation of firm and market behavior as improved economic models can supply, it may be necessary to bring noneconomic factors and the disciplines of other sciences to bear upon the problem.

Not only should specialized models deal with the special circumstances of individual firms or classes of firms, as they act in their factor and product markets, they should also be devised to explore the internal balance of the firm. Even though many of the internal balances of the firm are not directly related to the price and market allocation problems with which price theory deals, they are equally involved with the allocation of resources, which is the primary concern of economics. The internal relationships of the firm raise as many theoretical problems as they do practical problems. The whole area of managerial economics and the allied work in operations research offer interesting materials to the theorist.

In summary, we urge that economic theorists should concern

themselves with more detailed and more specific models, relating to particular firm or industry characteristics and dealing with internal resource allocation as well as external market behavior. The theorist should be heavily concerned with industry and company studies. In building theories of particular industries or even of particular firms, the theorist sacrifices generality, but this appears to be a necessary price for increased understanding. It is a general principle in science that where a set of phenomena is explained equally well by two competing theories, the simpler is to be preferred. Simplicity is no virtue, however, if it entails less theoretical understanding.

PART 2. *Biltmore Hotel Conference*

CONTRIBUTIONS FROM MATHEMATICAL

MODELS TO AN UNDERSTANDING OF

MARKET PERFORMANCE

DUAL PRICES AND COMPETITION

BY WILLIAM J. BAUMOL, PROFESSOR OF
ECONOMICS, PRINCETON UNIVERSITY, AND

RICHARD E. QUANDT, ASSOCIATE PROFESSOR OF
ECONOMICS, PRINCETON UNIVERSITY

In their recent work on economic problems mathematicians made a discovery which attracted a great deal of attention. It was found that for every economic problem which can be described as a linear program, and for many problems which can be described as nonlinear programs, there is an associated artificial problem which is known as the dual. That is, corresponding to each such programming problem, one can construct a second artificial problem called the dual of the first. The dual program has properties which are useful for computational purposes and interesting to the mathematician. But more remarkable and surprising is the fact that on closer inspection, the artificiality of the dual problem largely disappears. It becomes one which has a powerful and significant economic interpretation, one which seems to have "sneaked up" on the inventors of duality, rather than to have been placed there intentionally. To a considerable extent, the significance of the dual is the conservatism of its theoretical implications. Rather than providing a major revolution and a significant departure from neoclassical analysis, it has granted new authority to the mainstream of economic theory and the marginal analysis with which it is associated.

In this paper we shall try to assess the significance of duality for the understanding of pricing and competition, from the point of view of both the analyst and the practitioner. It should be stated in advance, however, that the significance of duality for these areas is not entirely straightforward. This theory has proved more helpful in dealing with competition within the firm, that is, among different segments and divisions of the firm, than it has for the analysis of competition among firms. Moreover, duality, and the pricing analysis which is derived from it, has been more directly relevant to the pricing of inputs than of outputs.

Unfortunately, there is no simple manner in which the structure of the duality analysis can be described. Once it is understood, it does have considerable intuitive appeal; but before that stage can be attained substantial preliminary effort must be invested in comprehension of the structure. For this reason, a substantial portion of our paper will be devoted to exposition, and those readers who are familiar with the general area may therefore wish to skip the first few sections.

Elements of Linear Programming

Before we can even attempt to explain the workings of the dual program it will be necessary to go into some detail on the linear programming problem itself. For this purpose it is convenient to concentrate on an illustrative economic problem. Consider a firm operating under pure or perfect competition which is selecting the items to be included in its product line; that is, for each potential product, the firm must determine whether it pays to produce that item and, if so, how much it is most profitable to produce. The firm is taken to be operating with a linear, homogeneous production function, that is, one where a doubling of all inputs will permit a doubling of all outputs. More specifically, our assumptions and notation may be described as follows: 1) The firm considers producing a number of products whose respective quantities are $Q_1, Q_2, \ldots, Q_n$ where Q_1 is the quantity to be produced of commodity 1, and so on. In particular, if the decision is to have $Q_5 = 0$, for example, this means that commodity 5 will not be produced at all. 2) It is also assumed that the profit per unit of output for each product is a given constant. These profits are respectively represented by π_1, π_2 ... π_n, so that, for example, π_1 is the number of dollars of profit earned by the production of one unit of commodity 1. 3) It is also assumed that the firm's production capacity is limited by a number of resource bottlenecks. That is, at least in the short run, there are several inputs, such as workers with specialized skills, certain types of machinery or raw material, each of which is available to the firm in fixed or limited quantities. The maximum availabilities of each of these scarce resources are represented by the quantities c_1, c_2 ... c_m, where m represents the total number of bottlenecks to which the firm is subject. Finally, 4) it is assumed that the production of one unit of any given product uses up a constant number of units of each resource. For example, if commodity 7 is shoes, and each pair of shoes uses up $\frac{3}{10}$ of a kilowatt hour of electricity in its production, where electricity is scarce resource number 2 for the firm, we designate the amount of electricity used per pair of shoes produced, by k_{27}. That is, we have in this case $k_{27} = 0.3$. Our linear programming problem may now be written as follows:

$$\text{maximize profits } \pi = \pi_1 Q_1 + \pi_2 Q_2 + \ldots + \pi_n Q_n$$
$$\text{subject to } k_{11} Q_1 + k_{12} Q_2 + \ldots + k_{1n} Q_n \leqq c_1$$
$$\cdot \quad \cdot \quad \cdot \quad \cdot \quad \cdot \quad \cdot \quad \cdot \quad \cdot \quad \cdot$$
$$k_{m1} Q_1 + k_{m2} Q_2 + \ldots + k_{mn} Q_n \leqq c_m$$
$$Q_1 \geqq 0, Q_2 \geqq 0, \ldots, Q_n \geqq 0.$$

The equation for π is the profit function. It tells us that the firm's total profit is equal to the profit per unit of output 1 produced times the quantity of output 1, plus the profit per unit of output 2, times the quantity of output 2, and so on. The firm's object, then, is taken to be the maximization of this total profit.

However, the circumstances of the firm do not give it complete freedom to make any decisions it wishes. The next set of inequalities, the ones involving the c_1 ... c_m, represent the company's limited resources. For example, since k_{11} tells us the quantity of input 1 that will be used per unit of output 1, $k_{11} \cdot Q_1$ then represents the total quantity of the first resource which will be used in producing product number one. Adding to this the quantity of the first resource which will be used in product number two, that is, adding to this $k_{12}Q_2$, and so on, we get the total quantity of resource 1 which will be needed by the firm. But any production decision which is feasible for the firm must not use up more of resource 1 than is available. That is, the total requirement of resource 1 must be less than or equal to the available amount, c_1. That is precisely what is specified by the first of our inequalities. The remaining resource-use in equalities obviously has a similar interpretation.

Finally, we have the nonnegativity conditions, $Q_1 \geqq 0$, and so on which tell us that it is impossible to produce negative quantities of any output, a stipulation which turns out to have more significance than at first appears. Specifically, these last inequalities point out one of the most obvious sources of difficulty in a more conventional analysis which uses differential calculus or straightforward marginal analysis to determine optimal product quantities. Specific numerical examples can easily demonstrate that these techniques may sometimes yield the absurd recommendation that negative quantities of various products be manufactured.

Let us turn now to a discussion of the definition and meaning of duality. It should be emphasized that, so far, nothing has been said explicitly about prices. Prices do occur implicitly in the assumption that unit profits for each output are constant. This, in turn, is usually interpreted to mean that the prices themselves are assumed to be imvariant with respect to quantity produced and supplied and, indeed, that is precisely what we would expect to result from our premise of perfect competition. Up until this point, then, our linear programming model would appear to have very little to say either about the determination of prices or the operation of the competitive process. And certainly, it would seem to say no more about these subjects than the most elementary of standard models of economic theory.

Definition of the Dual Problem

Before we turn to the economic interpretation of the dual, it will be desirable to describe the meaning of duality in a purely abstract manner, without any reference to meaning or interpretation. At the end of this section, given any linear programming problem, the reader should be able to recognize and construct its dual.

Suppose a mischievous gremlin were let loose on a linear programming problem, and decided that he would turn everything he possibly could on its head. There are a number of obvious things he would think of. For the word "maximize" he would substitute "minimize." For the symbol $\geq$ he would substitute $\leq$. Furthermore, a nice way to add to the resulting confusion might be to put the capacity figures, $c_1, c_2 \ldots c_m$, where the unit profit figures, $\pi_1, \pi_2 \ldots \pi_n$, used to be, and vice versa. For good measure, he might reverse the order in which the constants appear in the inequalities, or, better yet, he might rewrite them so that instead of reading across we would now read down. That is, where k_{12} was formerly the second constant in the first inequality, he would now make it the first constant in the second inequality. In other words, by reading across in the first inequality we would formerly have found the constants, k_{11}, k_{12}, k_{13}, and so on. Now we would find those same constants not by reading across from left to right but by reading down from the first inequality to the second to the third, and so on. Finally, to cap the confusion, our gremlin would probably decide to get rid of our original variables, $Q_1, Q_2, \ldots, Q_n$, altogether and substitute for them an entirely new set of variables, $v_1, v_2, \ldots, v_m$. Having done all this, he would find himself with the linear programming problem which may be written as follows:

$$\text{minimize } v = c_1 v_1 + c_2 v_2 + \ldots + c_m v_m$$
$$\text{subject to } k_{11} v_1 + k_{21} v_2 + \ldots + k_{m1} v_m \geq \pi_1$$
$$\cdot \quad \cdot \quad \cdot \quad \cdot \quad \cdot \quad \cdot \quad \cdot \quad \cdot \quad \cdot \quad \cdot$$
$$k_{1n} v_1 + k_{2n} v_2 + \ldots + k_{mn} v_m \geq \pi_n$$
$$v_1 \geq 0, v_2 \geq 0 \ldots v_m \geq 0.$$

This new program is what we call the dual. Let us list its characteristics explicitly. 1) If the primal problem involves maximization the dual involves minimization, and vice versa. 2) If the primal involves $\geqq$ signs the dual involves $\leqq$ signs, and vice versa. 3) The profit constants in the primal problem replace the capacity constants, and vice versa. 4) In the resource-use inequalities the constants which were found by going from left to right are positioned in the dual from top to bottom, and vice versa. 5) A new set of variables appears in the dual. 6) Neglecting the number of nonnegativity conditions, if there are n variables and m inequalities in the primal problem, in the dual there will be m variables and n inequalities.

Finally, it should be noted that if we were to let our gremlin loose again and have him do his work on the dual problem, he would again reach the problem with which he started. That is, if he were to take the dual problem and subject it to all the abuses which he had heaped on our original linear program, he would find that, in the end, he would have undone all his mischief. The dual of the dual problem is the original linear programming problem itself. It follows that given such a pair of problems it is entirely arbitrary which of them is referred to as the dual. Each one of them is the dual of the other.

These rules for the construction of the dual are illustrated in the following pair of numerical linear programming problems. The reader should verify that these problems do indeed constitute one another's dual, as follows:

$$\text{maximize } \pi = 2Q_1 + 6Q_2$$
$$\text{subject to} \quad 4Q_1 + Q_2 \leqq 5 \quad \text{(sky hooks)}$$
$$3Q_1 + 2Q_2 \leqq 7 \quad \text{(electricity)}$$
$$Q_1 + Q_2 \leqq 2 \quad \text{(wibblers)}$$
$$Q_1 \geqq 0, Q_2 \geqq 0.$$

$$\text{minimize } V = 5V_1 + 7V_2 + 2V_3$$
$$\text{subject to } 4V_1 + 3V_2 + 1V_3 \geqq 2$$
$$1V_1 + 2V_2 + 1V_3 \geqq 6$$
$$V_1 \geqq 0, V_2 \geqq 0, V_3 \geqq 0.$$

It will be noted, for example, that in our illustration the maximization problem involves two variables and, not counting the nonnegativity conditions, three inequalities, whereas the minimization problem involves three variables and two inequalities. It should also be pointed out that one feature is not tampered with in going from a linear programming problem to its dual—the inequalities of the nonnegativity condition retain their directions. That is, both in the primal and in the dual problem each variable is required to be greater than or equal to zero.

Interpretation of the Dual

We must now breathe economic life into the scrambled program which our gremlin produced for us. We started with a well-defined and meaningful economic problem which we wrote out mathematically as a linear program and out of that, arbitrarily and capriciously, we produced another program which is related to the first in a peculiar fashion. What possible economic meaning can this dual program have?

We shall show that the variables of the dual program, the V_1, V_2 and V_3 in our numerical examples, can be interpreted as the economic values of the firm's three scarce resources. Let us assume that our three scarce resources are, respectively, sky hooks, electricity, and wibblers, so that our original linear programming problem tells us that the firm has available to it 5 sky hooks, 7 units of electric capacity, and 2 wibblers. V_1 may then be described as the accounting value to the firm of a sky hook, V_2, as the accounting value of a unit of electrical capacity, and V_3 as the accounting value of a wibbler.

Tentatively accepting this interpretation, let us look at the first inequality in the dual problem and see what meaning it might possibly have. It will be remembered that the coefficient 4 of the variable V_1 in that inequality had a definite meaning in our primal problem. There it represented the number of sky hooks necessary to produce one unit of output 1. Similarly, the second coefficient, 3, in our dual inequality, that is, the coefficient of V_2, represented in the original problem the number of units of electricity needed to produce a unit of output 1. Finally, the coefficient of the V_3 in our dual inequality represented the number of wibblers needed to produce a unit of output 1. In sum, the three coefficients represent the quantities of the three different inputs which go into a unit of commodity 1. Now, if each sky hook is worth V_1 dollars, then 4 sky hooks would be worth 4 times V_1 dollars and, similarly, if each unit of electricity is worth V_2 dollars, the three units of electricity would be worth $3V_2$ dollars. Finally, the one wibbler would be worth 1 times V_3 dollars if each unit is worth V_3. We see, then, that the expression on the left hand side of our inequality, $4V_1 + 3V_2 + 1V_3$, has a straightforward economic interpretation, given the meaning which has tentatively been assigned to our variables. That sum is the total value of the inputs which are necessary to produce one unit of output of commodity 1.

Only one more step is needed to complete our interpretation of this inequality. We must now recall what is signified by the number 2 on the right hand side of that inequality. Going back to the original problem once more, we see that the 2 is the unit profit one obtains by producing the first commodity. Each unit of commodity 1 which is manufactured yields \$2 to the firm. Our first inequality can now be read to state the following: The value of the inputs used in the production of a unit of commodity 1 must be greater than or equal to the profit which the firm makes by producing a unit of commodity 1.

At first glance, this appears to be a curious requirement. It would seem to mean that the firm must always lose money, or at best break even, by producing commodity 1 because the value of the inputs used in its manufacture will always eat up the profits, and possibly, more. Actually, however, this last interpretation is a mistake which one makes all too easily. The number 2 is a profit figure and not a revenue figure. Hence, the fact that the value of inputs exceeds profits does not mean that profits are zero or negative. Profits are \$2 per unit of output, as stated, and that is all there is to it. Furthermore,

V_1, V_2, and V_3 are not cost figures; they are accounting values which have been assigned to our three inputs. One can assume that the firm has already acquired its sky hooks, electricity, and wibblers and that these now represent an overhead or fixed cost, so that their current value to the firm may be totally independent of their historic, sunk costs, incurred when these inputs were obtained. Rather, the V's should be interpreted as an accounting device designed to divide the profits of the firm among the three scarce inputs. We are saying, in effect, that the firm could not earn its $2 on each unit of output 1 without having any sky hooks, electricity, or wibblers available to it. In other words, these profits are ascribable or imputable to these three inputs and the question is, what valuation of each input appropriately imputes these profits. Our first inequality, then, states that we must assign to each of the inputs a value sufficiently great to impute all the profits of output number 1. If the inequality were violated, that is, if the values were so low that the sum of the values of the inputs were less than two dollars, we would still have some unimputed profits, that is, some profits which had not been ascribed to one of the inputs. Just as the first inequality of the dual program imputes the profit from commodity 1, so the second inequality imputes all the profit from each unit of output 2 to these inputs. It states that the values of the three inputs which are used to make a unit of commodity 2 must account fully for the $6 of profit which are yielded by a unit of commodity 2.

We will see presently why it is correct to write these as inequalities rather than equations, that is, why we do not require that the values of the inputs be exactly equal to the profits. One simple reason that appears at once follows from the fact that the number of variables and the number of inequalities need not be the same. We have three variables in our dual problem, and two inequalities. We could just as easily have had, say, six variables and fifteen inequalities. If we had attempted to write these as equations rather than equalities, we would have had a system involving fifteen equations in six unknowns and, obviously, this would be likely to run us into difficulties;

that is, usually it is impossible to satisfy a system of linear equations containing more equations than unknowns.[1] Since, therefore, in such a situation we may be forced to relinquish equality in part of the system, we have chosen between the two apparently less desirable alternatives, overimputation and underimputation, and have decided to favor the former. That is, we have said, if it is absolutely necessary to assign values to our inputs which make the imputed value of the inputs used in producing a unit of output either greater than or less than unit profits, let us assign values which are greater than unit profits.

But once we have stated the inequalities in this way, it would appear that there is no problem at all. We need only assign values as capriciously high as we wish to each of the inputs, to be sure that they will more than account for all of the profits. What prevents this sort of arbitrary solution is the fact that V must be minimized in the dual problem. V also has an economic interpretation. It will be recalled that we have 5 sky hooks, so that the total value of the sky hooks available to the firm will be $5V_1$ and similarly, the total value of the electricity available to the firm will be $7V_2$ because there are 7 units of electricity at the firm's command, and so on. Hence, V represents the total value of all the inputs which the firm has under its control. The dual problem then says that we are to find the smallest value for this stock of inputs which completely accounts for all the profits of each of the outputs.

So far, one may have the feeling that this interpretation is somewhat strained. We have forced an economic reading on our dual problem but that interpretation seems to have been picked out of the air and we have not indicated any reason why an economist, or anyone else, should really be interested in it. However, mathematicians have proved a number of theorems about the dual problem which add power to the entire construct. Before describing these theorems, we must emphasize that they deal exclusively, unless otherwise stated,

---

[1] I.e., unless sufficiently many equations are linear combinations of the remaining equations.

with the optimal solutions to the primal and dual problems. That is, they deal with the quantities of the various outputs which maximize profits in the primal problem and the imputed values of the inputs, the $V_1, \ldots, V_n$, which minimize the value expression, V.

THEOREM 1. The maximum value of π in the primal problem is equal to the minimum value of V in the dual problem.

The first theorem tells us that the imputation process will turn out to be more effective than we had any right to expect. We had set up our constraints in the dual problem in such a way that overimputation seemed very likely. It seemed entirely possible that for some commodities the value of the inputs used in their production would exceed their profitability. Hence, one might well expect that the accounting value of all the inputs used in the production process will exceed the sum of the profits which are available to the firm. In fact, Theorem 1 tells us that this will never occur—that if our problems are amenable to solution, that is, if the problems have any solutions at all, they will exactly impute away all of the firm's profits, no more and no less. We will return to the logic behind this result presently, for it has an entirely plausible explanation. But first, it will be necessary to examine several other theorems.

THEOREM 2. The imputed values of the firm's scarce inputs are exactly equal to their marginal profitabilities.[2]

This result is precisely in accord with the traditional notions of economic theory. It is a standard economic proposition that a scarce resource should be used up to the point at which its marginal contribution equals its price. That is to say, we should consider the utility of a scarce resource to be equal to the addition to our returns which would be offered to us by the acquisition of another unit of that item. And it can be proved that this is exactly what is meant by the V's in our dual problem. V_1, the accounting value which is assigned to a sky hook, is equal to the increase in the profits which would be

---

[2] For purposes of this theorem it is assumed that we deal with "nondegenerate" linear programs. For present purposes this may be considered a technicality which need not concern the nonspecialist reader.

earned by the firm if the number of sky hooks which it had available were increased from 5 to 6. In other words, an alternative way of finding V_1 might be to solve a second linear programming problem which was the same as our original problem, except that the number on the right hand side of our first constraint was 6 instead of 5. By comparing the profits to be earned in the two situations and finding how much larger is the profit in the second than in the first, we would have a value for our first dual variable, V_1. This is doubtless very reassuring. It shows us that all roads do indeed lead to Rome —that all methods of optimality analysis are, after all, good marginalism. And if this reassurance comes to us in an entirely unexpected way it is no less welcome, for it.

THEOREM 3. In the inequalities of the dual problem, any excess of the accounting value of the inputs used to produce some item over the profitability of that item can be interpreted as the opportunity cost of producing that item.

This is really a corollary of the preceding theorem. It states that if the accounting value assigned to the inputs needed to produce, say, commodity 1, is $9, then, on every unit of commodity 1 which is produced we suffer an opportunity loss of $7. True, we still obtain $2 in profits by producing that unit of commodity 1, but in so doing we are giving up even higher profits which could be obtained by transferring our resources from the production of commodity 1 to the manufacture of some other commodity. Indeed, the fact that the opportunity cost in this case is $9 − 2 = $7 means that if we transferred the resources from the production of commodity 1 to the manufacture of the most profitable of the products which the firm can produce, we would obtain an additional $7 for each unit of commodity 1 which we gave up. In particular, an item whose profits are precisely imputed by the values of our dual variables must be one of the goods whose production is most profitable to the firm. To understand this, we note that the value of the inputs of such an item must be precisely equal to the unit profits of that commodity so that the opportunity loss involved in producing that item must be zero. There must be no other way for the firm to use its resources more profitably. We can see intuitively how this opportunity cost interpretation follows from the preceding theorem, that is, from Theorem 2. If V_1 is the marginal profitability of a sky hook, $4V_1$ will be a rough measure of the profits which the firm would hope to earn from the four units of sky hooks which it uses up in the production of a unit of commodity 1. Similarly, $3V_2$ represents the profits which the electricity used in producing in a unit of commodity 1 could potentially earn for the firm, and so on. Thus, $4V_1 + 3V_2 + 1V_3$ represents the maximum profits which the firm could hope to earn from the resources used up in the production of a unit of commodity 1. If these potential profits are greater than the $2 which one actually earns from the production of a unit of that commodity, then, clearly, the firm is not doing as well as it could be. It is suffering an opportunity loss by misallocating resources to that particular output. This result should prepare us for the next theorem.

THEOREM 4. If the solution of the dual problem involves a positive opportunity loss for some commodity k, then the solution of the primal problem will contain a zero output level for that commodity k.

Going back to our illustrative case, if we have $4V_1 + 3V_2 + 1V_3 > 2$, the solution associates a positive opportunity cost with commodity 1. In other words, the firm would do better to reallocate resources away from the production of commodity 1 to some other output. Therefore, it is not surprising that in the corresponding primal solution, Q_1 equals zero. And, indeed, it is not too difficult to prove that this will always be the case; that is, that the solution of the primal and dual problems, even though calculated quite independently, will always mesh in such a way as to make good economic sense. Whenever the dual problem solution indicates that a certain commodity is unprofitable in the relative sense, that is, whenever it indicates that despite its possibly high unit profits the item involves an opportunity loss, then an independent calculation of the optimal solution of the primal problem will show that that commodity will not be produced. This, also, is a very comforting result.

Incidentally, this result also gives us some idea as to why Theorem

1 holds. Theorem 4, which we are now discussing, admits the possibility that the V's will imply a positive opportunity cost for some commodities. But those will be the commodities which are not produced at all. In other words, the output of those items will be zero and the resources going into their production will be zero. Thus, the only items which are produced are those for which the profits are exactly imputed by our dual calculation. Commodity 2 will only be produced if $1V_1 + 2V_2 + 1V_3 = 6$. In sum, when we consider only the commodities which are actually produced, it will be clear that the imputed values will be exactly sufficient to account for their earned profits. Hence, the total imputed values of all resources used must equal the total profits of the firm, which is what Theorem 1 states.

Theorem 4 also has the following interesting consequence. In linear programming, the difficult thing to determine is which outputs it will, and which outputs it will not pay to produce. Once we have determined which items will be turned out it is relatively easy to find out in what quantities they should be manufactured. Theorem 4 tells us that we can learn which commodities it will pay us to produce either by a direct calculation on the basis of the original linear program or by solving the dual problem. We thus have a strategic choice. We can solve one problem or the other, whichever happens to be easier or more convenient. Actually, this statement underemphasizes the degree of connection between the solution of the original problem and that of its dual. Once we have solved either of these problems it is a trivial matter to find the solution to the other. Usually, from the solution of the original problem the solution of the dual can be written out by inspection, or vice versa. Let us now turn to the final theorem.

THEOREM 5. Any input which is not fully used will receive an accounting value equal to zero.

Suppose we solve a primal problem and find that the most profitable output program requires the company to leave one wibbler unused. Since wibblers are the third of the scarce inputs, this last theorem tells us that the solution to the dual problem will yield the value $V_3 = 0$. Of course, this also makes good economic sense. Any input which is redundant must have, one would expect, a zero economic value. Or, looked at in terms of the interpretation of Theorem 2, if some input has a positive marginal profitability, clearly, no portion of that resource will remain unused in an optimal solution. Obviously, we could always increase profits by using the unemployed portion of that input.

It may be of interest to note that Theorems 4 and 5 are basically the same, one applying to the original problem and the other to the dual problem. They both state that if a constraint in one of the problems involves an inequality ($<$ or $>$), then the corresponding variable in the other problem will have the value zero. In the case of Theorem 5 we can see this as follows: The left hand side of the first constraint represents the number of sky hooks which will be used up in the production of commodities 1 and 2. If this total adds up to less than 5, it means that there will be an unused quantity of sky hooks. Only if $4Q_1 + Q_2$ is equal to 5 will the company's supply of sky hooks be used up completely, and only in these circumstances can the value of V_1 be unequal to zero, according to the theorem.

There are a number of other interesting and important theorems about duality which have been proved by mathematicians but most of these are of limited interest for present purposes and, in addition, they are much more abstruse and difficult to explain.

Illustrative Example

A rather interesting illustration of the workings of the duality relationships is presented by the following linear programming problem:

$$\text{maximize } pQ_1 + Q_2 + 2Q_3$$
$$\text{subject to } 2Q_1 + Q_2 \qquad \leqq 100$$
$$Q_1 - Q_2 + Q_3 \leqq 0$$
$$\text{and} \qquad Q_1 \geqq 0, Q_2 \geqq 0, Q_3 \geqq 0.$$

Interpretation: Production of the first commodity brings in p dollars of profit (p to be discussed later) and uses 2 units of the first and 1 unit of the second resource. Production of the second commodity brings in \$1, uses 1 unit of the first resource, and yields 1 unit of the second resource as a by-product. The third commodity involves only the sale of the second resource at a price of \$2 per unit. The interpretation of the first constraint is obvious. The second constraint says: The sales of resource 3 must not exceed the output of that resource, minus the amount which is used up: $Q_3 \leqq Q_2 - Q_1$. The dual of our problem is:

$$\text{minimize } 100V_1 + oV_2$$
$$\text{subject to} \quad 2V_1 + V_2 \geqq p$$
$$V_1 - V_2 \geqq 1$$
$$V_2 \geqq 2$$
$$\text{and} \quad V_1 \geqq o, V_2 \geqq o, V_3 \geqq o.$$

We conclude from the last inequality that our accounting price for the second resource (V_2) must not be less than the market price, \$2.00.

Second, one can prove that if $p < 8$, the first commodity will not be produced [3] and the imputed price, V_2, of the second resource will equal \$2, i.e., it will equal its market price, whatever the actual value of p.

Third, if $p > 8$, none of the second resource will be sold (since it is so valuable in producing output), and its imputed value will increase above 2 and will be higher, the higher is p. If $p = 8$, we are indifferent between selling or not selling any of the second resource.

All this makes good sense: as long as it is profitable to sell the second resource, its value to us cannot go above market price. When it is not profitable to sell because some commodity using it gives high profit, its imputed value must rise in accord with the increased marginal revenue product of the second resource.

[3] Proof: By the second dual inequality, $V_1 \geqq 1 + V_2$, so that if $V_2 \geqq 2$ then $V_1 \geqq 3$, and hence $2V_1 + V_2 \geqq 8$. Thus, if p is less than 8, we must have $2V_1 + V_2 > p$, and so production of item 1 will involve an opportunity loss.

Remarks on Duality and Nonlinear Programming

So far, the discussion has been confined exclusively to the simple case of linear programming. As we have already stated, this implicitly assumes that we are dealing with a situation involving pure or perfect competition. As soon as the firm's selling price becomes a variable whose value is influenced by the quantities of the commodities which it produces, we are automatically faced with a nonlinear programming problem. This is so because in the expression for the profit of the firm which is being maximized, we must have a term representing total revenue for each output, that is, price times quantity. But if the price of that commodity is itself a function of quantity, $f(Q)$, then price times quantity is given by $Q \cdot f(Q)$. In other words, we have an expression which is virtually certain to be nonlinear and may involve some complicated function of Q. Nonlinear programming involves a variety of computational and conceptual difficulties which lead to a temptation to employ linear approximations wherever this is reasonably justified. Unfortunately, as we have just seen, the absence of perfect competition normally destroys the justification for this sort of approximative calculation.

Happily, theorems very closely analogous to those which we have described for the case of linear programming apply to wide classes of nonlinear programming problems. Most of these developments rest on the work of H. W. Kuhn and A. W. Tucker, as well as on the earlier writings of John von Neumann. The analysis runs into serious difficulties only if the economic situation with which we are dealing involves significant discontinuities and important increasing returns. The presence of diminishing returns to scale or of negatively sloping demand curves which may essentially be interpreted as diminishing returns to marketing effort causes no important problems. Thus, with the warning that in dealing with problems of competition, and with most actual firms, one is likely to have to resort to nonlinear programming, and warned that the nonlinear case is somewhat less simple than the one we have just described, one may nevertheless proceed on the assumption that most of what has been said in this paper about duality is relevant for the subsequent discussion.

Usefulness of Duality Theory: Preliminary

We come now to the heart of this paper, the evaluation of the contribution of duality theory to the understanding of the competitive process and to pricing, in particular. Before we proceed to the details on this discussion several preliminary matters must be considered.

It is well known that linear programming calculations have been exceedingly useful in many industrial contexts and, in some cases, to government, and that the same has been true to a somewhat more limited extent of nonlinear programming, though the applicability of the latter is virtually certain to increase in the future, as computational methods improve. A wide variety of practical problems have been rendered far more tractable by the use of these techniques. There are many standard examples, including the selection of advertising media, the blending of animal feeds, the determination of transportation routes, and the scheduling of productive processes. Moreover, the wide variety and ingenuity of nonstandardized applications is also impressive. Particularly where there are concrete decisions to be made and specific numbers to be calculated, programming has often proved invaluable. In all of this, duality theory has played a role. By making clear the marginal calculations which lay behind the analysis, it provided better understanding of the problems. Perhaps more important for the practical man is the fact that duality provided for faster, more economical calculations in many cases. For, as we have already seen, in solving any linear programming problem we have the choice between solving either the original problem or its dual, and a somewhat similar situation holds in the case of nonlinearity. It happens that in many circumstances it is better strategy to conduct one's numerical calculations in terms of the dual than in terms of the original program, and a number of specialized computational approaches have been developed on this basis.

However, it must be emphasized that all of this is largely beside the point. No one, to our knowledge, has questioned the usefulness of mathematical programming and duality, and documentation of their helpfulness would be as simple as it would be uninteresting. None of the applications which have so far been listed has anything essential to do with either the structure of competition or the nature of the pricing process and, thus, it is outside the range of our present interest. It was suggested as a frame of reference for these papers that the usefulness of a technique might be evaluated in terms of the interests of four different classes of persons. These are the empirical investigator of economic institutions, the economic theorist, the businessman, and the maker of government policy. The relevance of duality to the interests of each of these will be discussed in turn, with the exception of the first of the four classes. We believe that duality theory is completely irrelevant for the work of the empirical investigator of economic institutions. The reasons for this are not difficult to determine. Programming is, by its very definition, an instrument for the calculation of optimal decisions, decisions which maximize or minimize the achievement of some objective. As a result, programming analyses and calculations are likely to yield prescriptive rather than descriptive results. They are apt to present advice rather than actuality. Though the economic theorist often finds it convenient and useful to proceed on the assumption that the members of the economy behave optimally, from their own points of view, that consumers maximize utility, and that business firms maximize profits, this is surely no safe premise for the empirical student. Departures from perfectly calculated behavior are his meat and drink. Habits, traditions, and psychological quirks which are sufficiently prevalent are of as much or greater interest to him than the degree of approximation to some normative ideals. A programming problem and its dual are empty of this sort of material. A programming calculation can therefore be expected to be of interest to him only as a matter of contrast, to show him how far what is, departs from what might have been; to enable him to evaluate the degree of "inefficiency" in the rough and ready operations of the actual economy, as compared to what might be achieved if optimal calculations were widely made and followed.

Duality and Government Operation

There is a fairly considerable body of literature which ties duality theory into the operations of government and the pricing mechanism. The antecedents of this literature are to be found in the writings of A. P. Lerner, Oskar Lange, and others, who produced a considerable body of work on the application of marginal analysis to the economics of socialism and governmental control of the economy. It will be recalled that these writers maintained, essentially, that socialism could achieve its economic objectives without giving up the independence and initiative of the individual decision maker. Following the standard analysis of welfare economics, they pointed out that competition provided a mechanism which closely circumscribed the decisions of the businessman and the other participants in the economy. In crudest terms, a businessman could not afford to produce anything for which there existed no profitable market and so, in Adam Smith's phrasing, "by directing . . . industry in such a manner as its produce may be of the greatest value, he intends only his own gain, and he is in this, as in many other cases, led by an invisible hand to promote an end which was no part of his intention."

The more sophisticated and complex analysis of modern welfare economics had extended these results and made them far more specific and rigorous. It was shown that if businessmen and consumers operated under a regime of perfect competition, then, given certain criteria of efficiency and consumer welfare, the economy would automatically and without any interference produce results which were optimal—in the limited sense of Pareto-optimality—for its members. This is a remarkable result, though, for a variety of reasons, its practical applicability is rather limited. It states that a perfectly competitive system is a giant analogue computer which calculates the decisions necessary to achieve maximal well-being and, indeed, which automatically sees to it that these decisions are made and carried out.

Lerner and Lange argued that where the economy departed from conditions of pure competition, these results could be achieved artificially with a minimum of governmental interference. By forcing managers to behave as though they were operating under perfect competition, by requiring that they produce up to the point where price equals the marginal costs of production, and by insisting that markets be cleared, that is, by lowering the price whenever there is an excess supply and raising the price whenever there is unsatisfied demand, it was suggested that the benefits of socialist planning could be obtained without the details and nuisances involved in the setting and enforcement of quotas, norms, rations, and the like. Each manager would be told that he was responsible for his own profitability and for his own decisions, provided only that he followed the simple rules of the game, the rules which called for marginal cost pricing and for clearing of the market. Certain difficulties for this proposal were noted, for example, in the case of economies of large scale production, but these are not relevant to the present discussion.

The mathematical programming and activity analysis literature has brought about a revival of interest in these ideas. It has been shown that the dual prices or values which are calculated from the dual programming problem can be used as the basis of a profitability requirement whose function would be closely analogous with that of the Lange-Lerner analysis. In allocating the economy's limited resources, the government need not set out specific quotas for the individual firms which constitute the economy. Instead, it need only set a price on each product, and a price on each scarce resource which is given by its dual value. We have already seen that any operation which produces some commodity that is not included in an optimal mix will necessarily suffer an opportunity loss in terms of these dual values. If the businessman is actually charged these dual prices, this opportunity cost is converted into a very real dollars and cents deficit. That is, if management were charged the dual values for all its inputs, it would find that it could break even only by concentrating production on those commodities which are optimal. Thus, we can crudely characterize the conclusion of this analysis as the assertion that one can achieve the advantages of detailed central planning and careful optimality calculation without telling the individual decision makers what they should do. A simple change in bookkeeping practices, together with the businessman's continued dedication to the pursuit of profits, would suffice to produce these ideal results.

There is no doubt that these results and this analysis are of great interest to the economist, but more careful consideration indicates that their practical application is likely to be highly limited, even in an economy in which central planning is an accepted goal. First of all, in the linear programming case there is a particular problem which is worth mentioning. It is true that in these circumstances if product managers pay for resources prices equal to their dual values, they will automatically produce a commodity if and only if its unit profit is equal to the value of the resources necessary to produce it. Thus, dual prices might indeed lead to correct decisions as to which items should be produced and which should not be produced. But dual prices do not, in these circumstances, indicate to management how much of each commodity which is included in the product line should be manufactured. In the linear programming case, since there are constant returns to scale and fixed prices, given that a product is profitable, it will be equally lucrative whether produced on a large scale or on a small. What prevents the indefinite expansion of the production of such a remunerative product is the scarcity of resources. Declining profitability of the production of an item as the market becomes saturated is not what brings production to a halt. Hence, in the linear programming case, dual prices, while they would direct production into the correct channels, would not necessarily yield the optimal relative utilization of these channels.

A second limitation of the use of duality as a device for preserving decentralized decision making is that the method appears to break down in the presence of important economies of large scale and significant discontinuities in production. Since these are important facts of industrial arrangements, one must not be surprised to find a variety of situations where so simple a scheme will run into serious and perhaps insuperable difficulties.

Finally, it must be emphasized that the degree of decentralization and extent of economy in decision making involved in dual pricing is largely illusory. As has been emphasized several times, solution of the original problem and of the dual essentially amount to the same thing; that is, if one is solved the other is automatically also solved. Hence, if the central planning board is to go to the trouble of finding the dual prices, it must, in the process, calculate quotas and norms for individual producers. The fact that these trappings of direct intervention may be kept in the background by means of dual pricing may be a psychological advantage but it involves no material change in the situation. The central planning board has made the complete calculation and whether it prefers to present it in one form or the other, there has been no economy in calculation, nor is there any real increase in the freedom of the individual decision maker. He is, in effect, given a choice but for all practical purposes, the choice is between following the desires of the central planning board or committing economic suicide. Dual pricing, in effect, tells him that any other action than that which the board desires will necessarily and rapidly lead him to bankruptcy. If this be freedom of choice for the decision maker then so, perhaps, is the choice between following the decisions of the central planning board and the option of a paid vacation in the salt mines of Siberia.

Duality and Business Decisions

It should now be easy to see why we made the earlier statement that dual pricing is of more relevance for the evaluation of inputs than of final commodities. The values which emerge from the solution of the dual problem have nothing to do with the market price of the commodity which is manufactured. Rather, they give the value to the firm of the input which it employs in its productive process.

This at once suggests an application which may be of use to the businessman. Indeed, it is an application which has been investigated recently. The users of an important agricultural commodity have been experiencing some difficulty in determining which grade or variety of this commodity to purchase for their purposes. Currently, the market prices of these different grades bear a very tenuous relationship to the usefulness of the different grades to the processor.

Moreover, a certain grade may be more useful to one type of manufacturer than to another. How, then, should a businessman decide which one of the available grades to purchase? An approach to this matter which should now be clear to the reader is the calculation of dual values for these different grades. Comparison of actual market prices with these dual values should enable the businessman readily to determine which grades are appropriate for his purposes. This approach is not only obvious, it is also promising. But even here it has its limitations and it is not quite as exciting as it might at first appear. It is not so very exciting, because all we are asserting here is that the firm's decision as to which inputs to purchase should be based on the marginal profitability of the alternatives. Comparison of the marginal profitability of the different items with their prices should tell at once which are desirable and which are not. Stated in this way, the result becomes much more familiar sounding and less impressive. Moreover, it points up the essential difficulty in the procedure, which is the problem of obtaining the data on which to base the calculation. The bulk of the work will be neither the formulation of the relevant programming problem nor the subsequent calculation, but the collection of the marginal profitability statistics in a form which provides sufficient accuracy and relevance to make the calculation useful.

A second application of duality to business decisions is analogous to the decentralized decision-making scheme which was discussed in the government policy section. Many large firms are composed of a considerable number of divisions operating partially or almost entirely independently. Very frequently these divisions compete with one another, either through inadvertence or as a result of direct decree by top management. But there is no reason to believe that even if these divisions were operated optimally from the point of view of the divisions themselves, they would produce results which would aggregate to an ideal situation from the point of view of the firm as a whole. This is the basic problem of suboptimization. The welfare of the whole is not the sum of the welfare of its parts. For example, if the divisions compete with one another, each may force down the profits of its rival and the end result may be a reduction in the total profits of the company. For the same reason that dual values may permit the semblance of decentralized decision making in an economy they may also preserve the same appearances to the division managers in a company. If central management is convinced that it can calculate the optimal programs for its constituent segments, dual values may represent the ideal instruments for their enforcement. Though in industrial applications many of the reservations which were raised in relation to the use of dual pricing in decentralized economic planning for the economy are also applicable, it is plausible that some exceptions will occur.

A suggestive illustration is provided by at least one large retail chain where, in continuation of long-established tradition, reordering for inventory is done entirely by the decision of the store managers. In the past, the store managers were the only ones who had a good and up-to-date estimate of inventory levels and, therefore, any attempt to centralize reordering decisions would almost certainly have produced inefficiency and waste. However, with the advent of the electronic computer, inventory record keeping has now been moved to company headquarters. Current information on inventory status is more readily obtained from the computer than from any other source. Today store managers still continue to make up orders, but these delivery requests are based on statistics which are obtained from company headquarters. This illustration is presented for two reasons.

First of all, it shows that it has now become possible to centralize decisions where that procedure would formerly have been uneconomical. Second, it has emphasized the need for managerial independence, at least to a degree, as a means for maintaining local initiative and morale. In such circumstances dual pricing may soon be given an effective role, for it possesses the essential requisites of the situation. It maintains the form of decentralized decision making while disposing of its substance.

Duality and Economic Theory

We turn finally to the topic closest to our own hearts—the relevance of programming and duality to the work of the economic theorist. From his point of view, the entire body of analysis suffers from two important limitations. First, as already stated, it is an instrument of optimality calculation. It is normative rather than descriptive. Thus, it should be more useful in welfare economics than in positive economics. Only to the extent that the behavior of individuals and firms is approximately optimal, will a linear programming calculation give a reasonably close description of actual behavior. Of course, this is a consideration which has always borne relatively little weight with economists. We have usually proceeded on the assumption that reasonably good predictions would be yielded by an optimality analysis. A second limitation of programming analysis is the fact that it is primarily quantitative rather than qualitative. Though the duality theorems which have been described previously have very important qualitative characteristics, most programming calculations can only be made in terms of specific numbers and specific examples. It is difficult to obtain qualitative programming results analogous with the very interesting comparative statics theorems of neoclassical analysis. It is as though we were forced, in the theory of production, to make all our analyses in terms of specific production functions, with specific coefficients and specific forms for the variables. This is a limitation which most theorists would have found intolerable until now. However, there are two things that can be done about it. First, as has been shown in the duality discussion and already mentioned in this section, with some degree of difficulty more general qualitative theorems can indeed be developed for programming problems. More novel, perhaps, is the approach which has been made possible by the availability of high speed electronic computers. These permit sensitivity analyses in which the effects of changes in values of the parameters in a problem can be examined by direct computation. In effect, what is done is shown by our last linear programming illustration, where the value of the price of the first output is permitted to vary. If a succession of different numbers is substituted for p in the profit function, successive calculations will show how the optimal solution will change and how the level of profitability will be affected. Thus we can obtain qualitative results by means of an inductive experimental approach, trying alternative values of the parameters and recording and analyzing their effects.

Aside from this, the main function of programming in economic theory and the light which it sheds on the competitive and pricing processes has, as already stated, largely consisted in an extension, further explanation, and confirmation of the standard marginal analysis. Duality has shown us that implicit in every optimality analysis and optimal decision process must be concepts of opportunity costs and marginal yield. It has shown this for a much wider variety of situations than was formerly covered and has offered us many new insights into the logic of the process.

One interesting consequence of all this has been the new position of marginal analysis in the Soviet Union. There, in recent years, the marginal apparatus has quite unexpectedly been restored to respectability and, interestingly enough, this has been the work of the mathematicians rather than of the pure economists. For the Soviet mathematicians have shown that many planning problems require for their analysis the entire apparatus of mathematical programming, and in investigating this apparatus, they independently came upon the structure and theorems of duality. Once it became apparent that programming works, and actually produces results, the rest was accepted more easily. It is interesting that recent writers have made no bones about the matter. In the Soviet publications it is now widely stated that marginal calculations are entirely necessary and appropriate for optimal decision making. Though there is some effort to interpret these results in a way which reconciles them with Marxian doctrine, those who accept them are in the ascendancy.

It is also noteworthy that the relationship of programming to economic theory is a two-way street. For example, some computational methods for nonlinear programming, which are based on some economic models of oligopolistic competition, are currently being explored. Methods somewhat analogous to the Cournot process, whereby the firms finally attain their equilibrium point, are proposed for the solution of programming problems. But, all in all, it must be conceded that duality has given us no brilliant and deep insights into the nature of competition and pricing. Largely, perhaps, this is because, by its very nature, programming theory is empty of empirical content. It makes no pretense at being otherwise. But, surely, without empirical premises we can hope to shed very little light on matters which are essentially empirical.

THE RELEVANCE OF GAME THEORY

BY DAVID W. MILLER, ASSOCIATE PROFESSOR
OF QUANTITATIVE METHODS, THE GRADUATE
SCHOOL OF BUSINESS, COLUMBIA UNIVERSITY

The title of this paper has the virtue of brevity but it hardly does more than raise the questions: Relevant to what? or, to whom? As a reasonably specific answer to these two questions, my "what" will be competitive behavior and my "whom" will be anyone interested in "behaving" in a competitive situation or interested in understanding such behavior. Thus expanded, the intent of this presentation is to consider the relevance of game theory to an understanding of competitive behavior. If I discover that game theory is relevant to something else I will note it in passing, but my primary interest will be as stated.

My conclusions are essentially negative. We find that game theory is not very relevant to competitive behavior, in any practical sense. Of course, this bald statement needs some qualification and it will be the intention of the following presentation to supply it. For convenience this paper is divided into four parts. The first part gives a general introduction, a bird's eye view of game theory, and an indication of the apparently game-like character of competitive situations. The second part considers the logic of game theory in a manner which is intended to demonstrate the inherent limitations of the theory. The third part is devoted to a consideration of actual competitive situations in order to discover how closely they correspond to games in the game theory sense. The last part tries to briefly indicate some positive results of game theory insofar as it may provide a deeper understanding of some aspects of competitive behavior.

An Overview of Games and Their Theory

My main concern is with the applications and applicability of game theory, or of the major ideas of game theory, to the great variety of real-world situations which we attempt to summarize with the phrase "competitive behavior." Let us ignore definitions for a moment and make a quick pragmatic survey of some fairly recent developments in one area where competitive behavior is frequently encountered: the business world.

A short description of the contemporary scene might be as follows. The past fifteen years has seen an enormous increase in the utilization of quantitative and mathematical methods for the resolution of complex problems which arise, for example, in the business world. Inventory theory may serve as an illustration. There are literally hundreds of articles in the literature which develop analytical methods for the resolution of the great variety of practical inventory problems. In correspondence with this effort, we find hundreds of examples wherein inventory theory has been more or less successfully used in practice. Two other equally good illustrations would be programming methods and queuing theory.

Game theory has approximately the same age as the mentioned uses of quantitative methods, since it can be considered, for all practical purposes, to have originated with the appearance in 1944 of the classic work of Von Neumann and Morgenstern.[1] It is relevant, at least in frequently stated intent, to a most important aspect of the same business world. Indeed, in many cases the same persons who are interested in the applications of inventory theory, programming methods, and so forth, are also devotees of game theory. Further, the literature of game theory is truly vast. One, therefore, expects to find

[1] John von Neumann and Oskar Morgenstern, *Theory of Games and Economic Behavior* (Princeton, Princeton University Press, 1947).

a comparable number of cases wherein game theory has been used for the resolution of problems in the area of competitive behavior. Unfortunately, this expectation is a vain one. A long and diligent search must be made in order to find even one example of the resolution of a real-world business problem by means of game theory. Furthermore, the want of such examples is certainly not due to lack of trying on the part of the proponents of game theory.

Now, if one were to use some kind of pragmatic criterion of relevance, this essentially negative appraisal would definitely suggest the conclusion that game theory is not very relevant to actual competitive behavior, at least in the business world. While such a criterion, and the resulting evaluation, is not to be ignored, it would be unfair to evaluate relevance solely on this basis. A theory may very well deepen understanding by raising questions, even if the answers offered by the theory are, for one or another reason, unsatisfactory. This last statement impels assent, perhaps because of its vagueness. But I think that it can be made more precise and it will be useful to do so for subsequent purposes. The usual way in which a theory deepens understanding without providing answers seems to be somewhat as follows. Some concept of ordinary speech—say "volume" or "social welfare"—becomes of vital importance for some structure of ideas. For purposes of ordinary communication the concept functions very well, but as structures are reared which include the concept, questions arise as to what it "really" means. Careful analyses are undertaken and it is discovered that the concept really masks various, and sometimes contradictory, meanings. Thus, we discover that we must be careful in thinking which incorporates this concept. The theory does not tell us which meaning we "should" use nor how we "should" think about those matters requiring that concept. It is in this way, by highlighting difficulties and ambiguities that the theory has deepened our understanding. The two cited examples are both of this sort. Careful mathematical analysis has disclosed such contradictions in the concept of volume and Arrow's famous impossibility theorem has shown the same kind of difficulties regarding the concept of social welfare.[2] Here are some other, similar concepts: "truth," "probability," and "rationality."

The appraisal of game theory which will be developed here is fairly well outlined in the preceding paragraph. I do not think that game theory is relevant to competitive behavior in the sense that any practical problem arising in this area can be resolved by the use of game theory. But more important, I think that there are good and sufficient reasons why no elaboration of game theory in anything resembling its present form will ever be applicable to competitive problems, in this sense. Arguments in defense of this statement will be offered subsequently. However, I do think that game theory is of great importance in the sense of deepening understanding. Now, with so much in the way of advance notice, we must proceed to the main task.

The primary concern, here, is the applicability of game theory. I am not, therefore, interested in any axiomatic description of game theory itself. Rather, I am interested in that part of the real world to which game theory is expected to be applicable, competitive behavior. Logically, I should begin with some definition of our subject matter. Thus, I might define astronomy as the study of extraterrestrial physical phenomena. Similarly, we would like a definition of the subject matter of game theory. It is not necessarily the case that the subject matter of game theory is games, no matter how these might be defined. This is no more necessary than it is that logic is the study of correct arguments. Clearly, logic has something to do with correct arguments and game theory has something to do with games. But perhaps logic is a study of what we mean by "truth" and perhaps game theory is a study of what we mean by "rationality." Granting, this, I will provisorily assume that game theory is the study of games.

This suggests that we need a definition of games. Here I must

[2] Duncan R. Luce and Howard Raiffa, *Games and Decisions* (New York, Wiley, 1957).

make a distinction. On the one hand, there are real-world situations which in some sense, more or less vague, seem to be game-like. This is my provisorily accepted subject matter and I will designate these "actual" games as A-games. On the other hand, there are games as defined and elaborated in some portion of game theory. These I will designate as T-games. It is easy enough to offer definitions of T-games. Indeed, there can be a considerable amount of arbitrariness in such definitions. Of course, the theoretician has one eye on A-games when he is elaborating his definition of T-games, so we would expect some degree of correspondence between the two. However, there is by no means an identity. Since we are not specifically interested in T-game definitions I will not give any, here. Insofar as an A-game definition is concerned, I do not think that a satisfactory one is possible. Therefore, we cannot begin our discussion with the logically desirable definition of subject matter. This is, of course, a common enough predicament. Consider the problem of defining, in the same sense, the subject matter of logic. Prior, for example, starts his *Formal Logic* with this statement: "The best way to discover what logic is about is simply by doing logic." [3] If a logician is forced to this recourse, surely we can do likewise.

Granting this much in the way of equivocation, let us follow Dr. Shubik in his informal characterization of a game.[4] Shubik suggests that the idea of a game is ordinarily associated with some other ideas. Specifically, he lists such ideas as rules, players, moves, strategies, payoffs, competition or cooperation, and some conception of the importance of information. Shubik instances bidding in the game of bridge and bluffing in poker as examples of the importance of information. As would be expected, most of us have some rather ill-defined conceptions of these various ideas. We refer to Shubik's book for a clarification and formalization of these key ideas. For our purposes, we will be content to rely on the intuitive understanding of them, subject to some elaboration and exemplification sub-

[3] A. N. Prior, *Formal Logic* (Oxford, Clarendon Press, 1955).
[4] Martin Shubik, *Strategy and Market Structure* (New York, Wiley, 1959).

sequently. A parlor game, such as poker, provides a sufficiently clear conception of the relevance of the ideas mentioned to the idea of a game. Let us briefly consider poker in the context of these various ideas.

Rules: Codified in Hoyle or Scarne, and specify how the cards will be dealt, the sequence of betting, the rank of hands, and so forth.

Players: Any number greater than one, with some practical limitations at both ends of the scale.

Moves: The rules specify the possible moves; essentially, bet or get out unless you are the first bettor, in which case you can check.

Strategies: The procedures by which we propose to play the game. Thus, I will never bet more than so much in draw poker with such a hand. Or, in such and such circumstances I will bluff in *x* percent of the cases.

Payoffs: Specified by the rules, as all the money in the "pot," except in such games as high-low, where there can be two winners.

Competition: Not so straightforward! It is clear that the spirit of the game is: "Every man for himself and the devil take the hindmost." Furthermore, most kinds of overt cooperation would be characterized as cheating. Yet, it is a common observation that the losers during a poker session have a tendency to cooperate to some degree against the winners and this is generally permissible, subject to sharp restrictions in terms of information.

Information: The importance of information is evidenced by careful specifications regarding information, in the rules. The whole character of the game changes according to the information specifications. Thus, in draw poker there is no information concerning the cards in the other players' hands. In stud poker there is partial information. Some information about the other players' moves is always available, namely, how much they bet.

Some information is never available, namely, precisely what their hands are—until the conclusion of the game. Between the two, there is room for the great variety of different poker games.

It seems clear that a description of poker in terms of each of these ideas is necessary in order to understand the game. It is less clear, but probably true, that an accurate characterization of poker in terms of each of these ideas is sufficient to completely characterize the game. We shall, therefore, remain content with this informal description of a game.

Poker is clearly an A-game since it is actually played in the real world. However, this kind of A-game is not what we ordinarily have in mind when we are considering important kinds of competitive behavior. What about competitive behavior in the business world? Does it correspond to a game, so described? The presence of competition is enough to characterize a real-world situation as game-like, but is the relationship closer than that? Consideration of this question quickly discloses that all the above ideas are important in the characterization of a business competitive situation. Suppose we consider a pricing problem. Two drug companies, say, have simultaneously reached the marketing stage with drugs both intended to fulfill the same purpose. Each company must set a price on its drug. Let us consider this situation in the context of the same ideas.

Rules: Each company must set its price without knowing the price being set by the other company. A company may change its price at any subsequent time. Other rules might be introduced in order to formally construct the game.

Players: Two.

Moves: A move consists of setting a price initially or changing the price subsequently.

Strategies: Cost plus pricing, with or without modifications depending on the competitor's price, or any other pricing policy.

Payoffs: Can be sales, profits, market share, or anything similar.

They will generally depend in a complex way on a variety of factors other than price, but price is one of the factors.

Competition: Supposed to be complete. The government endeavors to enforce a rule to this effect.

Information: Neither competitor can know the other's initial price in advance, according to the rule mentioned under competition. Each competitor discovers the initial price, and subsequent price changes, of its competitor, but generally does so after some time lag.

It is clear that some description of the competitive situation in terms of these ideas is needed. But it is certainly not true that such a description is sufficiently complete to truly characterize the competitive situation. I will return to this subsequently. For the moment, it is sufficient to note that there is some correspondence and that it is at this point that one's hopes are highest with regard to the applicability of game theory to competitive situations.

Let us, then, turn to game theory proper. We are immediately assaulted by an extraordinary number of new concepts: extensive form, normalized form, characteristic function form, minimax, equilibrium points, zero-sum, mixed strategies, composite strategies, behavioral strategies, imputations, core solutions, S-equivalence, superadditivity, Shapley values, and so forth. This water is just too cold for us to swim in! Perhaps we can find some alternative route which will give us a sufficiently clear picture of game theory for our specific purposes. Since game theory deals with quite a variety of games, and since the state of the theory is different for the different kinds, perhaps we can simply summarize the existing situation by type of game. We find that there are a series of highly important dichotomies by means of which games are classified.

Number of players: Two-person or n-person games. The importance of this distinction is that coalitions of some players against other players may form as soon as the number of players exceeds two.

Payoffs: Zero-sum or nonzero-sum. This distinction refers to the total of all payoffs to all players at the conclusion of the game. For some games the sum of all payoffs is zero. Most parlor gambling games are of this kind. Poker is an example. Essentially, it means that what one player wins or loses another player loses or wins. In particular, it means that if there are only two players in a zero-sum game there must be complete conflict of interest. A nonzero-sum game may be exemplified by a poker game in which the "house" takes a cut of each "pot." The basic point of a nonzero-sum game is that, somehow, payoffs enter or leave the game which do not respectively, come from or go to the players.

Competition: Cooperative and noncooperative games. A cooperative game is one in which it is both possible and profitable for players to select a jointly determined course of action. A noncooperative game is one in which it is impossible, not profitable, or both, for the players to jointly determine their courses of action.

Information: Games with and without preplay communication. Obviously, preplay communication permits the establishment of a joint plan of action if this is desirable. As a subclass of games with preplay communication, there is a split into games with and without enforceable agreements. This distinction is particularly relevant to discussions of the "double-cross" strategy.

Games with and without side payments: This might be better listed under the heading of payoffs but it seems actually to be more appropriate here. The distinction is only relevant to cooperative games. The question is: Can one player make side-payments to another player to induce him to cooperate in some course of action which may give the first player some greatly enhanced payoff?

There are various other dichotomies but these seem to be the major ones. The two most important of these differentiations are those relevant to number of players and to payoffs. Both of these distinctions are really related to the question of the degree of competition or cooperation which exists in the game. In game theory this is called, for short, the degree of conflict of interest. A two-person, zero-sum game has complete conflict of interest because what one player wins the other player loses. There is no possibility of cooperation, side payments, or anything else. A two-person nonzero-sum game may not have complete conflict of interest because, for example, the payoff coming from outside the game may be sufficiently large to justify the players taking joint action in order to share the profits. An n-person, zero-sum game may not have complete conflict of interest because it may be possible, and profitable, for some players to form a coalition and take common action against the other players. And, of course, an n-person, nonzero-sum game may fail to have complete conflict of interest in either or both ways.

With these classifications in mind, I can offer a quick summary of the state of the art. For two-person, zero-sum games there is a complete theory available and a general consensus that the theory is correct. Indeed, this theory is so solidly based that it is difficult to conceive that it could be incorrect. For two-person, nonzero-sum games there are a variety of theories and, hence, there is no consensus. These various theories, and the arguments for and against them, are enormously interesting and, or so it seems to me, a player could play some variants of such games better, for having studied the various theories. For n-person zero-sum games there are, again, a variety of theories. These theories are also highly interesting but it seems unlikely that a player's ability to play such a game would be much increased by studying the theories. Finally, for n-person, nonzero-sum games the situation is certainly no better than it is for n-person, zero-sum games. In short, there are a variety of possibilities and it is doubtful whether any one, or all, of them really contributes to a better playing of such a game.

How do business competitive situations, viewed as games, fall into these four classes? It is immediately clear that the overwhelming majority of such A-games are nonzero-sum. The only major exception to this statement is a competitive struggle for market share. Here, obviously, what one company gains in market share another company must have lost. Of course, a competitive struggle in which market share was really the payoff would hardly be in accordance with the usual precepts of good business sense but it might, and perhaps does, occasionally happen. When a well-established company enters, for the first time, an already established market the company sometimes intends to immediately achieve a share of the new market in ac-accordance with its "dignity" in other markets. Thus, there might arise a zero-sum, market-share game. However, it is certainly far more common to have profits as payoffs and this kind of situation will generally be nonzero-sum. The reason for this can be exemplified by considering a regional promotional war between two companies. The chances are that the total of their efforts will draw customers from other markets into their market. Thus, both companies may achieve increased payoffs and, in game theory terms, this means that the situation must have been a nonzero-sum game. Taking the other dichotomy into account, it is clear that most game-like competitive situations are n-person for the simple reason that there are generally more than two competitors in a market. Therefore, we conclude that the majority of such competitive business situations are of the n-person, nonzero-sum type. This immediately suggests that game theory would not have much to offer in terms of an understanding, and better playing, of this most typical kind of competitive situation.

This rapid, birds'-eye view of the state of game theory, in terms of its applicability to competitive business situations, conveys some information, but it seems to me that it leaves an overall wrong impression. Looked at in this way, the conclusion might be somewhat as follows. "It is true that, at present, there is no satisfactory and generally accepted theory of n-person, nonzero-sum games. And since most business competitive situations are of this type, it follows that, again at present, game theory does not provide any real means for improving a player's performance in such a game. However, this is undoubtedly only a temporary state of affairs. Game theory has produced an excellent theory of two-person, zero-sum games and it is only a question of time until it does likewise with the more general n-person, nonzero-sum game. Therefore, we may expect that at some time in the foreseeable future game theory will provide means for the understanding, and better playing, of the kind of game which arises in business practice." This appears to be the conclusion which our summary suggests.

It seems to me that this is a totally erroneous conclusion. I do not think that there will ever be a meaningfully applicable theory of games, in anything resembling its present form, which can be used in the analysis of actual competitive situations. I do not doubt the earlier distinction, that advances in game theory will frequently deepen our understanding of some key concepts. But the conclusion that it will ever do more than this, I categorically reject. Some careful argumentation is necessary in order to justify this cavalier attitude.

The Logic of Game Theory

To give some indication of the argument, a different approach to game theory will be useful. Perhaps a short detour will be justified, to put this approach in its proper perspective. Many signs point to the consolidation and rapid development, in the near future, of a new subject, which Kotarbinski[5] has dubbed praxiology, the science of efficient action. If this development occurs, one may expect to find that praxiology will subsume such subjects as economics, decision theory, game theory, organization theory, and others. One can define praxiology equally well, alternatively, as the rational utilization of resources to achieve ends or the rational selection of means to achieve objectives. There are a variety of ways in which the same idea could be formulated but I think that a key word in all of them

[5] Tadeusz Kotarbinski, "Praxiological Sentences and How They Are Proved," in Ernest Nagel, Patrick Suppes, and Alfred Tarski, eds., *Logic, Methodology and Philosophy of Science* (Stanford, Stanford University Press, 1962).

will be the word rational. For it seems that if praxiology will be anything, it will be the ultimate example of what John Maurice Clark has called the "irrational passion to be dispassionately rational." Now, the concept of rationality falls into that select class of concepts which apparently have an inexhaustible amount of ambiguity. Analogies from other areas of thought which have had to deal with such concepts suggest that the development of praxiology will be one long, increasingly refined commentary on the meaning of "rationality." "Truth" in logic, "value" in economics, "good" in ethics, "existence" in metaphysics, "probability" in probability theory—these are examples of such concepts. For subsequent purposes it is of no consequence whether the prognostication concerning praxiology is accepted or whether the remarks concerning the concept of rationality sound reasonable. This was simply a general background for our next step: the consideration of game theory as an extended commentary on the meaning of rationality.

We need some definitions. The concept of rationality is inextricably intertwined with the idea of the pursuit of values. Indeed, C. I. Lewis has maintained that rationality is derivative from the pursuit of values.[6] We will define them jointly and as positivistically as possible. Values, then, are those things which should be maximized. Disvalues, sometimes called costs, are those things which should be minimized. And rationality is the recognition of these two facts. By these definitions, a rational human being is one who always selects the largest value when he is given a choice among several. Let us, then, take a rational human being as subject and present him with the following choice situation:

$$A \quad 5$$
$$B \quad 2$$

He is told that the numbers represent values and that he will receive the indicated value for either of his two possible choices, A and

[6] Clarence Irving Lewis, An Analysis of Knowledge and Valuation (La Salle, The Open Court Publishing Company, 1946).

B, which he chooses. Obviously, in accordance with our definitions, the subject will choose A because this maximizes the value. This is obvious enough, but it should be remembered that economic theory is built on little more than this, plus a reasonable assumption to the effect that successive equal increments of an object with value will afford successively diminishing increments of value.

Let us extend the example slightly. The subject is given the choice situation:

$$
\begin{array}{ccc}
A & 5 & 7 \\
B & 2 & 4 \\
\end{array}
$$

In addition to his previous information, he is told that by some means one of the two columns will be chosen and that he will receive the value at the intersection of his chosen row and the chosen column. He is told absolutely nothing about the choice mechanism for the column—it may be a malevolent demon, a benevolent angel, a rational opponent, or a chance mechanism. Clearly, our definition of rationality dictates that our rational subject will select A. This is the case because no matter which column is chosen, he will receive a larger value from A than he would from B. This simple argument is summarized by the idea of dominance. We say that choice A dominates choice B because every value in the A row is larger than the corresponding value in the B row.

The easiest of all extensions of this choice situation is to the case where our subject is faced with a rational opponent for whom the same numbers represent disvalues. Let the two rational subjects be designated I and II and let them be presented with the following choice situation:

		II		
		R	S	T
	A	2	7	3
I	B	5	6	4
	C	6	3	2

The numbers represent values to I and disvalues to II. Since this is a game-type situation it is easy to think of the numbers as representing, say, dollars which II will have to pay to I. The single idea of dominance is sufficient to resolve this choice situation. For II, the numbers are disvalues, so he wants to make them as small as possible. Inspection discloses that II's S is dominated by his T. This being the case, he will never choose S and it can be eliminated from the matrix. With S gone it is evident that I's B dominates his A, so A can be eliminated from the matrix. With both S and A eliminated it can be seen that II's T dominates his R. Eliminating R it follows, finally, that I's B dominates C. From this argument it follows that I will always select his B and that II will always select his T. These are the only choices which are in accord with our definition of rationality. This is, of course, a two-person, zero-sum game. In game theory parlance, we say that this game has a value of 4, to I, and, of course, a disvalue of 4, to II. Not all two-person zero-sum games can be resolved by this kind of argument. The only ones which can be so resolved are those in which some entry is simultaneously the largest entry in its column and the smallest entry in its row. When this is the case we say that the game has a saddle-point. Some two-person, zero-sum games with saddle-points can be resolved by this kind of argument, but not all of them.

Unfortunately, we have gone as far as we can go with our pure and untrammeled definition of rationality. No other general class of choice situations can be resolved solely on the basis of our definition. In order to analyze other kinds of choice situations we need to further specify what it means to be rational, what we mean by rational, or something of the sort. It will be worth a little effort to discover exactly what kind of extension is needed in order to cope with the next class of choice situations. Fortunately, the self-same extension will permit the resolution of two kinds of choice situations: the remaining two-person, zero-sum games and the general kind of situation known as choice under risk. Suppose we present our subject, I, with the following choice problem under risk:

	R	S
A	5	2
B	4	7

I

The numbers, of course, still represent values to I. It will be noted that we have designated the columns by letters, as if they were strategies to be selected by some kind of rational agency. Here, however, the letters are only for convenience and no rational agency is assumed to be selecting the column. Instead, the subject is informed that a column will be selected by some chance device and he is told that the chance device is so devised that the probability that R will be selected is ¾. Hence, the probability that S will be selected must be ¼. The question now is: How should a rational subject make his choice?

It is immediately clear that our previous definitions do not provide sufficient means to answer this question. No relationship of dominance exists between the two choices. Something more is needed. The approach that is followed in current theoretical analyses, including game theory, begins with this proposition: The definition of rationality will remain unchanged. In other words, we are going to continue to say, simply, that the rational chooser is one who always selects the largest of a set of values subject to his choice. This leaves only one definition which can be changed or elaborated: the definition of value. To appreciate the difficulties involved, and the suggested solution to them, it is necessary to ask the preliminary question: How do the numbers we have been calling values actually represent values to the rational subject? So far it has been sufficient that they did represent values. Now, it is essential to discover how they represent values. There are a variety of difficulties to be considered. To fix matters for convenience, let us assume that the numbers in the preceding choice matrix represent dollars. Thus, if one chooses A, and R results from the chance selection, then one will receive $5. Clearly, the dollar amounts do not necessarily represent values to the chooser. Introspection is sufficient to demonstrate that a given number of dollars does not always have the same value to the same individual. Five dollars to a poor, hungry man is certainly worth more to him than it would be to a man who had thousands of dollars in the bank. What is needed, then, is a measure of the value—economists would call it utility—of the given number of dollars for the person making the choice.

The question of the measurement of utility has been lengthily discussed by economists for generations and game theorists are not unaware of the arguments that have been developed. Many of the conclusions of these arguments are accepted as bases for the procedures under discussion here. We need not recapitulate any of the reasons but we may mention two of the generally accepted results. First, utility is subjective—only the individual in question can judge his utility. Second, interpersonal comparisons of utility are generally impossible. These two presuppositions suffice to determine the way in which numbers can represent the individual's values or utilities. The numbers must function like the numbers we use in measuring temperatures rather than like the numbers we use in measuring length or weight. Technically, we say that the numbers used to represent utility will form an interval scale. The simplest way to call attention to the implications of such a use of numbers is in terms of the difference between the measures of utility for two amounts of dollars. Such a difference will not be a utility itself. Similarly, the difference between two temperatures is not a temperature, but the difference between two weights is itself a weight. This is the reason for saying that the numbers which measure utilities function like the numbers which measure temperature.

We need no more details than these. A method of measuring an individual's utilities—for example, for the dollar amounts in our choice problem—is available. It is known as the standard gamble, and it will, in fact, produce numbers which represent the individual's utilities and which function in accordance with the remarks of the preceding paragraph. Before we try to conclude anything from this very rough outline of a delicate argument, let us see how this approach accomplishes the resolution of the choice problem we are considering. Concisely, if the individual making the choice can and does measure his utility for the various dollar amounts in accordance with the recommended procedure, then it can be shown that his utility for each choice can be determined by taking the expected value of the possible utilities he may receive from that choice. Then, in accordance with the definition of rationality, it only remains for him to select that choice which has the largest utility to him. Returning to our example, the subject might find his utilities to be the following:

	R	S
A	.6	0
B	.4	1

Using the stated probabilities of selection of R and S, we can immediately calculate the expected utilities of each choice:

$$A \quad (\tfrac{3}{4})\,(.6) + (\tfrac{1}{4})\,(0) = .45$$
$$B \quad (\tfrac{3}{4})\,(.4) + (\tfrac{1}{4})\,(1) = .55$$

These expected values are, then, the subject's utilities for the two choices. Therefore, he will choose B. Any such choice problem can be resolved by the same procedure.

The same extension permits the resolution of all two-person, zero-sum games which cannot be handled by the idea of dominance. This requires the introduction of the notion of a mixed strategy. A mixed strategy is one which requires the player to select one of two or more of his possible choices or strategies in accordance with some chance procedure with predetermined probabilities. It can be shown that every two-person, zero-sum game has mixed strategies for each player, so that if one player is using his optimal mixed strategy, then the other player can do no better than to use his own optimal mixed strategy. Another way of saying the same thing is that every two-person, zero-sum game has an equilibrium point. To illustrate the idea, assume that the payoffs (to player 1) of a two-person zero-sum game are:

Player II

R   S

Player I   A   5   2
          B   4   7

It is clear that no relation of dominance exists between the strategies of either player. However, each player has an optimal mixed strategy. Player I should play his two strategies each with probability ½. Player II should play his strategy R with probability ⅚ and, of course, S with probability ⅙. The intention is that the players should select their strategies randomly, but with the indicated probabilities. Thus, player I might toss a coin and select A if the coin showed heads. Player II might roll two dice and select S if he got a seven, R, otherwise. We should note that it requires calculation to determine these probabilities. We are simply citing them as illustrations. With the introduction of this idea of mixed strategies, all two-person, zero-sum games can be resolved. We needed the extension of the idea of utility, in order to accomplish this purpose, so that we would be justified in calculating the expected value of a mixed strategy.

Now that we have seen how the introduction of these ideas about measuring values or utilities accomplishes its purpose, let us reconsider the logic of the procedure. An obvious question might suggest itself. Earlier in this paper it was said that we would undertake a consideration of game theory as a commentary on the concept of rationality. Yet, at the first difficulty, we have concentrated our attention on the idea of value or utility. What about rationality? To answer this question, I must raise a different one. In my procedure I have demanded that the rational subject shall undertake to determine his subjective utility for the various possible outcomes resulting from his choices. My question is: Why not have the subject simply determine his utility for his various choices directly? Let him introspect and decide which choice, as a totality, has the greatest utility for him. This, then, is the one he must choose. Since his utility is, by accepted

definition, subjective, it follows that no comment about the rightness
or wrongness of his evaluation would be justified.

The usual answer to this last question is as follows. It is false to
assume that a rational subject could introspectively determine his
utility for his choices as totalities. Balancing probabilities and utilities is a delicate business and the unaided subject typically cannot do
it successfully. How do we know the subject is unsuccessful since,
after all, his utilities are subjective? We give a subject simple choice
problems under risk, and then we present him with more complicated ones which are actually built up from the simple ones. We can
then frequently observe that his choices in the more complicated
choice problems are inconsistent with his choices in the simple ones.
The key word here is "inconsistent." This argument amounts to a
definition to the effect that a rational person would assign his values
consistently. And this is why I am still talking about rationality, even
though it appears that I am talking solely about values or utilities. In
summary, I claim, in following this approach, that a rational subject
should be consistent in assigning values to his choices taken as totalities. And, subsidiarily, I maintain, on the basis of experimental evidence and introspection, that he is not likely to be consistent unless he
is aided by some kind of measurement procedure.

We may note, parenthetically and in passing, that the notion of
consistency has its own ambiguities. It could mean—the usual intention—the consistency of choices to values. But it could also mean
the consistency of values to choices. These are by no means the
same. The latter alternative is generally frowned upon and I believe
that extreme adherents of this alternative are called, technically,
psychopaths. However, it may well be the case that this alternative,
maintained in less extreme form, is a typically human response to an
overly complex valuation problem. As such, it would have certain
characteristics analogical to Simon's idea of satisficing.

Returning to the main theme, the measurement procedure which
is used for expressing utilities in numerical form is exactly what one
would expect, granting the consistency argument. Consider the

standard gamble procedure as it relates to the example we used of a choice problem under risk. The method is to present the subject with another choice problem under risk for each possible payoff except for the largest and smallest. Thus, for the payoff of $5 we would give the subject this "standard gamble":

	X	Y
C	5	5
D	7	2

Here, the subject is told that X will be selected by a chance device with probability, p, and Y with probability (1-p). Depending on his choices for a series of such choice problems, where p is given various different values, the subject's utility for $5 is deduced. This is then done for $4, and our decision problem is ready for resolution. The details of the method are of no particular importance for our argument. What is important is that the utility measurements are obtained precisely by giving the subject a series of simplified choice problems of exactly the same kind as the original choice problem which must be resolved.

We must be a bit more accurate: The simplified choice problem is not "exactly" the same. There are two differences: 1) We are assuming that the subject's utility is not affected by presenting choice problems which put each individual payoff against some risk combination of the largest and smallest payoffs. 2) We are assuming that his utility is not affected by considering the payoffs one at a time, so to speak, rather than all at once. Both of these assumptions are covered by axioms in the axiomatic development of these ideas but, of course, axioms and reality are different things. Apart from these two differences, the simplified choice problems really are miniscule versions of the bigger problem. The same factors, subjective and objective, which affect the subject's utilities in one case, do so in the other. Therefore, I would conclude that this approach is a perfectly good one for choice problems under risk and that it ought to be usable in practice.

It would be burking the truth not to note explicitly that each of the two differences has severe consequences. One of the first suggestions resulting from the rationalistic approach to the measurement of utility was that of Bernoulli, to the effect that equal percentages of total resources should carry equal incremental utilities. This is tantamount to assuming that utility of dollar amounts, for example, should be measured by the logarithm of the amount. A good argument can be made in defense of the thesis that many rational individuals might well have such a utility for dollars. Nevertheless, the first difference rules this out as a possibility. In other words, a rational individual with such a measure of utility could not analyze his complex choice problems by the method under discussion. Another rationalist's suggestion was that the utility of dollar amounts should be measured by the square root of the amount. This was first suggested by Cramer, a contemporary of Bernoulli, but Stevens [7] has reported some preliminary experimental work which indicates that this might be a reasonable measure of utility. This one is also ruled out by the first difference. Here is another "reasonable" argument. Many an individual will recognize that he is faced with a series of such choice problems throughout his life. Such an individual, being perfectly "rational," might well maintain that his primary measure of utility should be the probability that he will be ruined at some point in his life. This kind of argument is particularly appropriate for corporations, which are immortal by legal definition. Now, the probability of ruin depends in a complex way on all the possible payoffs that could occur as a result of any specific choice. Therefore, this possibility is ruled out by the second difference. One further point may be made in this context. The first two examples would require that utility be measured by some other means than the standard gamble, but both would proceed by taking expected

[7] S. Stevens, "Measurement, Psychophysics and Utility," in C. West Churchman, and P. Ratoosh, eds., *Measurement: Definitions and Theories* (New York, Wiley, 1959).

values. The third example, the ruin probability, would not even take expected values. This may serve to illustrate that there are many ways of being rational, not all of them encompassed by this theory.

We have tried to show why this general procedure works, to the degree that it does, with regard to choice problems under risk. There remains the question of why it also seems to work with regard to two-person, zero-sum games. I suggest that the reason for this is that there are two more or less coincidental facts involved. First, the idea of mixed strategies demands that taking expected values of utilities should be justified. The procedure we have been discussing affords such justification. Second, as a result of the complete conflict of interest in a two-person, zero-sum game, there are no other causes arising which affect the player's utilities. As we shall see, this is not the case in nonzero-sum games.

Before we finally turn to nonzero-sum games, it will be useful to consider that kind of choice problem known as decision-making under uncertainty. Suppose our subject is given the same payoff matrix as before:

	R	S
A	5	2
B	4	7

This time, he is told that any conceivable mechanism or agency may be used in selecting one of the columns: benevolent, malevolent, chance, or any other. Often, this kind of choice problem is defined in terms of the subject's "complete ignorance" concerning the columns of the matrix. We are not assuming so much ignorance. Our subject knows that there are only two columns. The essence of the problem is that he does not have probabilities of occurrence of the columns. How should a rational subject make his choice? A variety of procedures have been suggested and it is no part of this presentation to review them. Worth noting, however, is the fact that for every suggestion there is a counter-example. In other words, a specific payoff matrix is presented for which the suggested procedure seems to fail in the sense that, seemingly, a rational person would use some other procedure. This has occurred so often that one is almost justified to enunciate a principle which we may call the paradox of rationality: for any criterion of rationality, it is possible to find a counter-example such that a rational person would not use the criterion. Such a principle would be analogous to the situation in logic, where it can be proved that for any reasonable comprehensive logical system, it is possible to construct statements which are true yet which cannot be proved within the system to be true.

What causes this failure, in terms of the point of view we have been studying? This kind of choice problem is relevant to game theory, since any two-person game for which the utilities of the opponent are not known degenerates to this case. Further, granted the assumptions of the theory concerning the subjectivity of utility, it is not at all unlikely that the opponent's utilities will not be known in real-world situations. The cause of the failure is not hard to find. The heart of the procedure, insofar as choice under risk is concerned, is to present the subjects with simplified choice situations which are similar to the choice problem to be resolved. "Similar" means that the same factors which determine the subject's utility in the complex case, but no others, operate in the simpler case. Therefore, his utility can be measured, and his utility for the various choices as totalities can be determined, under the requirement of his consistency. It is impossible to determine what simpler choice problems under uncertainty are equivalent to the original one. Any simplification introduces new factors which affect the subject's utilities. In short, the only way to determine the subject's utilities for the choices as totalities, is to present him with the self-same choice problem which we hope to analyze and to ask him which choice he will make. This, of course, means that the subject is resolving the choice problem and there is neither room nor need for analysis. Faced with this predicament, the theorists have recourse to attempts to prescribe the kinds of factors rational individuals should respond to, in determining their utilities.

Since the theory's presuppositions incorporate the idea of *de gustibus non disputandum est*, this is not a very rewarding approach. Hence, the difficulties and the paradox of "rationality."

We will now consider some aspects of two-person, nonzero-sum games. An essential distinction was mentioned earlier. This is the dichotomy of such games into cooperative and noncooperative games. The distinction between these two kinds of nonzero-sum games does not depend on the payoff matrix for the game. Any such game can be played either cooperatively or noncooperatively, depending on circumstances associated with the playing of the game. Specifically, to play a game cooperatively, generally requires the possibility of communication between the players in order to reach an agreement, and is facilitated by the existence of transferable utility so that side payments can be made. It is generally necessary that there be some means of enforcing agreements, or else the moral climate must be such that the players are convinced that agreements will be respected. If these conditions do not obtain, it will usually be the case that the game will be played noncooperatively. Of course, two-person, zero-sum games are noncooperative because there is no possible way for the players to benefit by reaching agreement.

We may begin by displaying some examples of two-person nonzero-sum payoff matrices, which will illustrate the kinds of difficulties which arise. Since the payoffs do not sum to zero, it is necessary to display the payoffs for each player. We will use the convention that the left entry refers to player I and the right entry to player II. Suppose we have this situation:

		Player II	
		R	S
Player I	A	6,5	3,2
	B	4,4	1,1

How should player I make his choice? Clearly, there is no difficulty in this example. Both players will achieve their maximum payoffs from the A-R cell and, since they are both presumed to be rational, this is certainly the payoff they will choose. For such an example as this, it does not matter whether the game is non-cooperative or not, nor does it matter whether the game will be played once or many times. The reason for this is that the game has an equilibrium point at (6,5) and it is the only equilibrium point in the game. It is an equilibrium point because if either player knew that his opponent was going to make his choice to achieve this equilibrium point, he could do no better than to make his own choice to achieve this point.

Difficulties arise when we consider a game such as this:

Player II

		R	S
Player I	A	10,10	2,15
	B	15,2	3,3

In this game (3,3) is the only equilibrium point and if the game is played noncooperatively there is an irresistible rational pressure to produce this as the outcome. However, if the game is played cooperatively and if there are protections against double-crossing, one would imagine that the players will agree to (10,10) as the desired outcome. The fact that cooperation is not always desirable is illustrated by the following game from Luce and Raiffa's *Games and Decisions:* [8]

Player II

		R	S
Player I	A	1,2	3,1
	B	0, −200	2, −300

If there were no preplay communication, the players would probably achieve (1,2), since this is the unique equilibrium point of the game. If there is preplay communication, player I can demand that player II should choose S, under threat that if he does not, player I will choose B. Obviously, player I can better sustain a payoff of 0 than

[8] Luce and Raiffa, p. 111.

player II can sustain a payoff of —200. This example illustrates one of the key themes of nonzero-sum game theory: the idea of threats in terms of cooperative games. Presumably, cooperation in such a game would consist of some bargaining as to how the total returns might be apportioned between the two players, in the case of transferable utility, or as to which joint choice of strategies would be agreed upon, in the case of nontransferable utility. In this bargaining, a player's strength will depend in great measure on the threats which he has at his disposal.

We cannot undertake a discussion of the details of the various solutions which have been proposed and debated for this kind of game. The general procedure is to suggest some canons of rational behavior and then to deduce from these the strategy which a player ought to follow. Alternatively, such games are sometimes discussed from the standpoint of arbitration. How should an impartial arbitrator assess the relative strengths of the two players in assigning a unique payoff to them? The various solutions do not generally give the same result in the analysis of a specific game. Consider an example discussed by Luce and Raiffa.[9]

		Player II	
		R	S
Player I	A	1,4	—1, —4
	B	—4, —1	4,1

The Nash solution to a game is based strictly on the fact that there is no interpersonal comparison of utility possible. The Nash solution is that the two players should coordinate their selection of strategies so that each of the two payoffs (1,4) and (4,1) is selected half the time. This would give each player an average payoff of 2½. Yet, inspection of the game shows that it is really quite unsymmetrical with regard to threats. Suppose player II threatens to play R. What alternative has player I, but to play A, which gives 4 units

⁹ Luce and Raiffa, pp. 139 ff.

to player II. To take this kind of situation into account, Raiffa has suggested an analysis which depends on the existence of a common unit of measurement for the players' utilities. Raiffa's solution to this game would be that the players should agree on the payoff (1,4). There are various other kinds of proposed solutions, and examples can be given wherein every solution results in a different strategy.

While we cannot even outline the arguments for and against the different proposed solutions, we may, nevertheless, be able to reach some general conclusions, by approaching this kind of choice situation from the same standpoint we used above. The first question that needs to be considered is, as before, the meaning of the numbers used in the payoff matrix for such a game. The specific question we want to consider is: Do the utilities include components representing the utility which results from disutility to one's opponent? Thus, in the example above, does the 4 in (4,1) include a component resulting from the value to player I of the fact that his opponent only received a payoff of 1?

There is a question of fact here and a question of measurement. The question of fact is: Does a player gain utility from his opponent's disutility? The other question is: How can his utility be measured, if he does? Let us consider the latter question first. Our presupposition is that an individual cannot call forth numbers, from his conscious or subconscious, which represent his utility in any meaningful sense of the word. The numbers only have meaning if it is known how they represent his utility and, hence, how they can be be manipulated in analysis. This requires the utilization of some measuring device, such as the standard gamble. Now, while the standard gamble is not appropriate to this kind of choice problem in the same sense in which it was appropriate to choice problems under risk, it does afford a measuring device with known characteristics. How might it be used in this context? Let us take the preceding matrix as an example and assume that the payoffs are given in dollars. We would ask player I to indicate the two outcomes which are worst and best, from his point of view. Suppose they were, respectively, $(-4, -1)$ and $(4,1)$. Then we would present him with standard gambles in the form

Player I	C	(1,4)	(1,4)
	D	(4,1)	$(-4, -1)$

The columns would be selected by a chance device with known probabilities. Depending on the changes in choice as the probability is varied, the player's utility for the outcome could be determined by the usual procedures. Some assumptions are needed to ensure that this procedure would work, but equivalent assumptions would appear to be required for any measuring device for this case.

Suppose, then, that the utility can be determined. What might the resulting utilities look like? This is a question of fact to be established in any specific case, but the gamut of possibilities would look like this, where only the utilities of player I are given:

	i		ii		iii		iv		v	
A	1	0	1	0	.5	.2	0	1	0	1
B	.2	.5	0	1	0	1	0	1	.5	.2

In i, player I is a complete altruist and he ignores his own payoffs, being only interested in having player II receive as much as possible. In ii he is a half-way altruist, valuing a dollar return to II as much as he values one to himself. In iii he is indifferent to the payoff which II receives and his utilities are based solely on his own payoffs. In iv he is a half-way malevolent agent, valuing a loss of one dollar to II as much as he values a gain of one dollar to himself. Finally, in v he is totally malevolent, ignoring his own payoffs in order to inflict the maximum possible damage on II. These possibilities are quite similar to some distinctions made by Boulding in his fascinating book, *Conflict and Defense*.[10] Our i corresponds to his saint, our v corresponds to his malevolent hostility, our iv is in rough correspondence with his nonmalevolent hostility, and iii corresponds to his

[10] Kenneth Boulding, *Conflict and Defense* (New York, Harper, 1962).

benevolent hostility. The world being what it is, we can probably ignore the gamut of possibilities which are left of center, but it is certainly possible that any position on the right hand side of the scale could occur. The amount of malevolence which exists between the players might be defined by the divergence, in some sense, of the actual utilities from iii, which would represent zero malevolence. That these possibilities are not totally irrelevant may be indicated by the fact that Raiffa's solution would follow if player II were type iv and player I were type iii, while Nash's solution would follow if both players were type iii.

Generally, the degree of malevolence will be determined by a great number of factors. Past experience with the same player is one, basic psychological characteristics is another. Resources available is a key factor, since a player may be unable to afford the luxury of malevolence. In any event, the important consideration from our present point of view is that even if we make the usual, and rather ruthless, assumption that each player knows the other's utilities for the various outcomes, it does not follow that either player knows the degree of malevolence of the other. This cannot be ascertained from the utilities as given in the payoff matrix.

Granting that the utilities have been measured by some such means as these, we can turn to a consideration of the threat situation. For this purpose we will use the somewhat simpler example:

Player II

		R	S
Player I	A	3,5	10,2
	B	1,—4	2,—8

It will be noted that this game has a unique equilibrium point at (3,5). However, with preplay communication, player I will use his threat of choosing B to try to force player II to agree to choose S. More generally, player I may demand a side payment as well, if it is permitted. In other words, he might demand that player II enter into a binding agreement to choose S and that, in addition, player II must pay him some amount up to 6 units, arguing that as long as the amount is less than 6 units player II will do better than he would have done if I chose B. Now, this threat, as any other, in itself generates another game. Player II has two choices: give in to the threat (choose S) or refuse to give in (choose R). Player I also has two choices: he will certainly choose A if II agrees to choose S, but if II refuses he can either carry out his threat or, himself, give in and choose A. The payoff matrix for this threat game is:

Player II

R   S

Player I	(A if S; B if R)	1,—4	10+c,2—c
	(A if S; A if R)	3,5	10+c,2—c

In advance of negotiations, player I must determine the c he will demand. Consider any specific value of c. The likelihood of player II giving in to the threat will depend strictly on his appraisal of the likelihood that player I will carry out the threat, his first choice above. This, in turn, depends on the degree of malevolence of player I, which II cannot know. In other words, player I cannot rationally carry out the threat unless he values the loss of 9 units to II as worth more than the loss of 2 units to himself. This is my definition of malevolence.

The threat game, therefore, either degenerates into choice under uncertainty or, more likely, the process of the negotiations is used by both players to give intimations of their respective degrees of malevolence to the other. Schelling, in his *The Strategy of Conflict*,[11] has given an excellent account of the numerous devices which the players may use to accomplish this purpose. In any event, the threat negotiations are not incorporated in the threat game matrix and, hence, the original game cannot be analyzed by any such approach.

[11] Thomas C. Schelling, *The Strategy of Conflict* (Cambridge, Harvard University Press, 1960).

The reason that the various proposed solutions seem to be effective is that they all are effective once a common assumption is granted. One assumption is explicit or implicit in all of the arguments leading to the different solutions. It is that the rational behavior of the two players must be symmetric in the sense, roughly, that both must agree that the solution is rational and act accordingly. Shelling [12] has called attention to the questionable nature of this assumption. It seems fallacious, to me, precisely because of one of the paradoxes of rationality: if being irrational produces a larger value, then it is rational to be irrational.

Similar arguments can be adduced for the proposed analyses of n-person games. Space requirements will not permit presenting them here. However, it should be clear that if two-person nonzero-sum games cannot be successfully analyzed by the arguments of game theory, then n-person nonzero-sum games certainly cannot.

The purpose of this lengthy section has been to demonstrate that the lack of applicability of nonzero-sum game theory to practical competitive problems is not due to insufficient development of the theory. Rather, it is due to some basic methodological considerations relating to the measurement of utilities, and to some paradoxical difficulties with the concept of rationality. If the argument sustains the conclusion, it would appear that we could conclude this presentation with a verdict of "not applicable." However, it might be assumed that for many kinds of competitive situations, dollar amounts, in one form or another, represent satisfactory measures of payoff. This assumption, plus some suitable qualifications, would escape the point of the preceding arguments. I think, however, that there are other reasons for concluding that game theory is not applicable to actual competitive situations.

The Games of Business Competitive Behavior

In this section I will be concerned with the degree of correspondence which exists between the games of game theory and the games

---

[12] Schelling, pp. 278 ff.

of the real world of competitive behavior in business. In the preceding section, I attempted to show cause for the conclusion that game theory provides no workable theory of nonzero-sum games. Here, I will consider whether game theory would be applicable to competitive behavior in business if it did have a valid theory of nonzero-sum games.

An example was given previously which attempted to demonstrate some parallels between the description of poker and the description of a pricing problem. That example was intended to present the best possible picture of the potential applicability of game theory to such a common competitive problem as pricing. Here, I will try to show that the structure of the games of business competition is quite different from that of the games of game theory. Indeed, the differences are sufficiently consequential to make it appear extremely unlikely that game theory could be applicable to business competitive games.

In my earlier example, I noted that there were two competitors and I proceeded to describe the competitive situation in terms of those two competitors as the players in a two-person game. But in reality, who are the players in a typical business situation? There are at least five kinds of players: 1) Competitors, 2) Government, 3) Stockholders (assuming a separate management), 4) Retailers, 5 Consumers. Other players may enter into specific situations: unions, suppliers, factions within the company, and so forth. Naturally, not all of these kinds of players are involved in every specific industry's competitive situation but typically, at least, competitors, government, stockholders, and consumers are so involved.

What kind of game are these players playing? It is tempting to assume that it is simply some kind of n-person game like, for example, one person (management) playing poker against a group of opponents (except, of course, that the game need not be zero-sum). Once this is assumed it follows that game theory should be applicable, at least in the sense that game theory does deal with n-person games. I question whether this analogy is at all appropriate. Here is one which seems to be more apt: imagine one person playing chess against three opponents (or more). There is one chess board for each opponent and each of the opponents has his own set of pieces and makes his own moves. The single player must make one move each time which is simultaneously played in all three of his games. In other words, the single player cannot make separate moves for the separate games—his one move applies to all games. Imagine, further, that none of the opponents is permitted to know the moves made on any other board. Now, expand this analogy so that each competitor is similarly involved—and, of course, the competitors play among themselves with similar rules—in such an interlocking set of games. This, I think, would more nearly approximate the business situation. Assuming, for the moment, that this kind of complexity is involved in the business competitive situation, could not such a game be represented in game theory terms? It certainly could. The extensive form of a game is apt for the representation of almost any thinkable game-like situation. But representation of a game and theoretical conclusions about it are two different things. There are at least two major differences between this kind of game and the n-person games of game theory. First, since the various opponents are playing in different games, the kinds of coalitions that might arise are quite limited, except among the competitors themselves. Further, the government enters into some kind of coalition occasionally, but usually for reasons connected with the government's perception of the true utilities of one or another of the players. In short, the coalition possibilities are quite different—and with quite different motivations—from those of n-person game theory. Second, no competitor knows which game his competitor is playing when he makes a move. Therefore, he has no possible way to estimate the utility of his opponent. With no estimates of utilities there is no possibility of game theoretic analysis. Thus, it would appear that there are insuperable difficulties in the way of applying game theory to such a game as the one described above.

Do business competitive situations resemble, in any noticable way, the game we have suggested? Perhaps the simplest way to try to show that they do is to use an example: pricing in the coffee industry. One of the largest and most successful of the coffee companies has recently given a huge, twenty cent cut in price to the wholesalers. Why? Was it in any way related to the company's competitors or to their past actions? No. Rumor has it that it was a move in the company game against the government, which was threatening one or another kind of investigation. It will be a hard blow to the competitors, nonetheless. Another highly successful company in this industry is famous for its aggressive entry into new geographical markets. This company advertises and promotes with tremendous intensity, and offers deals and label-offs with prodigious liberality. Is this a cast-iron hard competitor in action? No. The company is privately owned and it is a move in the owners' zero-sum game against the government vis-a-vis taxes. Another company in the same industry is not so successful. Yet this company's label-offs are almost never-ending. Is this a struggle against its competitors? Only in the most general sense. It is more nearly a move in the game against the retailers, since the velocity of the product has fallen until the retailers are squeezing it off the shelves.

Does this mean that there is no price competition, in the usual sense, in the coffee industry? Nothing could be further from the truth. It is a furiously competitive industry in terms of price. Why? In great measure, because of the effect which long-continuing games between local retailers has had on the game against the consumer. Weekly special offers by retailers have converted a sizable percentage of the consumer market into persons called brand tramps, in some circles, but whom Wesley Mitchell might have called adepts of "the backward art of spending money." Company pricing policies are fairly well dictated by this fact. Companies will typically respond to a price cut with one of their own. Other players enter here, also. Witness the recent confiscation by the government of a large shipment of somebody's coffee because at some point in the whirlwind of dealing, the economy size was priced a fraction of a cent higher than the regular size.

The point of this example is to illustrate the kind of game described above. One pricing move in any one of these separate games takes effect simultaneously in all of the games. It may have been motivated by a situation arising in any of the games, and no one outside the company knows which game was the determining factor. Therefore, it is impossible to estimate the utilities involved and, hence, impossible to use game theory to analyze the game. Too often, I think, this kind of difficulty disappears in discussions of the applicability of game theory under the "assuming we know the utilities" clause. In a situation such as we have described here, the utilities could not be known.

It is probably true that pricing games are somewhat less than typical in terms of the number of simultaneous games going on. However, there is another reason which, I suspect, explains why most actual competitive situations would not be analyzed in terms of game theory, even if on all other counts, they could be. The word "suspect" is intended to forewarn that this argument will not be proved, only raised. The question at issue has to do with the chance element in games. While we did not discuss the chance element in games previously, it is a fact that chance elements can readily be incorporated in the analysis of a game. It is equally true that chance elements affect the payoffs in actual business competitive situations. An important question, then, would appear to be: Which has the greater effect on payoffs, competitive behavior, in the game theory sense, or chance?

The relevance of this question can perhaps be illustrated by an example. Assume you intended to devote considerable amounts of time to playing two games: poker and Monopoly. Is there any difference in the way you would apportion your time in studying the theory of these two games? It seems clear that there is. Both games have competitors and both games have chance elements, but the weight of the chance elements in Monopoly so overwhelms the effect of competitive behavior that one would almost certainly ignore the latter in trying to deduce an optimal pattern of play. In poker, competitive behavior is more important and good players notoriously spend considerable time in analyzing the implications of their opponents' actions. Even so, it is probably true that a player who played poker solely in terms of the chance elements would go home a winner. If this kind of distinction is reasonable—and many more examples could be given to make it seem so—then it would follow that a rational business executive should give careful consideration to the relative weights of these two components before he apportioned his resources to their study.

I am not aware of any factual study of this question but my suspicion is that the chance elements have far more effect on payoffs than do competitive actions. If this seems like a shocking statement it may be so partly because of the word "chance." Strictly speaking, once the probabilities are known for a chance device, everything is known about it. This is not the way I am using the word "chance." I mean to include under this word all those cases wherein we do not understand the causal mechanisms which, as scientists, we assume are operative. In this sense, it is chance that accounts for the stunning success of a black eye-patch in selling shirts, but we may hope to understand some of the reasons for the success. In this sense, it is chance that accounts for the failure of a new drug which is effective against acne, and it is chance that accounts for the success of a build-it-yourself harpsichord kit. Obviously, we should eventually be able to understand and predict such occurrences. That chance plays an important role in determining payoffs can hardly be disputed although the relative importance may be. As to that, I am simply stating my opinion.

Game theoretic analyses of competitive situations are difficult and expensive to accomplish. If chance plays the greater role, where should the rational executive put his efforts? I think the answer is obvious. Which is of greater importance: analyzing the game theory

implications of an advertising battle or determining the optimal allocation of a given budget among media? Which is of greater importance: analyzing the game theory implications of pricing strategies
or trying to determine the elasticity of demand? A fast-dealing company in the coffee industry is reputed to have such bad coffee that
they lose customers every time they cut the price, because they
induce people to try their coffee. Allowing for some competitive
exaggeration here, is this company interested in game theoretic analyses? It is not relevant to answer that the company must first analyze
price elasticities, and so forth. Resources are still scarce and we are
not debating about Utopia.

Since the "commonsense" answer to this last argument seems quite
compelling I will devote a paragraph to its refutation. The common-
sense point of view goes like this. Companies wax and wane but
some achieve a commanding position and maintain it. According to
general observation and general consensus, these particular companies
are superb competitors, and no reasonable man would doubt that this
is the explanation for their success. There are two counterarguments
to this. First, there is no reason to believe that the management of
the successful companies is, or ever has been, in the slightest degree
superior to the management of their competitors. Or, in any event,
there is an alternative explanation which has never been refuted.
I will draw an analogy with the famous problem of survival of family
names.[13] Given a number of individuals with a common family
name, and given the probability that a male with this name will
marry and have a son, and so on, what is the probability of a given
number of persons with this name in subsequent generations? The
answer is surprising but indubitable. There is a reasonable probability
of a great number of persons with this name and there is a reasonable probability that there will not be any persons with this name.
But the probability of a moderate number of such individuals is essentially zero. I offer this translation. For the initial number of per-

[13] William Feller, *An Introduction to Probability Theory and Its Applications*
(New York, Wiley, 1950).

sons with the given family name, read initial capital. For the probability of a son, read the probability that the capital will produce an increment. Result: starting with a group of absolutely identical companies, we would expect that after a number of economic generations a few of them would be very large and the others would be out of business. Second, and more plausible, if the management of the successful companies has been superior it could be—and would be, from my point of view—due to their superior assessment of the chance elements, not their superior competitive behavior.

Finally, we may note a more general characteristic of most kinds of competitive business situations which militates against the applicability of the ideas of game theory. There is a basic, paranoid attitude built into most game theory analyses. This is perfectly fitting in zero-sum games but the same attitude carries over into the analyses of cooperative games. This paranoia is observable in the business world precisely in those areas which most closely approximate zero-sum games: games with the government and games with unions. Elsewhere, I think, it doesn't exist. In terms of the scale suggested towards the end of the second section, in most competitive business games the degree of malevolence is essentially zero. This fact somehow makes the game theory analysis distorted. I say "somehow" because it is difficult to verbalize the distinction. Does Chevrolet think, when preparing the next year's design: "This is really going to ruin Ford!" Or do they think that the design is a good one, consumers should like it, their sales should stay up, and they should bet a bigger share of the market? And, with reference to the last, do they actively desire Ford's injury? I think the attitude is more nearly: "We do our best, they do their best, and we'll see what happens." This philosophy, which I think is generally the true one, is just not reflected in game theory.

The Relevance of Game Theory

In planning this conference the gentlemen responsible made certain suggestions concerning the structure of this paper. One of these was that the relevance of game theory might be discussed in terms of business decision-makers, empirical researchers, government policy-makers, and economic theorists. Since I have evaded the spirit of this suggestion it is only fitting that in this last section I should briefly observe the letter.

The first three parts of this paper are devoted to the argument that game theory is basically irrelevant to business decision makers. This evaluation was broad-gauge and was in terms of any of the high hopes usually inspired by acquaintance with game theory. In some specific areas game theory can be relevant. Generally, the closer a given situation approximates a zero-sum game, the greater the likelihood that game theory will be useful. Contract bidding is an example of where game theory can be useful. However, even here, it is worth noting, one of the basic articles abstracts from the game aspects of the situation and treats the problem probabilistically.[14] A good example of a cooperative game is a company with various divisions. Problems of the assignment of joint costs, and related matters, can be handled by means of some of the ideas of game theory, as discussed by Dr. Shubik in a recent article.[15] Other specific examples are available but by no means in sufficient number to affect our already stated conclusion.

With regard to empirical researchers I have very little to say. It is certainly true that game theory provides them means to describe unambiguously even inordinately complex kinds of competitive situations—no mean feat. But actual research along game theory lines might better be directed toward an investigation of some of the basic presuppositions of the theory. For example, are utilities actually measurable on an interval scale in practical business decision situations? What is the typical degree of malevolence? How well does the estimate of an opponent's utility compare with his actual utility? These are some of the questions which need answering.

[14] Lawrence Friedman, "A Competitive Bidding Strategy," *Operations Research*, Vol. 4, no. 1 (February, 1956), p. 104.

[15] Martin Shubik, "Incentives, Decentralized Control, the Assignment of Joint Costs and Internal Pricing," *Management Science*, Vol. 8, no. 3 (April, 1962).

Government policy makers seem to me to be a curious lot. That game theory can be useful in understanding them, I take to be demonstrated by the recent book of Buchanan and Tullock, *The Calculus of Consent.*[16] However, this is not game theory as applied to competitive business behavior, which I am assuming was the intention of the suggestions mentioned above. In this more particular sense game theory is probably of no use to them in formulating policy, but it may be of use to them in defending policy. For example, game theory shows that games with side payments and other forms of overt cooperation can lead to better results for everyone, in some cases, than can noncooperative games. This fact was discovered long ago in practice, and I am sure that government policy will continue to ignore it in the future—for good reason. Many governmental functions are of the nature of arbitration procedures. If game theory provides support for an already taken decision it will probably be used. If it doesn't, then "public interest" will be used instead of game theory. It has been suggested that game theory has had major consequences for various kinds of governmental negotiations. One cannot help wondering whether the theory would have been so eagerly embraced if it were not so pessimistically inclined.

That game theory is of direct and important consequence to economic theorists is beyond question. Since I am not an economist, and since I am in the presence of professional economists, it would require boundless temerity for me to undertake to detail the contributions of game theory to economic theory. Therefore, I will be content to instance the already cited book by Dr. Shubik as an outstanding example of the relevance of game theory in this context. However, there are two questions which arise as a result of the position taken in this presentation and which, therefore, it behooves me to answer. First, if economic theory subsumes behavior in the business world, and if game theory is subject to some fatal strictures in terms of applications to the business world, then, how can game

[16] James M. Buchanan and Gordon Tullock, *The Calculus of Consent* (Ann Arbor, The University of Michigan Press, 1962).

theory be relevant to economic theory? My answer is that it is particularly relevant because of the deepened understanding, mentioned in the first section. Specifically, game theory has revealed the consequences of many assumptions concerning key concepts of economic theory: perfect information, rationality, values, utilities, and so forth. As a result, it has greatly clarified our understanding of some of the difficulties connected with these concepts. Second, if game theory is relevant to economic theory, and if economic theory is relevant to business behavior, why, then, is game theory not relevant to business behavior? Simply because "relevance" is not a transitive relation.

SIMULATION AND GAMING: THEIR VALUE TO THE STUDY OF PRICING AND OTHER MARKET VARIABLES

BY MARTIN SHUBIK, MEMBER OF THE MATHEMATICS DIVISION, IBM THOMAS J. WATSON RESEARCH CENTER, YORKTOWN HEIGHTS, NEW YORK

The advent of the high-speed digital computer is already having a profound effect upon economic life, although, with little doubt, its potential has barely begun to be realized. The fabric of economic life is being influenced. In the course of time this will become evident at many levels. This is being, and will be further reflected in the methods utilized by government policy makers, management and entrepreneurs, and empirical research workers, as well as economic theorists.

The four major areas of development brought about by the computer age which are of most interest to those involved in economic life are: 1) data processing; 2) analytical methods; 3) simulation; and 4) gaming. The first two have had their scope considerably extended and, as is often the case, sufficiently large quantitative changes have brought with them qualitative changes, as well. The last two scarcely existed before the computer age.

As a matter of historical interest, we may note that the London School of Economics has had, for many years, an hydraulic model of a macroeconomic system which provides an analogue simulation of the economy; furthermore, the armed forces have employed sand tables to provide a simulated environment for war games or have used maneuvers to supply a real environment for war games. Even so, simulation and gaming were so severely limited by the lack of methods for the manipulation of large-scale models of the environment that they were of little if any use to the investigation of economic affairs. It is my contention that this is beginning to change and will continue to do so rapidly in the years ahead.

Although advances in data processing and analytical methods are perhaps even of greater immediate importance to the current economic scene than are simulation and gaming, this paper will be confined to the latter two.

Simulation

A simulation of a system or an organism is the operation of a model or simulator which is a representation of the system or organism. The operation of the model can be studied, and from it, properties concerning the behavior of the actual system are inferred. Among the reasons for constructing a simulation are that the model is amenable to manipulations which would be too expensive, impracticable, or difficult to perform on the entity it portrays.

The word, simulation, and the phrase, manipulation of a model, are essentially synonyms except that the latter might be taken to include analytical methods, while the former is limited to operations by digital computer or analogue devices.

Computer simulation, man-machine simulation, gaming, and Monte Carlo methods are often all classed as simulation. It is important to make clear the distinctions between these very different methods designed for different purposes. Not all of them are of the same importance to economic affairs. Our major distinction is between gaming and simulation. Gaming is an experimental or training device which may or may not make use of a simulated environment, but is invariably concerned with studying human behavior or teaching individuals. In a simulation the behavior of the components is taken as given. The actual presence of individuals is not necessary to a simulation, but is to a game. We return, later, to a discussion of gaming.

MONTE CARLO METHODS AND TACTICAL SIMULATIONS

The highly technical developments of Monte Carlo methods are of least immediate importance to those interested in economic policy or operations. Their uses have been primarily in physics and engineering.[1] No further discussion of them is given here, other than to note that they form a part of the broad area referred to as simulation.

Simulation, as it is used in the behavioral sciences, is a tool for exploration and for the evaluation and comparison of many contingencies. It is a tool whose main power comes from its being a flexible instrument for the study of an organization. It provides a natural mechanism for the exploration of decision rules. The resemblance of the simulation to the relevant features of the organization being studied may often be important. The model itself, as well as the results of manipulating it, may be of considerable worth.

A distinction can be made between two broad categories of simulation of interest to the economist, policy maker, or management scientist. Suggested names for the categories are tactical and strategic simulation. The distinction between the two is between simulation used as a device to compare the results of alternative decision rules within relatively well-defined structures, and simulation used primarily to explore the behavioral properties and the validity of relatively ill-defined models. The distinction is not totally clear-cut; however, several examples will help to clarify it.

Certain problems in operations research and applied microeconomics can be specified clearly and described accurately, in mathematical form. The resultant systems can be simulated to provide the answers to many questions which, in general, could not be obtained as well, if at all, by analytical methods. Traffic scheduling [2] waiting-line,[3] and

[1] A. W. Marshall, "Experimentation by Simulation and Monte Carlo," Santa Monica, RAND, 1958, p. 1174.

[2] N. H. Jennings and J. H. Dickens, "Computer Simulation of Peak Hour Operations in a Bus Terminal," *Management Science* (October, 1958), 106–20.

[3] A. Cobhom, "Priority Assignment in Waiting Line Problems," *Journal of Operations Research Society of America* (February, 1954), 70–76.

production scheduling problems [4] provide examples wherein the physical system can be relatively accurately described, and questions asked, such as: What is the effect of a new production rule? What is the current mean waiting time for a free line of communication? What is the expected length of queue at a certain production position? These are economically valuable questions but, for the most part, not at the top managerial level. Tactical simulation has provided additional and worthwhile tools to quantitative economics and, as work progresses more knowledge is being added to specialized but highly useful subjects such as inventory theory and production scheduling.

STRATEGIC SIMULATION

The word "strategic" is used here to imply broad or general, and usually refers to situations which are not amenable to careful description or measurement. The construction of the model for a strategic simulation yields in itself much, if not most, of the benefit to be gained from the project. The preliminary operations of the model serve to validate the perceptions of the modelers. Given the description of the behavior of the decision units and the structure of the environment, does the model produce an output, under known conditions, that is a sufficiently good representation of the actions of the organization? This poses many difficult problems of validation.

The mass of institutional data which can be handled by a computer makes it possible to construct detailed micro-models of complex economic systems such as an industry or even aspects of a whole economy. It provides an opportunity for a union of mathematical and institutional approaches. Exploration, insight, "feel," and broad, casual empiricism have been the earmarks of much valuable work in economics and other fields concerned with human behavior. Especially with conjectures and speculations concerning the behavior of the firm in a market or the functioning of special markets or systems

[4] J. R. Jackson, "Simulation Research on Job Shop Production," *Naval Research Logistics Quarterly* (December, 1957), 287–95.

for decentralization, the work involved in checking even the simplest of conjectures may be prohibitively long and expensive. Quick, general simulations are now feasible and may serve as an aid to the intuition, inasmuch as they enable the individual to check more "hunches" and investigate more conjectures than would otherwise be possible.

There is little doubt that one of the most valuable contributions of simulation has been the discipline imposed by the necessity of precisely defining for the computer the model to be investigated. Fortunately, in some ways, the computer is literal minded and has little imagination. If it is fed a model which is logically incomplete or incorrect, it usually will return gibberish or will stop. It does not supply left-out steps, nor does it correct statements involving substantive features of a model. This means that as a checking device a simulation is of considerable value. Furthermore, the value is twofold, as the work to obtain an operational simulation imposes method not only upon the checking of models for consistency and completeness, but also on the design of consistent and efficient data-organization processes.

As an applied tool for the firm or governmental agency, the immediate value of a strategic simulation will be in the provision of a consistent data organizing system directed, toward decision making, rather than toward answering policy questions. The reasons are model building and data gathering. Large economic organizations are usually not short paperwork, statistics, reports, documents, and memos. They are, however, often short of statistics or paperwork deemed important by the decision maker or economist engaged in approaching old problems with new sophistication, or in approaching new problems. Sometimes the information is present in a plethora of documents, but the data-processing and information-retrieval costs make it economically unavailable.

It must be stressed that the short-run costs of gathering information and the long-run costs can be vastly different. The approach of simulation as an aid to management and policy is both organismic and oriented toward decision making. This means that once a simulator is in place, although it is designed to be of operational worth, it may be only after the information-processing system has been established for some time, that the cost of providing the information to the simulator becomes small. Furthermore, technological substitution takes place throughout the data-processing system. Reports are handled differently. Previously performed routines may be totally changed or abandoned. Until the method for handling new information is established, the organization of flows created and the usefulness of the new information demonstrated, the expense of the new approach is great and the offsetting immediate revenues are few, if any.

There is a sociology as well as a technology that accompanies the application of any body of knowledge or science. Not only must the new tools and techniques exist and meet technological standards, but organizations must be prepared to use them and individuals must be willing to change and adapt. In general this is a slow process. Thus, although there is no doubt that the tools and techniques for large-scale simulation are available, a lengthy and difficult process of integration into organizations must take place before much of the potential can be tapped.

TOOLS AND TECHNIQUES

The size, speed, and availability of computers, at least in the United States, is such that they do not provide the important limitations on the possibilities of simulation. Basic arithmetic and logic operations can be performed in times as short as millionths of a second, on the larger machines. Most major universities, government agencies, and large corporations now have these machines or have easy access to them. Technical staffs programmers and machine personnel were relatively short a few years ago; however, this bottleneck no longer exists.

A major barrier to the use of machine methods in human affairs has been, and to some extent, still is, the difficulty in communication between the man and the machine. There are still many improvements to be made in input, output, and display devices and techniques. As has already been noted, models have to be carefully formulated for a computer. It is not possible to communicate your desires by merely talking to it. The language problem presents an important obstacle. In order to proceed from a verbal description to a computer simulation, as many as five languages may be needed. The verbal description of the problem may be translated into a mathematical model and/or a set of flow diagrams, these in turn may be translated into a source language, which is then automatically translated by a machine program into an object language. The machine then operates the simulation from the last of these languages. It is possible to proceed directly from the verbal description to the machine language; however, in general, there are few individuals trained to use both and, furthermore, the process is wasteful in time.

Great advances have been made, during the past few years, in the design of special languages to make the task of modeling easier and more natural. FORTRAN,[5] SIMPAC[6] and SIMSCRIPT[7] are among the languages making the translation task easier. Flow diagramming and these special languages are now relatively easy to learn. One or two days is sufficient to obtain a reasonable proficiency in flow diagramming and two or three weeks suffices for a language such as FORTRAN. They are useful in themselves, inasmuch as they are more flexible than mathematical notation and more precise than English.

A SIMPLE EXAMPLE

The example presented here is, of necessity, very simple; however, it serves the purpose of demonstrating the methods of simula-

[5] IBM, "Programs Review for FORTRAN for the IBM 704," (New York, IBM, c. 1957).

[6] M. Lackner, "SIMPAC," Santa Monica, S.D.C., 1962, mimeographed.

[7] H. M. Markowitz, B. Hausner, and H. W. Karr, "SIMSCRIPT," Santa Monica, RAND, RM 3310-PR, Nov. 1962.

tion and serves as a basis from which to point out the difficulties
faced in dealing with business or managerial problems.

The verbal description of the problem is given first. There are
two competing businesses which sell substitutable shelf items in a
local market. They know that they cannot afford to charge different
prices, as their goods are regarded as undifferentiated to the customers.
During each period there is a nominal market split. We have observed that the first firm obtains a certain proportion of the market when both have the item on hand. However, if the stock of
one firm is depleted, all the additional demand is channeled to the
other up to its ability to fulfill that extra demand.

We wish to examine the effect of a change in inventory policy by
one of the firms. Suppose that both firms have started each week with
a constant inventory level and we have observed the result of this
policy. We now wish to consider what would happen if we change
our policy so that at the start of each week we have on hand an
amount equal to the demand made upon us during the previous week.

This problem can now be translated to a mathematical formulation. It is assumed that the total market demand at any period, t, is
a random variable, z_t, whose distribution has been determined from
previous information. When both have inventories the market is split
in segments of $a_t^1{}_{-1}$ and $a_t^2{}_{-1}$ where $a_t^1{}_{-1} + a_t^2{}_{-1} = 1$. At the beginning of any period t, the first firm will have an amount $x_t^1 = k$,
a constant. The second firm has $x_t^2 = d_t^2{}_{-1}$ which is the demand
made upon it in the previous period. The sales of a firm are the minimum of the demand upon it or its inventory. $s_t^1 = \min(x_t^1, d_t^1)$.

Suppose that we wish to study the behavior of the market for some
period of time, says, five years. The flow diagram below describes the
steps in the simulation. Each box represents a set of actions. The
ovals contain possible branches in the program. The flow thus indicates that the first event is the determination of the demand for the
initial period. In a case as simple as this, this may actually be performed by rolling a set of dice. After this has been done, the program
calculates the market share to be offered to each firm. The third item,

the first oval in the flow diagram, then queries to see if both can satisfy the demand. If they can, the program then checks on the inventory policies and makes the appropriate orders for the firms. The bookkeeping for the results of the period is then performed. The

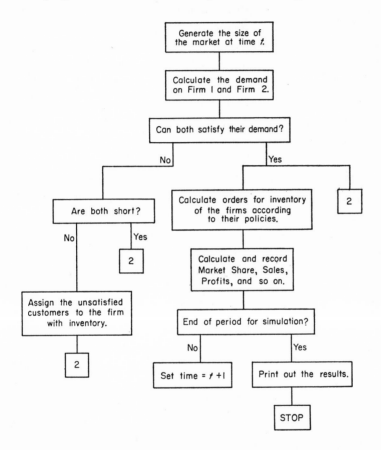

program then proceeds to check if this is the last period in the five years being investigated. If it is, the computer is instructed to print out the results and to stop. If it is not, then the "clock" advances to the next period, a new demand is generated, and the program is repeated, thereby generating a new period of history. If at least one firm cannot satisfy its demand, the program is questioned to find out if only one, or if both firms are in short supply. If both firms are short, there is nothing more to be done. The customers are left unsatisfied and the program returns to 2 for the inventory orders and bookkeeping. If only one firm is short, the customers are assigned to its competitor, after which the program returns to 2.

In order to obtain the fluctuating demand we suggested that a pair of dice could be rolled each period. Instead of using them, we might have used a roulette wheel with the compartments marked so that the probability of obtaining a number on the wheel would coincide with the probability of the market being a certain size. The roulette wheel as a method for generating events which occur randomly gives rise to the name of the Monte Carlo method.

Instead of obtaining the random numbers by hand, which can be done in this simple case, a digital computer can be used to generate the numbers and to run the program and record results. For this to be done, the information from the mathematical formulation and the flow diagrams is translated into one of the several possible source languages. The two instructions below are a translation of the second box in the flow diagram into FORTRAN language:

$$\mathrm{DEM_1 = A_1(NOW\text{-}1) \quad * \quad Z \ (NOW)}$$
$$\mathrm{DEM_2 = A_2(NOW\text{-}2) \quad * \quad Z \ (NOW)}$$

The machine takes a program written in this language, translates it into its own language, and from that the simulation is run. A history of the example given above is traced out for ten periods. This was actually done by rolling dice. In the calculation, sales have been rounded off to the nearest $\frac{1}{2}$ unit. It may be observed from Figs. 1 and 2 that the inventory policy of the second firm causes far greater fluctuations in orders than does the policy of the first firm.

In a problem in physics the precise form of behavior of, say, an elementary particle, may be known. The behavior of a complicated system based upon the interaction of many particles is not known, but by the use of Monte Carlo methods it is possible to evaluate it without having to solve the resulting system of equations.

Suppose $x_1^1 k = 20$ and $x_1^2 = 20$

Also $a_0^1 = a_0^2 = \frac{1}{2}$

Demand $Z_t = 5 x$ (number of spots on two thrown dice)

MARKET HISTORY

	Market Demand Z_t	Stocks Firm 1 x_t^1	Stocks Firm 2 x_t^2	Market Share Firm 1 a_t^1	Market Share Firm 2 a_t^2	Stock Order Firm 1 r_t^1	Stock Order Firm 2 r_t^2	Sales Firm 1 S_t^1	Sales Firm 2 S_t^2
$t = 1$	25	20	20	½	½	—	—	12½	12½
2	30	20	12½	½	½	12½	5	17½	12½
3	30	20	15	7/12	5/12	17½	15	17½	12½
4	25	20	12½	7/12	5/12	17½	10	14½	10½
5	40	20	10½	7/12	5/12	14½	8½	20	10½
6	45	20	16½	7/12	5/12	**20**	16½	20	16½
7	50	20	19	7/12	5/12	20	19	20	19
8	35	20	21	7/12	**5/12**	20	21	20	14½
9	40	20	14½	7/12	**5/12**	20	8	20	14½
10	40	20	16½	7/12	5/12	20	16½	20	16½

In the inventory competitive problem just described, the behavior of the market demand may be difficult to describe with any accuracy. There may be many other parts of the system which are difficult to portray. If the model is used without sufficient care, spurious conclusions may be drawn. However if the results are used for comparative purposes, even with models of dubious accuracy, it may be possible to perform a useful comparative evaluation of the gross characteristics of alternative policies.

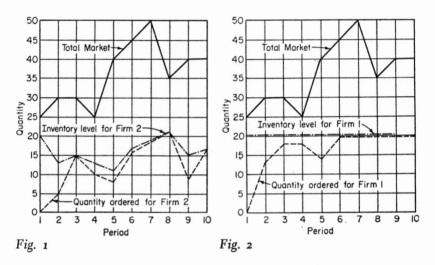

Fig. 1   *Fig. 2*

Gaming

Although it has been common to use the word "gaming" and "simulation" interchangeably, much confusion can be caused by doing so. In general, individuals are referring to gaming in a simulated environment when they use the word simulation in reference to a game. There are many types of game and many purposes for which games can be used. The three major divisions are games for teaching, experimentation, and operational purposes. All these are of interest to the economist or policy maker. Many games do not need computers in order to be played. Military games such as maneuvers, for example, make use of a real rather than a simulated environment;

other military games use an analogue simulation for the environment, such as a sand table. Several simple production games and marketing exercises have been designed to be played with pencil and paper. However, when the environment in which the game is to be played becomes complex and when the information to be presented to the players involves numerical displays, a digital computer becomes a necessity.

In many areas of economic investigation there are three major aspects of interest to the observer. They are: 1) an adequate description of the environment in which the activity takes place; 2) an understanding of the plans, strategies, and motivations of the decision makers; and 3) an ability to predict what will happen if the decision makers carry out their plans, given the environment. A simulation takes the first two items as given and provides a method for obtaining the third. Gaming in a simulated environment may be used as a method whereby the first is taken as given, the outcome of the game is observed, and inferences are made concerning the intents and motivations of the players. This would be so in experimental gaming.

In operational gaming, the environment may be taken as given and the players may then proceed to try out different plans and strategies in order to examine their outcomes. Returning to the simple example of a simulation provided above, this could easily be converted into a simple but useful operational game. Instead of writing the decision-rules for inventory-ordering policies and having the computer automatically follow these rules during the simulation, at each point when an inventory decision must be made it would be possible to have the program stop until an inventory order has been made by individuals gaming the role of the inventory manager of each firm. It may be advantageous to have new managers exposed to an intensive period of synthetic experience, in this manner. Furthermore, experienced managers are afforded an opportunity to try out "harebrained" schemes that they might want to experiment with, but feel would be too dangerous to risk in their real environment.

Other ways in which games may be classified concern the degree of control and formalization in the structure of the game, and the levels of richness of the environment. Many of the psychologists' experimental games tend to be extremely impoverished in environmental setting and highly controlled with respect to the rules and manner of play. At the other extreme, games designed as operational exercises for politico-diplomatic negotiations may be very loose in structure. In the latter case expert referees may decide upon rules and permissible strategies as the games progresses. The experimental controls may be few or nonexistent. The exercise may have more in common with a group psychodynamic process than with any formal theory of games.

Many of the business and market games fall between the two extremes noted above. They tend to have a relatively rich environment; however, the rules are fairly well known and the economic mechanism being portrayed usually gives a great deal of structure to the situation.

Some Examples of Simulation

Large-scale simulation in economics has been applied to problems at several levels. In order to provide a broad sketch of the work, six projects are discussed. They are the "Microanalysis of Socioeconomic Systems," by Orcutt, Rivlin, and associates; [8] Simulations of the Shoe, Leather and Hide Sequence, by Kalman Cohen; [9] the work in "Industrial Dynamics," by J. W. Forrester; [10] the Simulation of Market Processes by Balderston and Hoggatt; [11] a Simulation of Trust Investment by Geoffrey Clarkson; [12] and *The Behavioral Theory of the Firm* by Cyert and March.[13] Most of the work in simulation has been

[8] G. H. Orcutt, M. Greenberger, S. Korbel, and A. M. Rivlin, *Microanalysis of Socioeconomic Systems: A Simulation Study* (New York, Harpers, 1961).

[9] K. Cohen, *Computer Models of the Shoe, Leather, Hide Sequence* (Englewood Cliffs, Prentice Hall, 1960).

[10] J. W. Forrester, *Industrial Dynamics* (Cambridge, The M.I.T. Press, 1961).

[11] F. Balderston and A. C. Hoggatt, "The Simulation of Market Processes," Berkeley, Management Science Research Group, Working Paper 22, October, 1960, mimeographed.

[12] G. P. E. Clarkson, "A Simulation of Trust Investment," Pittsburgh, Behavioral Theory of the Firm, Working Paper 32, May, 1961, mimeographed.

[13] R. M. Cyert and J. G. March, "The Behavioral Theory of the Firm, A Behavioral Science—Economics Analysis," Pittsburgh, 1962, mimeographed.

done very recently as can be seen by observing that the earliest date on the published results of the projects noted here is 1959. In all of these projects the mere production of a logically consistent and relatively complete model of the economic activity being investigated is a major task.

Perhaps the most ambitious and the most important attempt at economic simulation has been that of Orcutt's group. In light of the published work, the simulation is more accurately described as a demographic model of the United States rather than as a general socioeconomic system. However, the authors point out that their study is "dedicated to the task of providing a means for bridging the gap between knowledge about institutions and decision units and prediction about socioeconomic aggregates."

They have constructed a simulation which provides a unified network for assembling the many separate studies done on varying aspects of birth, death, marriage, and divorce. The importance of this type of work to the construction of tools for policy making is stressed and, although the authors have not yet extended their model beyond its demographic parts, a discussion is provided indicating the lines along which models for the labor force, the demand for higher education, and debt and liquid asset behavior can be joined to the current model.

A representative sample of households was taken initially (the model has used approximately 4,500 households composed of 10,300 individuals). The sample for the experiments reported on was based on the 1950 Census and survey interviews administered by the Survey Research Center at the University of Michigan.

Given the initial composition of the sample population, a "pass" of the program consists in updating the monthly changes in every household. One after the other, each household is examined to determine the change in state called for by the various demographic routines. Each individual is examined according to his or her detailed characteristics, the "dice are loaded" accordingly, and rolled to determine the changes that may take place. For example, the probability of marriage of an eligible daughter will be given for age, race, and marital status, then a random drawing will determine if she is to marry during this month under consideration. As the months advance, the simulation provides a history of the changes of states.

An important feature of simulation used by Orcutt and associates, as well as others, is that it is possible to feed in certain values for variables and, thus, a certain amount of control can be exercised in the isolation of error generation. For example, the simulation may be forced to track an actual series. This means that if we were examining a simulation run and at the end of the first month, the simulated population would not necessarily match the observed population in a historical time series, we could then correct the simulated population, run it again for the next month, correct again, and keep on repeating this procedure. In this manner, errors are not permitted to accumulate. This is obviously not of use for long run forecasting but it is of considerable use in the examination of possible discrepancies caused by sections of the model. Discrepancies can be caused by poor models, or, when a very small population is used to represent a large one, by sampling variation (the scale-down factor here is approximately 15,000 to 1). Methods for correction are discussed. On the IBM 704 the demographic simulation has required 5 minutes per month; on large machines both the time and cost of this can be reduced considerably.

The model by Kalman Cohen used as its empirical basis the studies of Mrs. Mack.[14] The approach adopted was that of modeling the "typical firm." Each sector, retailers, manufacturers, and tanners, has been represented by behavior conditions for the representative firm. These are given as difference equations set down to represent features such as aggregate consumer expenditure on shoes, retailers' sales, anticipations, hide dealers' selling prices, and so forth.

In both his runs and discussion Cohen stresses the difference between "one-period change" models and "process models." These are

[14] R. P. Mack, *Consumption and Business Fluctuations: A Case Study of Shoe, Leather, Hide Sequence* (New York, National Bureau of Economic Research, 1956).

essentially the same as some of the distinctions made by Orcutt in this discussion of methods of tracking the time series. The time period used in this model was also a month, and on an IBM 650 the simulation required 1 minute for a period of the process model and 1¼ minutes for the one-period change models, in which corrections are made every period to prevent the propagation of certain errors.

Both the nature and the aim of the work by J. Forrester and his group differ considerably from the projects noted above. In order to appreciate the possible value of his approach, we must make several distinctions. Unlike most of the others working with large-scale simulation, Forrester's group has made a direct contribution to the computer techniques involved. Much of the book, *Industrial Dynamics*, is devoted to an exposition of a special computer language designed to facilitate the writing of certain types of computer simulation programs. This is the language known as DYNAMO.

The avowed intent of the industrial dynamics models is to provide simulation aid to the management of firms. There are several firms, including Sprague Electric and Hughes Aircraft, which have had projects utilizing these methods. The approach to questions to be answered by the simulation and validation of results is somewhat different from those of Orcutt or Cohen.

Six types of flows are identified for the firm. They are: information, material, orders, money, personnel and population, and capital equipment. Forrester's attitude to the problems of data gathering and statistics can be illustrated by his comment: "Many persons discount the potential utility of models of industrial operations on the assumption that we lack adequate data upon which to base a model. They believe that the first step must be extensive collecting of statistical data. Exactly the reverse is true." He stresses a cut-and-try approach heavily dependent upon the manager's insights and views of the environment. He argues that much of the worth of the models comes from their "precision," not their accuracy. The stated purpose of the work is "to aid in designing better management systems." It is pointed out that, to a great extent, the evaluation of improved managerial effectiveness rests on subjective judgments of managers in regard to the amount of help they have received. As Forrester views his work as an applied tool of immediate applicability to industry, his book even includes a chapter on the staffing of a group to construct models within a business.

The worth of the language, DYNAMO, depends upon several technical questions of modeling and computer operations (such as, does the system have simultaneous equations in it?) Details may be omitted here. For certain types of models which occur in economics and business the language may be good, for others this is not so. The selection of an appropriate language in which to program a simulation presents a technical problem, but it is sufficiently important that even a manager or executive interested in having a model of an operation made should be aware of some of the major limitations of different languages.

The work of Balderston and Hoggatt on the simulation of market processes differs from all three projects noted above. In many ways it is closer to the interests of the mathematical economist, microeconomic theorist, and marketing theorist. They investigate a three-level market with suppliers (modeled using Balderston's study of the West Coast lumber industry), wholesalers, and retailers. Their interests have focused on three types of variables in this model: the traditional economic features of prices, inventories, costs, and amounts traded; the features of more concern to marketing and decision theory, such as costs of information, organization, and volume of messages generated; and more sociological features, such as the formation of market segments and the isolation, evolution, and decay of these segments.

There are many results and insights of interest to the price theorist and student of market structure. Even behind the seeming purity of the most abstract and general economic theory, there are some implicit or explicit assumptions concerning the nature of the institutions comprising the market mechanism and the degree of efficiency with which they function. In this work they are made explicit and a start has been made in interpreting the effect of changes in this level of the market mechanism.

Although the authors comment that much of the general structure of the model was based on a particular industry and the parameter values for the experimental runs were selected from a study of the industry, no attempt was made to claim "realism" or any close fit to the specific industry, in its current state. Many approximations were made which served the authors' purpose producing a complex, but still sufficiently simple model to investigate the influence of broad economic, informational, and sociological factors.

Cyert and March and others at the Carnegie Institute of Technology, have been working on a behavioral theory of the firm. This differs from the more classical economic models of economic behavior inasmuch as it concentrates on the firm as an adaptively rational entity characterized by strivings in four areas. They are: 1) quasi-resolution of conflict; 2) uncertainty avoidance; 3) problemistic search; and 4) organizational learning. They stress that the firm as an organization has several decision centers; its goals are influenced by experience which modifies the aspiration levels of its members. The firm attempts to avoid uncertainty, hence, there is a concentration on short-term correction plans to deal with the immediate future, and short-run feedback rather than long-run anticipation. Plans, standard operating procedures, and industry tradition are all used as mechanisms to dampen the degree of uncertainty. The organization devotes its energies to search when confronted with a problem. Its desire to solve problems is motivated, and to a great extent the methods used are straightforward and relatively simple-minded. As the organization learns, there is an adaptation of its search rules, its goals, and its attention rules (i.e. rules determining which problems are to be attended to next).

The authors stress that the natural language to investigate the behavior of organisms with the properties sketched above is that of programming. In an application of a behavioral model to a department in a large department store, Cyert, March, and Moore have attempted to predict sales forecasts, advance orders, reorders, regular pricing, sales pricing, and markdown pricing. They report considerable success in their ability to do so. They were able to predict regular prices to within 1 cent 95 percent, sales prices 96 percent, and markdown prices 88 percent of the time.

The type of model they deal with is closely related to the more general models being dealt with by Simon, Marvin Minsky,[15] Ashby, and others, addressed to the problems of artificial intelligence.

The record of prediction, though impressive, raises questions concerning the differences between the normative and descriptive theories of the firm. The accuracy of prediction may imply that some fairly well-defined rules of thumb concerning price change are being used by the firm; however they do not deal with the possibility that if the members of the firm were aware of the implications of the work of Cyert and March, or of other studies in pricing, they would not be taught that some other pricing policy is better.

The last work to be noted is the Ph.D. thesis of Geoffrey Clarkson, on a simulation of trust investment. A model of the behavior of a trust investment officer is constructed. This model is then used to generate portfolios of several customers of the trust officer. These portfolios are then compared with those selected for the clients and are also compared with the performance of random-selection or simple-selection devices (such as selecting stocks on the basis of the greatest growth over a specified period of time). In four portfolios the agreement is 4 out of 5, 7 out of 9, 7 out of 8, and 6 out of 7, in issues and quantities selected.

Some Examples of Games

The largest and possibly most impressive game used for teaching is the Carnegie Tech. Management Game.[16] This has been a cooperative endeavor by many of the faculty, in the belief that the

[15] M. Minsky, "Artificial Intelligence," *Proceedings of the IRE* (January, 1961).
[16] "The Carnegie Tech. Management Game," "Players Manual," Pittsburgh, 1960, mimeographed.

more realistic a business game they could construct, the greater would be its uses as a tool for teaching and reseach. They selected a specific industry upon which to base their model, that of the packaged detergent. This selection was based upon considerations of the existence of a national market, a small number of firms, and differentiated products. The game has three firms, each with a raw-materials warehouse, production facilities capable of producing different product mixes, a factory warehouse, facilities for research and development, and leased warehouses in four market regions. The game starts with each firm in possession of one product; after this the firms may differentiate, using a basic set of seven raw materials to produce different detergents characterized by washing power, sudsing power, and "gentleness." There are a realistic set of production, research and development, and sales decisions, as well as many basic financial features. The financial conditions of the firms are initially set, depending upon the educational goals of the run. Many of the usual financial instruments are open to the management. Stock can be issued under certain conditions, debentures can be floated, long- and short-term financing can be arranged. Investment in plant is feasible, however, new market locations are not considered.

The players are called upon to analyze the output of the computer and to make their decisions accordingly. They find it necessary to develop both accounting and information processing procedures for the data on manufacturing, marketing, and finance. It is possible to spend for information, via marketing research. Surveys may be purchased and even laboratory tests can be obtained for new products.

This game is aimed at teaching undergraduates and graduate students by developing an environment in which the players could learn at least some managerial skills. The designers emphasize the roles of the manager as an information processor, a planner, a generalist, a specialist, and as an individual in interaction with others.

In order to bring out these features, for each simulated month of play (a move) there are many pieces of information supplied, upon which players may base up to 300 decisions in each period. Various measures of performance are also presented, and these are not always consistent. This calls for consideration of goals by the teams. There is sufficient richness and complexity to permit ten-man teams to play the game, hence internal organization becomes important.

At the end of each simulated year the teams are required to write annual reports to their stockholders, covering much the same type of features as are covered in actual reports. They must also answer to their boards of directors, who may be composed of members of the faculty. The directors also serve to monitor long-range plans which must be made for several reasons, including realistic time lags in financing, plant construction, and marketing effects.

The separation of function in the firms in the various areas of production, finance, and marketing serves to provide the players with specialist as well as generalist training. This is often difficult to obtain with simpler games.

Apart from a concentration upon more or less well-recognized managerial methods and activities, there is an advantage in using a complex management game of this variety, inasmuch as new methods and, possibly, unusual schemes can be tried. Hence, a certain amount of valuable experimentation can be done without the dangers attached to doing so in an actual, operating firm.

The designers have also intended the game to be used as a research instrument, and list oligopoly, aspects of organization theory such as team size, team structure, timing and spacing of moves, information flows, and stability of team membership. Finance, production, and marketing are also amenable to experimentation within this framework.

The game designed by Levitan and Shubik [17] is far simpler than the Carnegie game and is, currently, designed more specifically for investigation and exploration into aspects of oligopolistic behavior and into oligopolistic market structure. The teams make only six

[17] R. Levitan and M. Shubik, "A Business Game for Teaching and Research," Parts I, IIa, New York, IBM, RC-730, 731, July, 1962.

decisions per period in the current program; these include decisions on price, production, advertising, dividends, investment, and inventories. Firms may be bankrupted and new firms may enter the game, according to different profitability criteria. The game has been run under varying information conditions in order to investigate the plausibility of various theories of oligopolistic behavior. Given the market structure programmed within the game, predicted solutions under different oligopolistic conditions have been calculated. By the appropriate selection of the model for the gross aspects of market structure, it is hoped to obtain econometric estimates of the parameters which may be used to characterize a class of actual markets.

By restricting values of parameters, it is possible to use this game to carry out simple learning and organizational experiments. The emphasis throughout is upon the ability to analyze the structure of the game and its output. In its current, relatively simple state, the teaching uses are somewhat limited for functional purposes, although special subroutines, which will overcome some of this limitation, are being added.

The University of California at Los Angeles has a game whose complexity lies between the two games noted. There are also several general management games which can be played without the use of a computer, although it must be noted that as soon as a game attains a degree of complexity, the bookkeeping becomes tedious, and the probability of error becomes great if it is played without the aid of a computer.

There are many games designed to concentrate on single functional areas, such as materials management, production and inventory, logistics, and manpower management. A large game exists for teaching and training students in aspects of international business operations; this is INTOP, designed by a faculty team at the University of Chicago, with Professor Hans Thorelli as coordinator. Several games have had more or less detailed stock-market features attached to them, such as the G. E. Marketing game, run in conjunction with a stock market, by G. J. Feeney and M. Shubik. In this game there are four stocks being traded at four specialist posts where open books are maintained.

Present and Possible Future Uses of Gaming and Simulation: Teaching

The use of gaming in teaching has been sufficiently widespread that it is possible, at this time, to make some assessment of its worth. On the whole, games used in conjunction with courses of study appear to have had educational value. They are of use in teaching procedures, in organizing disparate features of decision problems, and in illustrating principles (there is a danger that they may be used to do this when no principle exists). For business schools, they appear to offer the advantages of "dynamic cases." Although their use to economists has not been as extensive, nor does it appear to be quite as general as their use in teaching, nevertheless, they do offer a method to investigate and illustrate more of the fine structure of the firm, and this is of considerable importance to the future development of theories of microeconomic decision making.

Large computer games are, in general, not cheap to construct. Unfortunately little has been published about the economics of games as teaching devices. From my own observations, costs are an important consideration, but at this time many games for teaching appear to be economically worthwhile.

Simulation is more of an operational and research tool than a didactic device, unless one wishes to include the topic of model building in this category. There is great teaching value to be derived from the constructions of small simulations for computer operation, even if they are never actually run. The discipline of being forced to completely and carefully define the operation of a system, down to the details of initial conditions and the types of inputs, and outputs required, is invaluable. Even merely as a testing device, to find out where an individual's model of a system is logically false, or where a system may be logically correct and complete, but where its behavior indicates important omissions of variables, the discipline of the construction of simulations cannot be overestimated. The added kinesthetics of constructing a simulation, as compared to constructing mathematical models, appears to make it a broader and more easily grasped instrument for understanding the nature of model construction than formal mathematical economics.

RESEARCH

Experimentation with gaming models ranging from very simple duopoly pricing games to complex models with distribution systems has helped to yield insights into some of the economic problems of pricing, bargaining, and market mechanisms. However, at this time, it is likely that there are more immediate difficulties to be faced in the characterization of market structure, the description of distribution systems, and the overall modeling of the economic environment, than in gaming human behavior. The work of Orcutt, Cyert, and March, Balderston and Hoggatt, and others, have all contributed to research in the description of economic systems. It is my belief that this type of work is at the beginning of the growth of mathematical institutional economics which, in the course of its development, will offer opportunities for the classification of general economical structures, and market structures in particular, as well as for the development of the appropriate theory to accompany them.

BUSINESS DECISION MAKING AND GOVERNMENT POLICY MAKING

The methodologies we have discussed are relatively new, and even if they were to prove undeniably successful, it would take many years before they had their impact on operations. The bringing in of radically new approaches and techniques usually takes a sizable fraction of a generation. The mere problem of long-run economies in data gathering makes the value of simulation depend heavily upon the current revolution in the computerization of record-keeping, at the levels of the firm and the government. It is not unreasonable however, to expect that within twenty years many large firms and sections of the government will have detailed simulations of different aspects of the environment in which they operate. If they do so, they will be in a position to explore policy alternatives and, in some cases, will also find it worthwhile to use their simulations to provide the environment for operational games in the same way as military operational games are used today. There is no royal road to this state of affairs, nor will it necessarily herald the millenium. A new methodology is becoming available at the appropriate time, when the increase in speed of technological change, joined with the size of population and the complexity of modern society, make it imperative for us to be in a position to examine and integrate models of economic fine structure.

Some of the work already performed has shown that it is possible to simulate, with a fair degree of accuracy, certain detailed aspects of behavior in setting prices. Computer programs are currently being utilized to calculate bids on oil leases and on municipal bonds.

Gaming, utilizing varying amounts of information, has illustrated many of the difficulties in obtaining meaningful definitions of concepts of competition, collusion, and communication in oligopolistic markets. A combination of simulation of oligopolistic environments and gaming within these environments, to understand the relationship between motivation, environment, and behavior, should eventually be of importance to social policy, in general, and to control of industry, in particular.

Simulations of distribution systems and transportation systems are feasible and give promise of supplying the tools to investigate industrial and social costs, to evaluate the worth of policy and structural changes, and to estimate the changes in price structure that may result.

The Effect of Simulation and Gaming on the Study of Markets.

In the previous sections an exposition of the nature of simulation and gaming has been presented, together with an overview of much of the work in progress. In this section we address ourselves to interpreting the effect of this work upon our understanding of price and, somewhat more generally, markets.

The advance of work in operations research as applied to marketing and the work on pricing exemplified by that of Cyert and March have begun to remove the aura of mystery about pricing, sales markdowns, and the general area of tactics and infighting over price. In many ways the work may be regarded as a natural successor to the technique of scientific management. The Gantt chart and the stopwatch are no longer the symbols of investigation, but in the new and more sophisticated environment they are replaced by flow diagrams and heuristics (another name for a formalization of a rule of thumb). Although we still lack satisfactory theories to explain why prices or advertising budgets are set in a certain manner, we are at least beginning to find out, in a systematic manner, how prices are set, sales determined, and markdowns selected. The economy is run, and it is not run by supermen; when thousands of prices must be set, someone sets them with dispatch. When an advertising manager is faced with submitting a budget he does so and meets his deadline, although his actions may not conform to all the laws of rational behavior. In the process of doing careful microeconomic work, the understanding of how pricing processes work has begun to provide leads to an understanding of why they work, and even to provide the appropriate considerations for those who wish to construct normative theories. Thus, for example, the cost of decision making and the sheer magnitude of the number of decisions have been shown to be far more important than is indicated by most writings in microeconomic theory prior to 1950.

The direct and relatively short–term effect, upon business executives and upon operations research workers, of the work to date is that many of the actions and routines of lower and middle management which were previously regarded (at least in popular utterances) as being peculiarly human, can be performed by computer programs. Flow diagrams, formalized protocols, and heuristics are about to become standard methods for explaining and unveiling many levels of decision processes. In each attempt to trace through a process there may no doubt be an extremely important unexplained residual. It is toward a better understanding and control over that residual that the energies of the affected managers should be channeled.

The empiricist is affected directly, inasmuch as it is now becoming feasible to gather, classify, and study a sufficient number of cases to begin to present a detailed picture of tactical behavior, at least, in many markets.

The mere growth of the appreciation and knowledge of the fine structure of the operations of firms and markets is having a direct impact upon the economic theorist. There is no single supremely rational theory for oligopolistic behavior. Many competing normative theories can be constructed. What are the criteria for choosing among them? They reflect not only value systems, but beliefs concerning the structure of the markets, and the importance of variables and relations in these markets. Even the purest of normative theorists is now confronted with the need to reexamine his selection of variables in his attempts to explain market behavior. A glance at the literature of economic theory of marketing, advertising, distribution, product variation, and intermediate markets indicates the size of the gap in our knowledge. It is the filling of this gap that is beginning to provide the material for the construction of better theory; and work both on the simulation of decisions and on the simulation of market structure is providing the material.

In any oligopolistic market there is a continuum of states between complete cooperation or collusion and outright warfare. There are many possibilities for different degrees of collusion to exist, and the level of collusion reflects sociological communications and information features concerning the economy. Experimental gaming, which, as applied to economic problems, is still in its infancy, has started to provide some insight into the plausibility of various theories of oligopolistic behavior and the possibilities of enforcement of market states under varying information and communication conditions. In the past few years attempts have been made to construct some measures of the cooperation in experimental games and in game theoretic structures. These attempts may be regarded as harbingers of the eventual construction of measures to evaluate the degree of collusion in a market.

What added insights have been gleaned by the new methods, and what old observations and ideas have been reinforced? In the realms of behavior, it has been shown that it is possible to model, in some cases, actual current pricing practices. In modeling of markets and in gaming, from observations, operations research work, and experimentation, price appears to be a competitive variable which is used less than is usually indicated by the role assigned to it in economic writings. Product variation, innovation, and other market variables account for most of the dynamic aspects of oligopoly. In many markets, price is regarded as too dangerous a weapon to be used extensively. The spread between price and costs serves as a gauge which activates the pressure for internal controls of the firm, such as a cost drive. As has been noted by Cyert and March, uncertainty surrogates are sought. Inasmuch as it is possible, both environmental and oligopolistic uncertainties are to be avoided.

Experimental gaming results have shown the tendency for the emergence of a noncooperative equilibrium level of prices and the theoretical basis for this type of policy is essentially inner-directed. In some games, especially where the monetary rewards to the players have been low, "beat-the-average" behavior offers a reasonable explanation of the observations. This type of behavior comes from using as measures of performance the firm's status relative to its competitors.

The nature of the noncooperative equilibrium and beat-the-average solutions can be seen from their formal definitions. Suppose that there are n firms in competition; each firm has a set of strategies, S_i, where the goals or payoff to the ith firm is denoted by P_i $(s_1, s_2, \ldots s_n)$, where s_i is a strategy from the set, S_i. The strategies

$(\bar{s}_1, \bar{s}_2. \ldots \bar{s}_n)$ form a noncooperative equilibrium point if for all the firms i

$$\text{Maximum} \quad P_i (\bar{s}_1, \bar{s}_2. \ldots \bar{s}_{i-1}, s_i, \bar{s}_{1+i}. \ldots \bar{s}_n)$$
$$s_i \text{ in } S_i$$

is such that $s_i = \bar{s}_i$. This states that if each individual assumes that the strategies of his competitors are given and unaffected by his own decisions, he will select that strategy $\bar{s}_i$ which maximizes the achievement of his goal. If the competitors were to engage in collusion they could earn even larger profits, but in the absence of cooperation by other firms $\bar{s}_i$ is the best that i can do for itself.

This concept of a noncooperative solution, with modifications to take into account entry and exit, is basic to many economic models, including those of Cournot, Bertrand, Edgeworth, Mrs. Robinson, Chamberlain, and Stackelberg. When the number of firms is large, and other conditions are appropriate this is equivalent to competitive conditions in a market.

The beat-the-average solution has the individual firm measuring its performance against that of its competitors. If the profit of the firm i, which is one of n's competitors, is denoted by P_i, then the average profit of the other competitors is given by:

$$\frac{1}{n-1} \sum_{j \neq i} P_j$$

If firm i is to beat this average yield, its own profit must exceed the average figure. Indeed, it will seek a strategy, s_i, which makes the difference between the two as large as possible. Formally, this is defined as the equation:

$$\text{Maximum} \atop s_i \text{ in } S_i \quad \left[P_i - \frac{1}{n-1} \sum_j P_j \right] \quad \text{where } j \neq i$$

Let us consider a set of parameters, θ_{ij}, which measures the degree of cooperation between firms i and j. Then suppose each firm were trying to maximize

$$\pi_i = \sum \theta_{ij} P_j$$

then the noncooperative equilibrium is characterized $\theta_{ii} = 1$ and $\theta_{ij} = 0$. The firms are "inner directed"; only their welfare counts. The beat-the-average solution is characterized by $\theta_{ii} = 1$, and $\theta_{ij} = -1/(n-1)$, which indicates a competitive regard for the profits of others.

It can be shown in game models of markets that there easily may be considerable ranges of price levels which are in equilibrium. This indicates the possibility of a certain amount of leeway in prices, bounded only by new entry. Thus, although to a certain extent, in game analysis and in gaming the predictions of Cournot, Edgeworth, Chamberlain, and others are confirmed, they are also modified and extended.

Experimentation, together with theoretical work in bargaining and bidding, has begun to indicate the importance of the role of information conditions. These conditions include lack of knowledge concerning moves of the competition, lack of knowledge concerning costs of the competition, or their evaluation of items of competitive interest, and also the amount of customers' understanding and knowledge of a product. In all categories, it has been indicated in the results of Seigal, Fouraker, Hoggatt, Balderston, Shubik, Vickrey, and others, that the variance in the range of prices is inversely related to the numbers of competitors and to the numbers of the types of information.

The simulation of intermediate markets and the actual use of bidding-evaluation programs in the municipal bond market have stressed the role of intermediate market mechanisms as information and evaluation brokers. There is a price and cost structure to information and evaluation which is, of itself, an important factor in the determination of price.

With considerable pomp, it has been observed that war is far too important a subject to be left to generals; it is my opinion that generals may help in the study of war. Economic policy is far too important a subject to be left to lawyers and legislators; I believe that economic analysis may help in the study of economic policy. The work described here is by no means refined, but it does represent a step toward the development of techniques and measures for understanding markets and price structure, and as such should be fostered, supported, and followed by governmental agencies such as the Department of Justice, in attempts to enforce an economically meaningful policy for social control of industry.

The methodological tools provided by gaming and simulation are making it feasible to uncover and examine in an organized manner much of the important fine structure of the firm and markets in which firms operate. Methodology and techniques alone do not provide answers or cure-alls. However, the progress to date and the costs of the progress in gaming and simulation indicate that they can be of immediate and direct use in business operations, that they are beginning to supply data and enlarge the knowledge of both the empiricist and economic theorists, and that they are beginning to provide a base for the construction of aids to guide in the framing of policy.

INTERACTIONS OF ECONOMIC THEORY AND OPERATIONS RESEARCH

BY GEOFFREY P. E. CLARKSON, ASSISTANT PROFESSOR IN THE SCHOOL OF INDUSTRIAL MANAGEMENT, THE MASSACHUSETTS INSTITUTE OF TECHNOLOGY

In the last few years an increasing amount of attention has been paid to the theoretical and technical developments that have evolved from the interaction of economic theory and operations research. During this period a number of papers have appeared which review the advances in economic theory as well as in the techniques of operations research.[1] Some of these papers have been directly concerned with the interplay between these two bodies of knowledge.[2] It would be redundant for me to devote this paper to retracing developments that have already been well noted and discussed. Hence, I shall not present a complete history of these interactions but, instead, I shall focus upon two important innovations that have occurred as a direct consequence of the activity of economic theorists and operation research-

[1] See, for example, the excellent review articles of H. A. Simon, "Theories of Decision-Making in Economics," *American Economic Review*, XLIX (June 1959), 253–83; and R. Dorfman, "Operations Research," *American Economic Review*, L (September, 1960), 575–623.

[2] See the papers presented by W. W. Cooper, W. J. Baumol, and C. J. Hitch and R. N. McKean for the symposium, "Managerial Economics: A New Frontier?" to be found in the *Papers and Proceedings of the AEA, American Economic Review*, LI (May, 1961), 131–55.

ers. The first of these innovations is the modified concept of rational behavior known as "satisficing"; and the second is the technique of theory and model construction known as "heuristic programming." Customarily these two notions are presented and discussed independently. But it is the combination of these two ideas that has led to what I am going to take the liberty of calling one of the major advances in our knowledge of organizational and individual decision-making behavior. In order to point out the effects that these two concepts have had both on the economic theory of the firm and on the practice of operations research, this paper is divided into three main sections. The first part is devoted to a brief description of some of the important changes in the theory of the firm that have been brought about by the introduction of the satisficing concept of behavior. The second contains a brief description of the development of heuristic programming, as well as an actual example in which the satisficing concept and the technique of heuristic programming are conjoined in the solution of a complex business problem. And the third section is devoted to an attempt to assess the implications of these two innovations both for general economic theory and its policy considerations as well as the practice of operations research.

Developments in the Theory of the Firm

To be able to trace a change or development in a theory, one must have a point at which to begin. For our purposes, the starting point will be the classical or conventional theory of the firm. Unfortunately, there is considerable disagreement among economists as to precisely what is the "Theory of the Firm." Since no one theory has been graced with this title for any length of time, I shall present what I consider represents a reasonable consensus of opinion.

CLASSICAL THEORY [3]

The classical theory of the firm is a theory of market behavior. It is concerned with explaining, at a general and aggregated level, the

[3] For a more detailed and extensive description of the classical theory of the firm see J. M. Henderson and R. E. Quandt, *Microeconomic Theory* (New York, McGraw-Hill, 1958), especially pp. 42–84.

allocative process of the market place. In particular, the theory takes as its objective the explanation of the behavior of firms and, consequently, the allocation of resources among firms under varying market conditions, e.g., pure competition, oligopoly, and monopoly. The firm, in this theory, is an entity whose objective is to maximize its net revenue (profits). The firm sets out to accomplish this objective by taking the prices of its inputs (labor, materials, equipment, and capital) as being given to it by the market place. It then examines its production function which is taken to be determined by the current state of technology. To maximize its net revenue, the firm decides upon the particular combination of inputs and outputs that is optimal with respect to the given prices and the production function.

In the market condition known as pure competition the firm is allowed to sell at a given price whatever quantity of finished product it produces. In this situation the theory is concerned with specifying the conditions under which such an optimum can be attained. In particular, when we are dealing with firms that only produce one product, the theory states the optimum position will be reached if the output of each firm is adjusted so that the marginal cost of producing this number of items is exactly equal to the marginal revenue derived from their sale. The theory also extends to multiproduct firms and specifies the optimal procedures whereby these firms can decide how much of each good it should produce. After specifying the conditions under which firms engaging in pure competition can maximize their net revenue, the theory then explains the effects of changes in the prices of products and factors of production which result from alterations in the equilibrium position of the total market.

Because all markets do not meet the conditions of perfect competition, the theory extends to meet cases where either the market for the factors of production is imperfect, or the market for final products is imperfect, or both. One case in particular has received a considerable amount of attention. This is the market condition called oligopoly, where a small number of producers effectively dominate the market for a product or a specific set of products. In this case there are a number of contending theories whose primary object is to specify the manner in which, for example, firm A takes into account the pricing and output decisions of firms B and C.[4] However, in all these extensions to different market conditions the theory retains the same internal decision-making process—namely, it is the object of each firm to maximize its profit. Thus, while the classical theory of the firm has been extended to meet various market situations, its primary purpose has remained unchanged. Its object is to specify the mechanisms by which resources are allocated in the market place.

Lately, this theory, or collection of theories, has come under attack from a number of quarters. Some critics have argued that firms do not decide how much to produce by equating marginal cost with marginal revenue. As evidence, they point to the difference between the economic concept of cost found in the theory as against the accounting concept of cost used in actual business firms.[5] Other critics have noted that the theory does not view the firm as an organization and ignores the existence of such items as management planning, budgets, standard operating procedures, and the host of other components which they argue should be included in a theory of a firm's decision-making process.[6] These and many other criticisms reflect the central fact that the classical theory of the firm was constructed to explain, at a general level, the behavior of firms within a given market, and not the behavior of individuals within a particular firm. Consequently, these criticisms not only reflect the disparity between the behavior of actual firms and the firms of the theory, but also the directions in which the theory ought to be revised if it is to become a vehicle for explaining and predicting the variety of behavior exhibited in the market place, as well as inside the firm.

[4] For a survey of some recent theories of oligopoly see: Franco Modigliani, "New Developments on the Oligopoly Front," *Journal of Political Economy*, LXVI (June, 1958), 215–32.

[5] See, for example: R. L. Hall and C. J. Hitch, "Price Theory and Business Behavior," in T. Wilson and P. W. S. Andrews (eds.), *Oxford Studies in the Price Mechanism* (Oxford, 1951), pp. 107–38.

[6] A. Papandreou, "Some Basic Problems in the Theory of the Firm," in B. F. Haley (ed.), *A Survey of Contemporary Economics* (Homewood, Illinois, 1952), 2, 183–219.

As noted above, the many critiques are not so much comments on the inadequacy of classical theory to meet its stated goals as they are suggestions to guide the development of a new microtheory of the firm. That is to say, the majority of suggestions pertain to the construction of a theory that describes and predicts the internal decision-making process of a firm. Most of these suggestions have come from economists who, while engaged in consulting and operations research capacities, found that the classical theory was not suited to their needs. For example, to quote a leading economist: "I can say quite categorically that I have never encountered a business problem in which my investigation was helped by any specific economic theorem." [7] As one might expect, the disparity between theory and observable practices has stimulated economists to propose several new theories. And we shall now examine two of the principal classes of revisions that have taken place.

Market theories. The first major revision was proposed by Professor Baumol. From his observations of business behavior Baumol arrived at the conclusion that firms do not devote all their energies to maximizing profits, but rather, that as long as a "satisfactory level" of profit is maintained, a company will seek to maximize its sales revenue. This theory, which is worked out in some detail,[8] differs sharply in some respects from the classical theory out of which it grew. One obvious difference is that total sales revenue has been substituted for profits. But what is much more important is that the theory includes two decision criteria or objectives—namely, a satisfactory level of profit and the highest sales possible. In other words, the firm is no longer viewed as working toward one objective alone. Instead, it is portrayed as having to balance two competing and not necessarily consistent goals.

[7] W. J. Baumol, "What Can Economic Theory Contribute to Managerial Economics?" *Papers and Proceedings of the American Economic Association,* p. 144.

[8] W. J. Baumol, *Business Behavior, Value and Growth* (Macmillan, New York, 1959), especially pp. 45–53.

From this principal hypothesis Baumol draws several important conclusions, which are more consistent with observed behavior than the conclusions drawn from conventional theory. The first of these is that firms faced with an increase in fixed costs will either pass these costs directly to the consumer in the form of higher prices or will try to reduce an expense over which they have some control, e.g., advertising expenditures. Conventional theory, on the other hand, asserts that changes in fixed costs (overhead) should not lead a firm to alter either its output or its prices. A second and rather important conclusion that Baumol draws is: "Sales maximization makes far greater the presumption that businessmen will consider *non*price competition to be the more advantageous alternative." [9] Classical theory asserts that businessmen will consider price cuts or increases as the primary mechanism for increasing profits, but observations of business behavior do not support this dictum. On the contrary, firms appear to go to great lengths to set their prices at the same levels as their competitors, while devoting their competitive energies toward advertising, product distribution, servicing, and the like.

While Baumol's theory is clearly more consistent with observed behavior, its primary focus is upon the behavior of firms in the market place. The theory does not describe in any detail the decision procedures whereby firms are able to maximize their sales subject to their satisfactory-level-of-profit constraint. That is to say, even though a firm may wish to maximize its sales, if it is not aware of the particular set of decisions and procedures that will lead it to this goal, then it is unlikely to succeed. Skepticism with respect to this and other basic premises of the decision-making process in these market theories stimulated a second major type of revision.

Behavioral theories. Even though operations researchers have not been concerned with conducting large surveys of business practice, their exertions have produced samples of data on business decision making which are strikingly at variance with the decision processes postulated in classical market theories. This divergence between the-

---

[9] W. J. Baumol, *Business Behavior*, p. 76.

ory and data has led some economists to abandon nomative formulations—that is, rules by which price and output decisions should be made—and concentrate on developing a body of theory that describes and predicts the actual decision processes found in business firms. Instead of focusing on market mechanisms these theorists consider the firm as the basic unit. Their objective is the analysis and prediction of a firm's decision-making behavior on price, output, internal resource allocation, and so on. To create such a theory, however, requires a knowledge of the major classes and attributes of business decisions. It is easy to see how these researchers have been led, from such a research committment, to investigate the variety of alternatives facing business decision makers as well as the processes by which choices are made. In brief, the object of this research is to discover how organizational objectives are formed, how decision strategies are developed, and how, on the basis of these strategies, conflicts are reduced and decisions made.[10]

The minute one abandons the classical notion that all firms have a single, universal goal, to maximize net revenue, and substitutes for it the notion that firms have a variety of goals, then a decision mechanism must be introduced that permits conflicts between objectives to be resolved. As noted above, Baumol retained the principle of maximization in his market theory but made the pursuit of maximum sales revenue contingent upon the firm's realizing, at the same time, an acceptable level of profit. But for a theory that intends to describe as well as predict the internal decision behavior of firms it is not sufficient merely to name a decision mechanism, e.g., maximize sales subject to a profit constraint. If the object is to describe decision behavior, then the processes included in the theory must be defined in sufficient detail to allow the relevant decisions to be traced through

[10] For examples of the literature on this research, see: R. M. Cyert and J. G. March, "Organizational Factors in a Theory of Oligopoly," *Quarterly Journal of Economics*, LXX (1956), 44–64; R. M. Cyert, W. R. Dill, and J. G. March, "The Role of Expectations in Business Decision-Making," *Administrative Science Quarterly*, III (1958), pp. 307–40; and R. M. Cyert and J. G. March, "Introduction to a Behavioral Theory of Organizational Objectives," in M. Haire (ed.), *Modern Organization Theory* (New York, 1959).

the organization and tested against observable behavior. Mechanisms must be introduced that account for the processes by which a search for new information is initiated, the order in which alternatives are considered, and the order in which decisions are made.

The inclusion of these and other, similar decision processes into a theory of firm behavior has led to the development of what has been entitled the Behavioral Theory of the Firm.[11] This is a theory of how an organization makes decisions on the basis of the information that is available at any given point in time. It is a theory of decision-making behavior which has substituted the notion of a satisfactory level of performance for the classical principle of maximization.

By abandoning the classical principle of maximizing for the behavioral principle of satisficing, the theorist can add to his theory as many goals or objectives as are consistent with observed behavior. Each goal now enters the theory as a single constraint, and current performance on each goal is evaluated with respect to past and expected performance. Hence, the total number of objectives defines a set of satisfactory performance figures. A satisfactory level of performance on sales, for example, represents a level of aspiration with respect to sales which the firm will use to evaluate alternative decisions. The level of aspiration can rise or fall over time, but in the short run it performs the task of measuring the success of present performance. Current results are either satisfactory or they are unsatisfactory. And each goal enters the decision-making process with one or the other of these values.[12]

For example, consider the decision mechanisms included in a model that was designed to describe and predict the behavior of a firm

[11] For a complete statement of the theory and of the empirical research that has been conducted so far, see R. M. Cyert and J. G. March, *The Behavioral Theory of the Firm* (Englewood Cliffs, Prentice-Hall, 1963).

[12] For a more extensive discussion of the need for, as well as the characteristics of a satisfying decision mechanism see: J. Margolis, "The Analysis of the Firm: Rationalism, Conventionalism, and Behaviorism," *Journal of Business*, 31 (July, 1958), 187–99; H. A. Simon, "A Behavioral Model of Rational Choice," *Quarterly Journal of Economics*, LXIX (February, 1952), 99–118.

entering a market previously dominated by one major producer.[13] In this duopoly model, Cyert, Feigenbaum, and March outline the decision-making procedures used by each firm. The decision process consists of a sequence of individual decisions which finally result in each firm setting its output for the coming period. The output decision is made by first considering the competitor's reactions to any proposed changes in output over the previous period. Estimates of the demand for and the costs of producing this output are made, and the estimated profits are calculated to make sure that this profit is at an acceptable level. If a satisfactory level of profit is not obtained, then the firm searches for ways of reducing costs, revises its estimates of the demand for its product, and, if necessary, lowers the profit goal so that it is consistent with the revised cost and output figures. Although this model was not developed to reproduce the behavior of any particular firm, it was tested against the recorded history of the tin can industry. By specifying parameter values for the model, a stream of behavior was generated that closely paralleled some of the notable features of the behavior of the Continental Can Company from the time it entered the market as a competitor of the American Can Company.[14] Since a classical model of duopoly does not exist that can generate roughly comparable outputs on the basis of roughly comparable inputs, it is not possible to compare the performance of a classical model with this behavioral one. But it is possible to compare, at a fairly general level, the behavior of this model with the behavior of two specific, existing business firms. Whether this advance could have been made without the introduction of a satisficing mechanism is difficult to determine. That it was made with its inclusion is, of course, a matter of historical fact.

The Development of Heuristic Programming

At the same time that these revisions were taking place in the economic theory of the firm, advances were being made by opera-

[13] R. M. Cyert, E. A. Feigenbaum, and J. G. March, "Models in a Behavioral Theory of the Firm," *Behavioral Science*, 4 (April, 1959), 81–95.

[14] *Ibid.*, Figs. I and II, pp. 91 and 92.

tions researchers in the application of such techniques as linear and dynamic programming to business problems. Many production, scheduling, and inventory problems are now being tackled and solved by the application of these and other mathematical tools.[15] But, a significant proportion of management's problems—namely, those whose structure is elusive and whose importance requires special treatment by middle and top management—are too complex to be successfully handled by current operations research techniques. Even though heroic simplifications can always be made there are a striking number of decision problems which are simply not amenable to current mathematical treatment. The answer appears to lie in the theory and technique of heuristic programming. To understand what is meant and implied by this technique we must first briefly examine the theory of human problem solving from which this technique has evolved.

A THEORY OF HUMAN PROBLEM SOLVING

The theory of human problem solving that we shall consider was developed by Newell, Shaw, and Simon,[16] to explain and predict the decision-making behavior of humans engaged in solving specified tasks. The object of the theory is to explain the problem solving process by identifying the types of decision processes that people use as well as the various decision mechanisms that permit these processes to be employed. A basic assumption of the theory is that thinking processes can be isolated as well as identified, and that they can be represented by a series of straightforward mechanical operations. This is not to say that thought processes are simple or easy to represent, but rather that they can be broken down into their elemental parts that, in turn, consist of collections of simple mechanisms. When these operations are recorded as a set of statements (decision rules) which describe the behavior under investigation, that behavior is said to have been "programmed."

[15] These techniques are discussed and many applications are noted in C. W. Churchman, R. L. Ackoff, and E. L. Arnoff, *Introduction to Operations Research* (New York, Wiley, 1957).

[16] A. Newell, J. C. Shaw, and H. A. Simon, "The Elements of a Theory of Human Problem Solving," *Psychological Review*, 65 (1958), 151–66.

Programs, however, can contain a wide variety of decision rules. When operations researchers apply their mathematical techniques to a business problem the programs they construct to produce a solution almost invariably employ algorithmic decision rules. These decision rules describe a set of procedures and calculations which guarantee that the required minimum or maximum will be found.

Humans, on the other hand, when engaged in solving complex problems do not employ these algorithmic techniques. Instead they use "rules of thumb," or heuristics, to guide them in their search for solutions. For example, in a game of chess a good player may look three or four moves ahead on a number of possible plays. And by evaluating the consequences of these possibilities he will decide on his next move. If, however, algorithmic decision rules were employed to search for the "best" move he would now have to examine every possible move and its consequences before coming to a decision. If there were thirty possible moves that he could make and he examined each alternative for two moves ahead, then he would need to examine 30^4, or roughly 800,000 possibilities before he could be sure that he had found the best move.[17] Clearly, chess players, like other human beings, are unable to consider 800,000 possibilities in a few minutes. Thus, the importance of rules of thumb or heuristics is that they frequently lead us to solutions which we would otherwise reach much more expensively, if at all, by algorithmic and other analytic techniques.

When a program is constructed that attempts to reproduce the decision processes of a human problem solver the decision rules are in the form of heuristics. These programs are called heuristic programs and have two important characteristics. The first is the ability to determine, at any point in the decision process, its subsequent action by making choices between the alternatives that are available to it at that particular point in time. This property, called branching, or conditional transfer, allows a program to adapt itself to changes in

[17] For an excellent discussion of existing chess programs as well as the problems involved in constructing a heuristic chess program, see A. Newell, J. C. Shaw, H. A. Simon, "Chess-Playing and the Problems of Complexity," *IBM Journal of Research and Development*, 2 (October, 1958), 320–35.

the alternatives. Hence, heuristic programs can follow strategies. The second important characteristic is the capacity to use any set or sets of operations repetitively and recursively. In other words, a specific operation can be employed over and over again to perform the same function on a stream of inputs; or a decision rule can be applied to itself, to form a hierarchy of the same operations to be applied to a specific set or sets of inputs. In this manner a heuristic program can use the same decision mechanisms to process different pieces of information or to solve quite different sets of problems.

Heuristic programming, then, is an attempt to incorporate into the theoretical structure of a model the selective, rule of thumb processes that humans employ in solving complex problems. It is a technique that has been used to reproduce parts of the thinking or problem-solving process.[18] And more recently it has begun to be used as an aid in management decision making.[19]

HEURISTIC PROGRAMMING: AN EXAMPLE

To illustrate these remarks let us consider for a moment a heuristic program which was developed to solve assembly-line balancing problems.[20] Although no direct attempt was made to simulate a particular, human assembly-line balance, this program was modeled on the decision processes used by skilled human schedulers. The object of the program is to schedule, or balance, an assembly line.

The problem of scheduling an assembly line is similar to many other types of industrial scheduling problems, e.g. the scheduling of orders in a job shop, the routing of traveling salesmen, and the assigning of a given number of men to a given number of machines. The essence of these tasks is a combinatorial problem in which the ele-

[18] For an excellent example of the growing literature of this subject, see A. Newell and H. A. Simon, "The Simulation of Human Thought," W. Dennis (ed.), *Current Trends in Psychological Theory* (Pittsburgh, University of Pittsburgh Press, 1959), pp. 152–79.

[19] See, for example, H. A. Simon, *The New Science of Management Decision* (New York, Harper and Brothers, 1960).

[20] F. M. Tonge, *A Heuristic Program for Assembly-Line Balancing* (Englewood Cliffs, Prentice-Hall, 1961).

ments of a set (the pieces that go to make up the final article, the orders in a job shop, and the like) are ordered or grouped on the basis of one or more criteria. While some of these problems have been tackled by standard operations research techniques,[21] they are frequently too large and complex to be solved by algorithmic procedures. For example, if the product to be assembled contains one hundred parts and we are looking for the most efficient way to assemble them, then to be cetrain we had located the best way we might have to inspect each of $100! = 9.3 \times 10^{157}$ possible arrangements. Now, if we employed a high-speed computer and inspected 10^6 orderings each second it would take 3×10^{114} years to cover them all. Clearly, blind-search techniques of this sort are simply not feasible methods for solving combinatorial problems of any size.

The task of scheduling an assembly line consists of assigning the components making up the total assembly to work stations along the line. In order to consider an actual problem, Tonge's program assumes that the speed of the conveyer belt is fixed, e.g. there is constant production rate, and that the time required to assemble each component part is known. The goal of the program is to discover the minimum number of workmen that are needed to keep up with the given production rate and to meet the partial ordering constraints imposed on the assembly operation. Heuristics are employed to sufficiently simplify the task so that it can finally be solved by straightforward methods.

The program consists of three main phases. The first is concerned with ordering the elemental tasks into fairly large subassemblies. Each of these subassemblies contains its own partial orderings between its elements, and each requires a certain amount of operating time. Hence, at the end of phase one, the program has constructed a hierarchy of subassemblies. The second phase takes these subassemblies and assigns to them the required number of workmen. It then treats

[21] For an excellent discussion of the application of linear programming to many of these problems, see A. Charnes and W. W. Cooper, *Management Models and Industrial Applications of Linear Programming* (New York, Wiley, 1961).

each subassembly as a separate scheduling problem and assigns the workmen to the various components of each subassembly. After this rough scheduling of men and component parts is completed, phase three is employed. This phase consists of a "smoothing" operation. It adjusts the components and the men among the work stations set up by the first two phases until the distribution of assigned time per worker is as even as possible.

Since this program was not designed to reproduce a specific scheduler's behavior, it is somewhat difficult to directly compare its performance with that of an industrial scheduler. However, the program was tested on a 70-element problem that was roughly similar to a particular industrial assembly line. Even though the industrial engineer had to contend with a few extra constraints, the program's performance compared very favorably with that of the engineer's. For the 70-element problem the heuristic program required 23 men to complete the assembly operation, as against the 26 men assigned to the task by the industrial scheduler. While this result by no means demonstrates the superiority of the heuristic program it is striking evidence of the power and versatility of this technique.

Implications of These Innovations for Economic Theory and Operations Research

From the foregoing discussion it should be readily apparent that the introduction of the concept of satisficing and the technique of heuristic programming have already had a significant impact on the fundamental research conducted in the economic theory of the firm and in operations research. It should also be clear that the chief object of this research is to be able to explain, as well as improve, the decision-making behavior of individuals and organizations. Although most of this research is of very recent origin, sufficient progress has been made to tempt me to try and outline some of the implications this research should have on the development of economic theory and on the guiding of business decisions.

ECONOMIC THEORY

It is my belief that the principal effect of the researches in decision-making behavior will be noticed in economic theory itself. For example, in the first section it was noted that the empirical investigation of business decision procedures has led some economists to propose extensive revisions in the classical theory of the firm. These revisions were stimulated by the manifest disparity between classical theory and observed practice. One of the more notable of these differences is exemplified by the way the pricing mechanism is employed. In the classical theory, firms are supposed to maximize their profit. And the pricing mechanism is declared to be the most efficient method of allocating resources in the market place. But if, as in Baumol's theory, firms only maximize sales revenue subject to a satisfactory-profit constraint, or if, as in the Behavioral Theory of the Firm, firms no longer maximize any criterion function, then the classical assertions about the efficacy of the pricing mechanism may also require revision.

As a further example, consider the assumptions, contained in classical theories, that have been called into question by these researches into decision-making behavior. In particular, consider the assumption that firms, or individuals, make decisions by maximizing a clearly defined decision function. All the evidence collected so far by these investigators supports the hypothesis that individuals and organizations make decisions by paying attention to a limited number of objectives, and by doing what they can to see that they meet these goals most of the time.[22] The objectives, however, are not stated as clearly defined decision functions. On the contrary, they are usually stated in terms of past behavior, and current performance either is or is not up to these fairly flexible standards or objectives. If this is a reasonably accurate statement of the case, then the setting of prices, for example, can only be one of a number of organizational objectives. As

[22] For an extensive and stimulating discussion of organizational decision-making behavior, see J. G. March and H. A. Simon, *Organizations* (New York, Wiley, 1958).

a result, a firm will only consider the altering of prices as one of the possible alternatives facing it at any point in time.

A corollary of this conclusion is that changes in the prices of a firm's inputs will also not have the effects on their decision processes that are asserted by classical theory. Firms do not equate marginal cost with marginal revenue. And even if they had some idea of how to make these calculations, the pressure of satisfying competing goals would probably prevent them from carrying out and making use of such calculations.

It is apparent, therefore, that as behavioral theories are developed and tested, the conflict between the classical and the new will probably sharpen. And as I am reasonably convinced that the evidence will support the behavioral theories, I would expect to see some rather large and basic revisions being made in many branches of economic theory. These changes will not be induced because the revised theories are simpler or more elegant than classical ones. On the contrary, theories of individual and organizational decision-making behavior are almost certain to be more complex and less esthetically pleasing than their classical counterparts. But what will cause the changes to occur is the simple fact that as more is learned about decision processes, theories will be constructed which will explain and predict a large part of many decision procedures.

As evidence for this claim and as an example of the manner in which these revisions may take place, consider the following example of a behavioral theory of the trust investment process.[23] The object of this research was to construct a theory that would describe and predict the portfolio selections of a particular trust investor. The theory was built by observing and incorporating the decision processes of the trust investor into a program for computer simulation. The theory was tested for its ability to predict the actual behavior of the trust officer by requiring it to select a series of portfolios for an actual set of trust accounts. These accounts were processed both by the trust

[23] G. P. E. Clarkson, *Portfolio Selection: A Simulation of Trust Investment* (Englewood Cliffs, Prentice-Hall, 1962).

officer and the theory during the first and third quarters of 1960. The portfolios chosen by the theory compared very favorably with those chosen by the trust investor. As a further test, the decision processes by which the theory generated its portfolios were compared with the trust officer's recorded decision behavior. Even though it is not possible to say that the theory completely reproduces the recorded behavior, the evidence from these tests strongly supports the hypothesis that the theory explains a considerable portion of the trust investment process.[24]

A theory that describes and predicts one trust investor's portfolio selection process is still a long way from becoming a general theory of trust investment. But the evidence is there that theories can be built that explain and predict, to a considerable level of detail, the decision processes of human decision makers. Hence, if the success in building theories of individual behavior can be translated into theories of organizational and market behavior, then many branches of economic theory will undergo substantial alterations.[25]

So far, I have been discussing the changes that may take place in the theories of various economic units, e.g., the firm. But if my prognoses are correct, then revisions that are made in the theory of the firm, for example, must also be reflected in the aggregate theories of market behavior. That is to say, if the firm is no longer to be pictured as a static, profit-maximizing entity, then the theory that accounts for the aggregate behavior of firms must also undergo some change. Clearly, if firms are more accurately represented as complex organizations confronted with the task of satisfying many competing goals, the theory that accounts for their aggregate market behavior will have to take account of this fact.

As yet there is not a sufficient amount of data to suggest in any

[24] For an extensive analysis of the results obtained from these tests, see *ibid.*, chs. 6, 7.

[25] For a detailed examination of the way in which the economic theory of consumer behavior might be revised to accommodate a behavioral theory of consumer behavior, see G. P. E. Clarkson, *The Theory of Consumer Demand: A Critical Appraisal* (Englewood Cliffs, Prentice-Hall, 1963).

detail how such a revised market theory should be constructed. However, one component it would have to include is the apparent lack of interest on the part of large corporations in engaging in price competition. For example, Baumol has already observed that oligopolists will consider nonprice competition to be the more advantageous alternative. Also, the behavioral theory of the firm suggests that large firms, whether oligopolists or not, prefer to have a stable environment to work with. And one way to keep the environment stable is to avoid price competition. Hence, whatever form the revised theory finally takes, it no longer is likely to represent the market as a place where firms struggle fiercely to meet price competition. Instead, the theory should provide us with a more accurate picture of the nature of competitive markets and of the forces that influence the behavior of individual firms.

ECONOMIC POLICY

If we accept, for the moment, the supposition that the evidence will largely support the behavioral theories, then what will be the effect of these theoretical revisions on policy considerations? In particular, can we say anything about the amendments that may have to be made to our conception of how pricing policies should be regulated?

Classical theory, as mentioned earlier, asserts that competitive pricing is the most efficient way to keep the prices of finished products, e.g. consumer prices, as low as possible. Consequently, when competitive pricing appears to have vanished and one or two companies dominate an industry, antitrust measures are invoked with the intent of restoring competitive pricing to that particular market. But if, as investigations of business behavior suggest,[26] the pricing decision is only one of a firm's decision problems, then increasing the number of firms in the market may not have the desired effect. In other words,

[26] For further discussion of this point, see H. A. Simon, "New Developments in the Theory of the Firm," *Papers and Proceedings of the AEA, American Economic Review,* LII (May 1962), 1–15.

unless it can be shown that the number of firms in the industry has a direct effect on the prices that are set, it does not make much sense to invoke antitrust measures whose purpose is to increase the number of competing firms.

For example, it has been observed in a number of cases that increases in internal administrative costs frequently lead firms to centralize their allocative processes.[27] In effect, these firms replace internal pricing mechanisms with central planning. Departments no longer maintain their own profit and loss figures, but instead work from allocated budgets and set prices. A further stimulant to centralized decision making has been provided by the high-speed computer, and it is clear that many firms are making full use of their data-processing abilities. If most prices and budgets of large corporations are set by a central plan, this plan will not be sensitive to external changes. The vast amount of coordination required by central planning precludes the possibility of its being very sensitive to external disturbances. Hence, if prices within an industry are judged to be too high and antitrust measures are invoked, then for these measures to be effective they must somehow directly affect some of the principal components of a firm's internal plan. Unfortunately, not enough is yet known about the planning process to suggest effective procedures for inducing the desired change. But the evidence is sufficient to call into question many of the traditional beliefs about the efficacy of market mechanisms in controlling prices.

As a further example of how policy conclusions may have to be revised, consider the traditional conception of a firm's reaction to various tax policies. In particular, let us examine the effect of levying a lump-sum or poll tax on all corporations.

Under classical theory, the assessing of a lump-sum tax is supposed to be one of the most effective ways of taxing a corporation without having the cost of this tax passed on to the consumer. This conclusion

---

[27] For example, see J. G. March and H. A. Simon, *Organizations* (New York, Wiley, 1958), especially, ch. 7; H. A. Simon, *The New Science of Management Decision*, ch. 5.

is supported by the classical assertion, referred to earlier, that changes in fixed costs should be ignored when setting prices and output. But observations of business behavior do not support this assertion. On the contrary, firms have been observed to raise prices to compensate for increases in overhead costs. And, in Baumol's analysis, increases in overhead costs, such as a poll tax, will be shifted, at least in part, to the consumer, because, "when they are levied on him, the oligopolist will raise his prices and reduce his selling costs to a point where his profit constraint is once again satisfied. . . . Since no one seems to deny that businessmen do, in fact, often raise prices when their overheads increase this point must be accepted by someone who questions the sales maximization hypothesis." [28]

If the classical conclusion concerning the poll tax is in error, it is reasonable to suppose that other conclusions about tax policies may also be erroneous. And if our conclusions about the efficacy of the price mechanism are also substantially correct, then it would appear that many of the standard notions about appropriate policies are also in need of reexamination. Manifestly, it would be pleasant to be able to point to all the errors and indicate the necessary corrections. But until a great deal more is learned about organizational behavior such a procedure is simply not feasible. The best that can be done is to point toward a few of the most likely candidates and hope, by this approach, to generate an attitude of healthy suspicion toward the remaining, unexplored conclusions.

BUSINESS DECISION MAKING

If it is possible to point out the likely revisions in economic theory and its policy conclusions, then it is pertinent to inquire into the effects these changes may have on the business decision maker. If and when our understanding of decision processes reaches the point where the "best" procedures can be prescribed, then the advances in economic theory will be of great importance to the businessman. But

[28] W. J. Baumol, *Business Behavior, Value and Growth*, p. 78.

until the requisite knowledge has been acquired, it is perhaps more fruitful to examine the implications of current research for operations research. In other words, it seems more reasonable to examine the effects of recent research on the techniques of decision making rather than on the process itself.

When operations researchers first tried to employ traditional economic models to solve business problems, they discovered that important changes had to be made. Out of this search for new analytical techniques, innovations like linear programming, game theory, and statistical decision theory evolved. These techniques have been successfully applied to a large number of business problems, and the application of operations research techniques has become an established tool in management's decision process.

The advent of heuristic programming, however, opens up an important new class of problems. It will allow operations researchers to tackle problems that previously were far too complex and ill structured to be solved by standard techniques. For example, one of the earliest uses of this technique was in the analysis and synthesis of electric motor design. Ten years ago, in one company, engineers worked out the designs for standard and special order electric motors. Today, a computer, programmed with a relatively simple heuristic program, takes customers' orders for many types of electric motors, generators, and transformers, and sends the design specifications to the factory floor.[29] Earlier, we described Tonge's line balancing program which, by combining heuristics and some simple mathematical techniques, was able to schedule assembly operations as well as, if not more efficiently than, skilled industrial engineers. Indeed the technique of heuristic programming has made it possible to develop programs which will solve many of the problems that traditionally have been the concern of middle management.

The fact that it is now technically possible to begin replacing man-

[29] G. L. Goodwin, "Digital Computers Tap out Designs for Large Motors Fast," *Power* (April, 1958), pp. 102–4, 190–92.

agers with heuristic programs does not imply that it is yet economi-cally desirable to do so.[30] For example, consider the case of the trust officer at a bank. The evidence gathered so far suggests that his job of selecting portfolios for trust accounts could be taken over by a suitably programmed computer. The evidence also suggests that the computer can be programmed to select its portfolios for the same reasons as the human investor. Presumably, the computer could even be taught how to improve upon its performance. But, before a com-puter will ever replace a trust investor, it must be demonstrated that it is either more efficient or cheaper to employ a computer instead of the trust investor. As yet the evidence on this point is far from clear. And the flexibility of the human problem solver is still orders of magnitude greater than that of current com-puter programs. But, as our programming abilities develop and our understanding of problem solving behavior grows, I am convinced that heuristic programming will become one of the primary tools in management's decision-making apparatus.

Conclusion

In the last few pages I have made a number of strong statements about the current state of economic theory. I have also pointed out some of the effects that the proposed revisions of economic theory may have on government policy and business practice. And I have noted that the current state of our knowledge is insufficient to iden-tify and assess these changes with any significant degree of accuracy. However, the reason for this state of affairs is easy to identify. Econ-omists have an abundance of theories but a dearth of facts. Until this situation is corrected the best we can do is point to the difficul-ties and hope for the best.

Consequently, if we are to understand decision processes, and if we are to use this knowledge to assist in public and private decision

[30] For an extremely interesting analysis of the future role of computers in management decision making, see H. A. Simon, "The Corporation: Will it be Managed by Machines?" in M. Anshen and G. L. Bach (eds.), *Management and Corporations 1985* (New York, McGraw-Hill, 1960).

procedures, a large amount of effort must be devoted to empirical research. This research will have to focus on the decision-making processes of individuals and organizations, and, unlike a good deal of previous research, it will have to be conducted in a reasonably systematic way.

For example, most of the information we have about business behavior is derived from economists' and operations researchers' anecdotes, and sample surveys of business behavior. Neither are very reliable sources of information. The former are subject to bias by the observer's preconceptions. And the latter often contain scanty pieces of ill-supported and unverified data. As a result, whether we are satisfied or not with classical theories, there is no solid foundation of data from which to develop and test.

However, the scarcity of reliable data is not a result of a paucity of ways for collecting it. On the contrary, intensive interviews, detailed observations, and the techniques employed in simulation studies are all useful methods for gathering and sorting data. Since the number of untested hypotheses far exceeds the available data it is toward this objective that the emphasis on empirical research should be placed.

INTERPRETATIONS AND CONCLUSIONS

BY ALFRED R. OXENFELDT AND
RICHARD B. TENNANT

The two Columbia conferences reviewed approaches currently used to analyze the operations of markets and the nature of competition. Interpretations and Conclusions of Part 1 presented our evaluations of the standard market models of price theory, based upon the first conference. The present chapter seeks to relate the results of the second conference, which dealt with the newer mathematical models of operations research, to our findings in Part 1. In this chapter we will focus our attention on the marginal contribution of the new techniques to an understanding of markets and competition. Specifically, how much additional light do they throw on antitrust policy, business decisions, industry studies, or economic theory?

The Market Models Intact

Our first conclusion is that the mathematical techniques of operations research are no substitute for the standard market models. Within their area of relevance, the market models remain intact. The newer models do not deny or replace them and indeed incorporate their concepts. Marginalism and oligopolistic interdependence—the notions that underlie the Marshallian and Chamberlinian analysis— are also central in the mathematical models of operations research. The most important concepts used in analyzing market and industry behavior are still those developed by economic theorists several decades ago.

Contributions of the Newer Models

Although the market models retain their central importance, the incremental contributions of the newer models to economic understanding are significant in two quite different directions: they provide methods for finding numerical answers to some concrete business problems and they provide theoretical illumination.

SPECIFIC ANSWERS TO BUSINESS PROBLEMS

Operations research techniques seek to apply analytical techniques drawn from many scientific disciplines (including economics) to the making of better decisions. The substantial successes of these methods have been of two major sorts. In some problem areas, operations research techniques are essentially computational devices that use available data and apply the concepts of neoclassical economics to arrive at a determinate numerical result; in other problem areas, assistance is given by analytical tools from other discplines, especially mathematics.

An example of computational assistance is the use of linear programming in an input-mix problem. The nature of this problem is well illuminated by ordinary techniques of marginal analysis. The technological constraints of imperfect substitutability are reflected in convex equal-output curves, and the optimal solution is that for which marginal rates of substitution of input factors in production are equal to marginal rates of substitution of the same factors in the supply market. Linear programming methods applied to the same problem express substitution restrictions in terms of limits specific to the particular situation and indicate the best mix in terms of given input and output prices. Because of computers and the development of the simplex algorithm, it is possible to solve highly complex mix problems by this method. The solution reached is, however, consistent with the criteria derived from marginal analysis.

The two approaches differ in nature and accomplishment. The marginal analysis of the theory of the firm is general, while the linear programming application is specific. Marginal analysis is simplified in that few facts (even assumed facts) are included, while linear programming requires substantial factual information. On the other hand, linear programming is simplified in that it is limited to linear relations, while the models of the firm are not so limited. Finally, marginal analysis provides concepts for the problem and gives it analytical structure, while linear programming yields a specific result. In view of these characteristics of linear programming, it is easy to see why it is of substantial assistance in solving some kinds of business problems.

The other type of assistance is illustrated by the application of probability theory to a range of decision problems under uncertainty. Inventory models and waiting-line models have made important contributions to inventory and production management.

In problem areas like these, business decisions have gained more from operations research techniques than they have from explicit applications of the market models. However, in other problem areas of broad business strategy such as pricing, integration, and acquisitions, operations research techniques are not widely applied, and we doubt that they will be. For many business problems, mathematical concepts or computational devices are less important than an understanding of industrial structure and competitive forces or an efficient framework of analysis. And, as we concluded in Chapter 7, the market models provide this kind of economic perspective and analytical framework.

THEORETICAL ILLUMINATION

We believe that the models of operations research have also cast light on important aspects of firm and industry behavior. They have made this contribution primarily because they have been devoted to different kinds of problems than were attacked with the market models and also because the assumptions differ from those underlying the market models.

The application of probability theory not only has helped to solve inventory and production problems but also, by illuminating behavior in this area, has provided additional insight into firm behavior. The market models ignore uncertainty, are not suitable for taking it into account, and to this extent are partly blind.

Still another deficiency of the market models—their lack of dynamic analysis—has been partly compensated for by developments in simulation and gaming. These developments, like others in operations research, are intended to help in the making of practical decisions, but we expect that the kind of understanding of markets and competition that we would like from a better theory of the firm will be advanced by these means.

In the analysis of oligopolistic interdependence, the standard models have considered a limited number of special cases of which differentiated and undifferentiated oligopoly are the most significant. With these simple tools it was possible to demonstrate the possibility of competitive behavior ranging from complete price identity at a monopoly level to extreme price warfare. The development of game theory has added significant perspectives. The mathematical structure of strategic opposition is better understood, and even the practical questions of strategic decision making are made somewhat easier by the use of game trees or the idea of a payoff matrix. Even though game theory has been an area of major frustration and has produced less in operations research applications than some other techniques, it seems to add significantly to the understanding contributed by the market models.

If the contribution of the mathematical models of operations research is primarily to specific business decisions and secondarily to illuminating some blind spots in the theory of the firm, it follows that their principal contribution is to the interests of business management with some secondary gains for economic theorists. It is difficult to see, at this stage, any substantial contributions that these methods would provide either to antitrust problems or industry studies. All applications, of course, will eventually gain if the power and scope of economic theory is increased.

Outlook and Needs

At the conclusion of our review of these two conferences, several principal findings stand out. First, the existing market models remain as useful tools for many purposes. Despite the many, legitimate criticisms to which they are subject, their substantial value must be acknowledged. They represent an imposing intellectual structure and are useful in understanding the complex conditions observed in real markets.

Second, these models cannot be applied, just as they are, to produce practical conclusions of any sort, without further analysis. For specific applications, they must be regarded as the basis for building further specific models; they must be given factual content before they can be brought to bear on concrete problems.

Third, we must look forward to substantial improvements in the existing models, achieved by a number of different methods. There is serious need to examine the problems of distribution, financial needs, and dynamic change that are assumed away in the standard models. As suggested above, some improvements in these directions have already been realized and more may yet come from the continued development of new sophisticated models of a mathematical type.

Fourth, we would expect that future progress will not be the sole property of mathematical methods. Our problems in better understanding are of many sorts, and many kinds of tools will be required. Marginal analysis has been helpful in illuminating subtle functional relationships that are not apparent to observation and intuition. The powerful computational methods of modern linear and dynamic programming and the resources of electronic computers make it possible to deal with voluminous data and complex relations. Probability theory is helpful in problems of uncertainty. Simulation enables us to deal with problems too large, too complex, or too uncertain for analytical solutions.

But when we have carried our application of such methods as far as they can go, we are still left with major problems of understanding and of decision. The world that we try to understand as economists, make decisions in as businessmen, or establish policy in as citizens confronts us with complexity beyond the capacity of the formal tools we have available. This complexity is of a type which can only be described as "messiness." The world is difficult to deal with because of the combination of nonquantifiable irregular personal, institutional, and historical factors that control it. Yet in the disorganized and complex world that we face, we have to make decisions and we strive for better understanding. In so doing we must derive many kinds of models. For many purposes, the best tools may not be models of increased sophistication but relatively naïve tools, simple models and analogies by which small increments of understanding and insight can be won.

APPENDIX: ARDEN HOUSE POETRY

BY KENNETH E. BOULDING

1 It's hard to praise with proper fervor
The nonparticipant observer
Who looks on each competing faction
From icy summits of abstraction.

2 The economist, then, may be at best a
Kind of businessman's court jester,
Or, if professor, is confined
To propagating his own kind.

3 The fogginess in man's relations
Escapes the model's clear equations,
But economics wasn't made
To serve the grubby hands of trade.

4 Businessmen are rather dumb,
Their model is a rule of thumb.
Economists, it should be said,
Prefer to have a rule of head.

5 But when the head is blank inside,
The thumb at least can hitch a ride,
And so one model comes in view—
To do what all the others do.

6   This model's fine, 'til there's rumor
     That all the others made a bloomer,
     And then we may be forced to face
     Another theory of the case.

7   Economists may think it's nice
     To set one greatest-profit price.
     But businessmen have cute devices
     To play their games with teams of prices.

8   The businessman had seldom missed
     The skills of the economist,
     Until he heard computers sing
     Of Lovely Linear Programming.

9   Just to know his A B Cs
     Once put the businessman at ease,
     But now he's sunk, unless he knows
     His Deltas, Sigmas, 'Pis, and Rhos.

10   Models help us see our way.
     Model-building's here to stay.
     But ultimately only God'll
     Formulate the perfect model.

11   Price agreements are illegal,
     Antitrust's an eagle-beagle,
     Guiding courts to shotgun-firing,
     Warning folks to stop conspiring.

12   Then, tired of empty exhortation
     Judges try an innovation,
     Finding models most enticing
     That prescribe a full-cost pricing.

13   Lawyers have a clear position,
They all believe in competition.
But even though they emphasize it,
They find it hard to recognize it.

14   Economists would be content
With structure rather than intent,
Though lawyers find they sometimes win
Their cases on *intent to sin.*

15   No business manager observes
The world as intersecting curves.
Still less does he perceive relations
As n-dimensional equations.

16   And yet, when all is done and said,
His actions come from off his head,
And so, from studying his illusions,
We draw behavioral conclusions.

17   The market in pure oligopoly
Can never do anything properly,
    For either collusion
    Or simple confusion
Will turn out to be its Thermopylae.